Wise Parenting Principles from Proverbs

Wise Parenting Principles from Proverbs

Chris R. Cutshall

ISBN: 154044449X
ISBN 13: 9781540444493

Praise for
Wise Parenting Principles from Proverbs

Chris Cutshall's *Wise Parenting Principles from Proverbs* is top-notch! More than a how-to parenting book, it is a manual on how to *be* a parent. Starting with foundational biblical truths and building on those principles in God's Word, it is a feast for those parents who long to train up their children in the way they should go. This has become my go-to reference and gift for parents.
Missy Horsfall, Author, speaker, radio host, pastor's wife

I've known Chris for thirty-five years, and through observing him raise his girls, I can testify that he practices what he preaches. This book was such a terrific read! He made the important point that the Bible needs to be the most important book from which we derive parenting principles. I appreciate the way he supported his wise parenting principles with pertinent illustrations and practical suggestions. I plan to recommend this practical and biblical book to everyone who will listen!
David Brewer, Missionary with Life in Messiah International, Bible teacher, Hebrew professor

Chris Cutshall speaks from the heart as well as from experience. His book, *Wise Parenting Principles from Proverbs*, is biblically sound and parentally motivating. I wish this book had been available when my four children were growing up. It

contains such truth and is written in easy-to-understand language with practical suggestions for putting these examples into action.
Becki Reiser, Speaker and author of THROUGH MY TEARS: AWASH IN FORGIVENESS

Intentional parenting is the pervasive theme of *Wise Parenting Principles from Proverbs*. The book offers guidance not only for parents but for all Christ-followers striving for faithfulness in their lives. Chris Cutshall convincingly reminds the reader that the window of opportunity for influencing our children is painfully short. Readers who desire their children to grow into faithful Christian adults who are confident in Jesus Christ's love and promises for their lives will find this book full of gems of wisdom for family life.
Chuck Ellis, President and co-owner of Pearl Valley Cheese Co.

As a mother of three young children, I believe this book is an essential "must read," as well as a book to continually reference throughout the various seasons of childhood. It's biblical and spot on as to what God's Word says about raising children God's way!
Julia Fisher, Homemaker, mother, and wife

Acknowledgements

I WISH TO EXPRESS MY deep appreciation to those who made this book a reality:

To my brother in the Lord, Chuck Ellis, for encouraging me in more ways than one to take the sermon series by the same title and make it into a book.

To our elders, Dwight Jarboe and Dave Shelly, and deacons, Greg Fisher, Kerry Patterson, Larry Leindecker, and Lynn Eiler, for their unflinching support of this project.

To my church family, Fresno Bible Church, for their faithful prayer and financial support. Without their love and encouragement, this book wouldn't be possible.

To Angela Brillhart, for her tremendous help in taking the original material from sermon form to book form. Her suggestions were critical to the early stage of the process.

To Rachel Overton of Wordscapes, our professional freelance editor, for her expert direction and edits. Without her, this work would be far too wordy, cumbersome, and, at times, off-point. It was a privilege to work with one so wise and so good at her craft.

To my mom, Roberta, who introduced her five children to Christ and made sure we were raised in a church where Jesus Christ was preeminent and God's Word was basic to our faith. At eighty-three, she's still not retired from serving the Lord.

To my daughters, Kerry and Lindsay. They are tremendous testimonies of God's grace and power, despite the mistakes their mother and I made in raising them. I'm proud of the daughter Kerry is and the mother she has become to her children—our grandchildren.

To my sons, Ben and Jason. Even though Jason and Lindsay died before they were married, Jason will always be a son to me and Ben will never be an in-law. I'm proud of the man Ben has become in Christ.

To my beloved wife, Kathy. We are truly one in marriage, and we were one in raising our children in the Lord. We grew together, blew it together, and succeeded together. Without her wisdom, beauty, and love, I would be only half the man I am today.

Finally, and most importantly, to our triune God. Without Him, life would be pointless and parenting would be powerless. During this project, I was often reminded of how desperate we are for His wisdom and power. May He be praised and pleased, and use this book for His everlasting glory.

Preface

This book originates from a sermon series that I preached to my beloved church family in Ohio at Fresno Bible Church. My primary method of preaching is expositional. In crafting the series into a book, I deliberately maintained much of its original sermonic form. The primary reason for this is that I am convinced that expository sermons are an excellent way for God's people to comprehend His Word and to grow by and in it.

With that said, there are two characteristics of Proverbs that I followed in my sermonic style. First, Proverbs practices what has been called "the art of repetition." It often repeats itself, offering either the near exact principle or artfully adding helpful nuances to the ones already stated. Therefore, you will no doubt notice that some of the principles given in this book may seem repetitive. But look further and you will see that they build upon one another in a powerful and most helpful manner. I trust you will find the art of repetition in this work useful for implanting God's principles deep within your heart and mind.

Second, the original sermons—and now this book—follow the language of Proverbs. In that biblical book of wisdom, many of the parenting proverbs specifically portray a father instructing his son or sons. Accordingly, the principles in this book follow the same style. Obviously, in our twenty-first century culture, we are far removed from the family dynamics of Solomon's day, when fathers and sons were the more prominent members of families. Also, not every family today follows the traditional format of husband, wife, and children. I realize that many of our Christian homes are led by single parents, whether widowed, never married, or divorced. If this describes your home, please understand that these parenting principles most certainly apply to you in bringing up your children in the Lord. You may feel very much alone in raising your children, but know that you have the same divine power, resources, and teachings available to you as do more traditional family units.

My prayer is that the principles taught here will help you and every parent who reads this book, regardless of circumstance, to become the wise parent-leader God has called to you to be—parents that He can effectively enable and use for your family's eternal benefit and His everlasting glory.

Table of Contents

INTRODUCTION

The Death of His Godly Ones

Have you ever thought about your children's deaths? I don't ask you that out of a morbid sense of doom, but out of parental experience. I have a child who died young. The Lord willing, your children will live long lives on the earth. But whether they die early, late, or somewhere in between, think forward to when they die and ask yourself these questions: Will they be ready? Have I done everything humanly possible in the power of Christ to ensure that they are ready? The Bible says, "Precious in the sight of the Lord is the death of His godly ones" (Psalm 116:15). My prayer for you as a parent of your beloved children is that the thought of their future deaths will be precious to you because they are His godly ones.

In August 2004, my daughter, Lindsay, and her fiancé, Jason Allen, were brutally murdered on a California beach north of San Francisco near the small coastal town of Jenner. They were serving as staff members at a Christian adventure camp located between Sacramento and Lake Tahoe on the South Fork of the American River. The murders occurred while they were taking a weekend sightseeing break near the end of the summer camping season. In fact, it was one week before Lindsay was to fly home to Ohio to make final preparations for their wedding, three weeks before her twenty-third birthday, and three and a half weeks before the wedding. Jason was twenty-six. Both sets of parents are convinced that our children were at the peak of their Christian experience. Of course, from the perspective of any parent, their lives were way too short, especially considering the means of their deaths—they were shot execution-style at point-blank range for no known reason.

There is not a day that goes by that my wife and I don't profoundly miss our daughter, but we are eternally grateful to God for the time we had with her. We regard our time together as foundational years that prepared her for an eternity with her heavenly Father, "who [was] able to keep [her] from stumbling, and to make [her] stand in the presence of His glory blameless with great joy" (Jude 1:24). It takes divine power and grace to do that. It also takes preparation. Like many Christian parents, we were committed to raising our daughter to be prepared for her last moment on earth, and we found that Lindsay herself was just as committed to being ready. At almost twenty-three, she wasn't thinking so much about being prepared for death as she was about being prepared for worship and service, but in the end, she discovered that they are one and the same.

As a husband, father, and pastor, I believe with all my heart that the Lord prepared me beforehand for this cataclysmic event by solidifying my faith in the doctrine of His sovereignty. Over time, God in His grace strengthened my faith in the belief that He not only cares for His creation, but He is in control of it as well. In particular, He cares for His children who belong to Him by grace through faith in Jesus Christ. Lindsay's and Jason's deaths did not teach me to trust in the Lord more, but rather to trust Him always, in every circumstance—even in the worst of times and circumstances. But perhaps what their deaths taught me the most was the urgent need to be prepared.

Urgency, I believe, was my greatest lesson. We often say that time is of the essence, but do we believe it? God made me believe it. Lindsay's death taught me that life truly is short. Whether we live twenty-two years or ninety-two years, life on earth is short, and time is of the essence. So here's how I see it: God has given me the gift of urgency. He has moved His Word in James 4:14, that life is "just a vapor that appears for a little while and then vanishes away," from my head to my heart and has fixed it there. It is no longer "head knowledge," which, when it comes to spiritual matters, is dangerous knowledge. Urgency only comes when the knowledge of God has taken root within the heart. That urgency within is the great and gracious gift God gave me.

This gift shows up in my teaching and counseling ministry, but especially in my preaching. I'm more than sixty years old. I don't know how much time I have left before I join Lindsay and Jason to stand in the presence of our heavenly Father and Christ Jesus our Lord, but I know it is not much time. And I don't know how much time you have left to instill biblical principles into the minds and hearts of your children. I don't know how much time you have to prepare them for a life of worship and service and eventual death, but I know it isn't much time; it never is. And we all know that the competition for their time and attention is stiff—the world vies for as much of their time and ours as it can get. I'm sure you will agree with me: time is of the essence. We must set aside anything that belongs to worldly wisdom and replace it with biblical principles that accomplish the righteousness of God, so that both the lives and deaths of our godly children will be precious in the sight of the Lord.

In August 2014, we marked the tenth anniversary of Lindsay's and Jason's deaths on the Northern California beach where they were ushered into the presence of Jesus Christ. It is hard to believe that it has been twelve years now, as I prepare to publish this book. But believe me, the urgency and burden within me to help parents make the most of their parenting time before it is too late has not waned. Rather, it has led me to preach a series of expository messages from the book of Proverbs, where we glean forty wise parenting principles. That sermon series, now much expanded and in the form of this book, is my urgent plea for Christian parents to allow these principles from God's Word to transform their lives. Urgently seek to be wise Christians who translate biblical wisdom into living and parenting God's way because, ultimately, any other way but God's way is of the world and is destined to miserably fail. As you give yourself to the application of God's Word, He will bless your obedience to His Word. Furthermore, you will give your children the opportunity they desperately need to be ready for life in Christ, which is the best preparation for their death when it comes. I cannot overstate the truth: *time is of the essence.*

During the last months before Lindsay left to serve the Lord in California that summer, she and her mother were doing a book study together, and Lindsay was journaling on her own. However, we didn't know she was keeping a journal until after her death. One of her entries said, "I sometimes think of myself as a pilgrim in a foreign land, traveling through life. Don't waste time."

Okay, sweetheart—I won't!

My prayer is that as you read this humble offering, you will take care to heed God's urgent plea from Proverbs that says, in effect: "Don't waste time, for time is of the essence!"

CHAPTER 1

The Pursuit of Wisdom

When I think about parenting, I can't help but note the contrast between those parents who follow God's Word and those who don't. Many of us older parents, now in our grandparenting years, are fully churched and Christianized and, therefore, well principled in God's Word. Our marriages are intact and thriving. Our children, for the most part, have turned out pretty well, though there are prodigals who refuse to be helped. On the other hand, there are also older parents who are full of the world and its ways and wise only in their own eyes. They have no guidance or wisdom from above, and many of their marriages have disintegrated. Their children are adrift on the sea of worldliness, wandering toward the precipice with little hope of making it to heaven. My purpose in writing this book is to help those who are just beginning this journey to travel it well, with Bible in hand and eyes on the ultimate example of parenting—the all-wise and loving heavenly Father.

The apostle Paul tells us in 1 Timothy that people who reject the faith consequently "suffer shipwreck in regard to their faith" (1:19), and a shipwrecked faith produces a shipwrecked life. What a difference it makes to be fully churched, Christianized, and principled in God's Word.

John Rosemond, a Christian psychologist, wrote in the introduction of his book, *The Well-Behaved Child*, "Never in any culture at any time has parenting been more stressful than it is in today's America. The problems began in the late 1960s, when parents stopped taking their cues from their elders and began following the advice of people like me: psychologists and other mental health professionals" (Thomas Nelson, 2009, xiii). I know that is true, because I was there. When Kathy and I started parenting in the 1970s, we had a copy of Dr. Benjamin Spock's book, *Baby and Child Care*, which for fifty-two years topped best-seller lists nationwide—second only to the Bible in sales. The book contained helpful advice about caring for infants; however, much of its counsel on raising children contradicted what our elders taught and what God authoritatively commands.

We were inexperienced young parents who lacked knowledge and wisdom for raising our children; thus, it was only by the grace of God that we set aside the second best-selling book and picked up the best seller, the Bible, and began to ask, "What does God say about parenting?" Not "What do the *experts* say?" but "What does *God* say?" And in time, these not-so-wise young parents—again, only by God's grace—laid hold of the wisdom of God.

The book of Proverbs is the quintessential wisdom book of Old Testament Scripture. Our aim in this study of Proverbs is to become wise Christians who translate biblical wisdom into living and parenting God's way. If we are going to be wise parents who know the favor of the Lord upon our lives and homes, we must acquire the wisdom of God, knowing full well that worldly wisdom will not do.

In my careful study of this book, I discovered three necessary steps we must take to lay hold of God's wonderful gift of wisdom. The first step is to deliberately and diligently *seek* wisdom. The second step is to deliberately and earnestly learn to *fear* the Lord. The third step is to deliberately and sincerely *receive* God's Word.

1. Deliberately and Diligently Seek Wisdom

The Hebrew word for wisdom is *chokemah.* As it applies to the spiritual realm, *chokemah* is the God-given knowledge, ability, and skill to live life right and to make wise decisions that produce right and righteous outcomes in line with God's Word. Because God wants to give it, *chokemah* comes to those who desire it, pray for it, and pursue it.

I remember reading James 1 as a young man and being arrested by the truth laid out in verses 5 and 6: "But if any of you lacks wisdom, let him ask of God, who gives to all generously and without reproach, and it will be given to him. But he must ask in faith without any doubting." I began praying this prayer, in faith asking God for wisdom, without realizing that the prayer was set in the context of suffering. The verses that immediately precede 5 and 6 are enlightening: "Consider it all joy, my brethren, when you encounter various trials, knowing that the testing of your faith produces endurance. And let endurance have its perfect result, so that you may be perfect and complete, lacking in nothing" (1:2–4). Now read verse 5 again. "If any of you lacks wisdom"—in other words, if you're not complete in wisdom— "let him ask of God." Little did I know that gaining the answer to this prayer for wisdom would involve a process that included suffering to break my will and then to build my faith. All I knew at the time was that I kept praying that prayer because I lacked wisdom and desired to have it.

The prayer of James 1 is a necessary one to bring to the beginning of a study in Proverbs. The first nine chapters of this Spirit-inspired book present a single, sustained exhortation to seek the gift of wisdom. Proverbs 4:7 (NIV) says, "The beginning of wisdom is this: Get wisdom. Though it cost you all you have, get understanding." Verse 13 continues: "Hold on to instruction, do not let it go; guard it well, for it is your life." The terms *wisdom*, *understanding*, and *instruction* here are synonymous. One can't read those verses without recognizing how precious and important it is to gain wisdom. It is paramount, so get it. It will cost you all you have, but get it anyway. Hold on to it. Don't let go. Guard it with your life because it *is* your life. Gaining wisdom from God does not come without testing and trials and consequent pain, but it is that important.

Solomon, the primary author of Proverbs, often used the poetic device of personification; he breathed life into wisdom by depicting it as a woman. We see this clearly in Proverbs 8:1–31 (NIV), where he builds a case for why we should pursue this pure "lady" called wisdom. In verses 13 and 17, wisdom says, "To fear the LORD is to hate evil; I hate pride and arrogance, evil behavior, and perverse speech." But, wisdom continues, "I love those who love me, and those who seek me find me." Verses 32–36 exhort us, therefore, to find her, listen to her, and wait patiently for her:

> Now then, my children, listen to me; blessed are those who keep my ways. Listen to my instruction and be wise; do not disregard it. Blessed are those who listen to me, watching daily at my doors, waiting at my doorway. For those who find me find life and receive favor from the LORD. But those who fail to find me harm themselves; all who hate me love death.

Life and death are in the balance. Those who choose life know the blessings of God, and those who do not choose life choose death and bring harm to themselves. I see this all the time in my ministry. I see people choose God and pursue wisdom with a passion, and then I watch them find life and experience the manifold blessings from above. Unfortunately, I also see those who are not willing to give themselves up to the process of gaining the pleasure of God and His wisdom, and I watch them bring great harm to themselves as they are separated from the bountiful blessings of God's goodness.

The emphasis throughout the book of Proverbs is upon the absolute necessity of gaining biblical, spiritual wisdom, as well as upon God's readiness to give it to all who will take the steps necessary to obtain it. The New Testament also teaches that wisdom is required of Christians. Ephesians 5:15–18 says:

> Therefore be careful how you walk, not as unwise men but as wise, making the most of your time, because the days are evil. So then do not be foolish, but understand what the will of the Lord is. And do not get drunk with wine, for that is dissipation [NLT: "that will ruin your life"], but be filled with the Spirit.

Then, in Colossians 1:9–10, Paul writes,

> We have not ceased to pray for you and to ask that you may be filled with the knowledge of His will in all spiritual wisdom and understanding, so that you will walk in a manner worthy of the Lord, to please Him in all respects, bearing fruit in every good work and increasing in the knowledge of God.

"Every good work" would include raising our children in the Lord. This is what spiritual wisdom and biblical understanding do for us, but we must want it badly enough to pursue it. This holy desire is beautifully expressed by people who understand that obtaining the wisdom of God may cost them everything, but knowing its value, they passionately pursue it anyway.

Are we that passionate for God and His wisdom? It will cost us, but, oh, the blessed payback of gaining it! Jim Elliot, a missionary martyred for the cause of Christ in Ecuador, said it best: "He is no fool who would give up what he cannot keep in order to gain what he cannot lose." Amen.

2. Deliberately and Earnestly Learn to Fear the Lord

The second step in gaining the wisdom of God is learning to fear Him. There are two foundational verses that clearly teach this truth in Proverbs. The first is Proverbs 1:7: "The fear of the Lord is the beginning of knowledge; fools despise wisdom and instruction." And the second is Proverbs 9:10: "The fear of the Lord is the beginning of wisdom, and the knowledge of the Holy One is understanding." Again, *wisdom* and *understanding* are synonymous. The gaining of wisdom must begin and continue with the fear of the Lord.

But what does it mean to fear the Lord? What does it look like? To have the fear of the Lord is often explained as possessing a holy reverence for Him—having the deepest, reverential awe and respect for God. But there is more to it than that. In Old Testament times, fear of the Lord meant holy reverence *and* fear—that is to say, the dread kind of fear. When God visited the nation of Israel at Mount Sinai, He descended upon the mountain in fire. Smoke ascended to heaven like a great furnace, and the whole mountain quaked. The sound of a trumpet grew louder and louder, and God spoke with thunder. Let me assure you, there was much holy dread involved in that! Exodus 20:18–21 tells us:

> [The people] trembled and stood at a distance. Then they said to Moses, "Speak to us yourself and we will listen; but let not God speak to us, or we will die." Moses said to the people, "Do not be afraid; for God has come in order to test you, and in order that the fear of Him may remain with you, so that you may not sin."

And that is the context in which God gave them the Ten Commandments. Moses told them they needn't be afraid for their lives, but they should be afraid of the God to whom they were accountable. A proper fear of the Lord would protect them from sin, including irreverence. It will protect us as well and will, in turn, allow us to approach life without fear. There's much wisdom in that!

Some people insist that this fear was only expected of Old Covenant Israel. New Covenant Christians should not fear the Father. In the New Testament, Jesus is revealed as being full of grace. So, they say, we should not be afraid of God.

It is indeed true that during this age of grace, Jesus has been revealed to us as being "full of grace" (John 1:14). But Jesus also said to His disciples in Luke 12:4–7,

> My friends, do not be afraid of those who kill the body and after that have no more that they can do. But I will

> warn you whom to fear: fear the One who, after He has killed, has authority to cast into hell; yes, I tell you, fear Him! Are not five sparrows sold for two cents? Yet not one of them is forgotten before God. Indeed, the very hairs of your head are all numbered. Do not fear; you are more valuable than many sparrows.

In the context of God's care for His own, Jesus underlines the need for us to fear Him. When we fear the Lord, we don't have to be afraid, because He greatly values His own.

Along the same lines, in Acts 4:32–5:5, the Lord was marvelously and miraculously building His early church in Jerusalem. Yet, in the middle of such wondrous grace, He gave His New Testament saints a grave warning. The congregation was experiencing unprecedented unity. So much so that no one was claiming personal ownership of their properties; instead, they sold them and brought much of the proceeds to the apostles for distribution among those in their number who were in need. One man stood out among them:

> Now Joseph, a Levite of Cyprian birth, who was also called Barnabas by the apostles (which translated means Son of Encouragement), and who owned a tract of land, sold it and brought the money and laid it at the apostles' feet (4:36–37).

A couple within the congregation, Ananias and Sapphira, wanted the same esteem Barnabas had received, but without equal sacrifice. So they devised a plan to sell a property, withhold some of the proceeds for themselves, and then bring the rest of the money to the apostles, pretending to give the full amount. But the apostle Peter had inside information—their deception was supernaturally revealed to him. When Ananias arrived with his offering, Peter asked,

> Why has Satan filled your heart to lie to the Holy Spirit and to keep back some of the price of the land? While it remained unsold, did it not remain your own? And after it was sold, was it not under your control? Why is it that you have conceived this deed in your heart? You have not lied to men but to God (5:3–4).

Holding back some of the money for himself was not a sin; the sin was lying about it in the face of God so that he could look as good and godly as Barnabas. "And as he heard these words, Ananias fell down and breathed his last" (5:5).

After about three hours, Sapphira showed up, and not knowing what had happened to her husband, she told the same lie. She too fell down dead. The result of their deaths is reported in Acts 5:11: "And great fear came over the whole church and over all who heard these things." We may rightly assume that God made an example of Ananias and Sapphira before the newly established church so that the church would walk wisely and fearfully before Him.

You noticed, I'm sure, that the fear the church experienced here was more than what we think of as holy reverence—it was what we know as *fear*! The awe-inspiring holiness of God ought to strike a healthy balance in us—not only holy reverence but holy fear as well—so we will walk wisely before Him. If you want to be wise in the sight of God, you must learn to appropriately and thoroughly fear Him.

However, the fear of the Lord is not fear that is meant to drive us away; it's a fear that calls and attracts us. When we fear Him, we may then draw near to Him. We don't have to be afraid, for He is full of grace. He invites us to come near, to live near, and to delight in nearness with Him.

If you are wise, you fear the Lord. If you are growing in wisdom, you are growing in your fear of Him because the fear of the Lord is the beginning of wisdom. If you are foolish, like Ananias and Sapphira, you do not fear the Lord—but you should. And one day, you will! According to Proverbs, wisdom begins with the fear of the Lord; this is the foundation upon which we build a wise life.

3. Deliberately and Sincerely Receive God's Word

This is the third step in the process of gaining wisdom. The wisdom of God is given only to those who diligently apply themselves to divine revelation. Psalm 119:97–99 (NIV) says,

> Oh, how I love your law! I meditate on it all day long. Your commands are always with me and make me

> wiser than my enemies. I have more insight than all my teachers, for I meditate on your statutes.

God's laws, commands, and statutes are all synonymous with His Word. The psalmist's love for the Word of God is evidenced by his continuous meditation on it. He learned that his love for the Scriptures made him wiser than his enemies and enabled him to deal with them wisely. He could even say that he was wiser than his teachers because he had the dynamic edge of meditating on God's statutes. He was in the Word, and he meditated on it until it was deep within him.

The apostle Paul also talked about how important meditating on the Word of God is for obtaining wisdom: "Let the word of Christ richly dwell within you, with all wisdom" (Colossians 3:16). To Timothy, he said that the Scriptures "are able to make [us] wise for salvation through faith in Christ Jesus" and to make us "thoroughly equipped for every good work" (2 Timothy 3:15, 17 NIV). *Thoroughly equipped*? That's what the Word of God says!

How long has it been since you read straight through the Bible? How long has it been since you've had a consistent quiet time with the Lord, where you've meditated on His words of wisdom? Do you spend as much time with the Bible daily as you do on social media? I fear that far too many of us who belong to Christ have fallen short of effectively growing in wisdom through a diligent, consistent study of God's Word. How foolish!

Furthermore, we remain foolish because we do not do what we should—we do not take hold of the wisdom of God by taking hold of His Word. God graciously offers us His wisdom, but we have responsibility in this. We must deliberately, sincerely, and consistently receive God's Word.

If we are going to be wise parents who raise wise children, we must acquire the wisdom of God. To acquire God's wisdom, we must take deliberate and diligent steps to seek wisdom, to fear the Lord, and to receive His Word. The Lord is waiting and wanting to give His wisdom to those who desire it, pray for it, and pursue it. Only then are we ready to take hold of and apply the wise parenting principles from Proverbs.

In chapters two through nine, I will lay out forty parenting principles. My prayer is that you are ready to take hold of them because you have taken the time to lay the strong foundation that was given in this chapter.

CHAPTER 2

Wise Parenting Principles 1-5: A Teachable Spirit

Proverbs 1–5

We would all agree that experience is an important quality to bring to the parenting process. But how many begin this adventure with experience? None! Every parent on the planet begins this job with absolutely no personal experience. Thus, before young parents gain valuable, on-the-job experience (which will hopefully translate into making consistently good decisions), they can count on making their fair share of poor decisions. We older parents certainly can relate to that. I remember hearing Howard Hendricks, many years ago, say something like, "About the time we get a handle on the job of parenting, we are out of a job." Isn't that the painful truth?

So what is there to be done? Experience is valuable, but our beloved heavenly Father places an infinitely valuable soul into the care of woefully inexperienced Christian parents. This tells me that, from God's perspective, a teachable spirit that is in pursuit of wisdom from above is more important than experience. Further, that teachable spirit must be rooted in humility of mind and heart. Pride is a significant barrier between us and a teachable spirit. The admonition in 1 Peter 5:5–7 is ever true:

> Clothe yourselves with humility toward one another, for God is opposed to the proud, but gives grace to the humble. Therefore humble yourselves under the mighty hand of God, that He may exalt you at the proper time, casting all your anxiety on Him, because He cares for you.

A teachable spirit is rooted in humility before God and others. This allows God to lavish His amazing grace upon us. And, oh, how much we need that as we parent our children!

God, in His grace, has placed in our hands the best parenting advice possible—the Bible. Further, no book in the Bible contains more wise principles that apply to parenting than the book of Proverbs. The fact that you are still reading *this* book is solid evidence that you have a strong desire to be a wise parent. So now, let's go to the source to gain the wisdom of God. The first five chapters of Proverbs give us the first five wise parenting principles.

Before we go any further, however, I want to be sure you personally understand the surpassing value and necessity of having a teachable spirit. I encourage you to bow right now in prayer and humbly open your heart and mind to the Holy

Spirit. Ask Him to teach you His eternal truths from His eternal Word.

Parenting Principle 1
Wise Parents Train Their Children to Walk in the Truth of God's Word

For the Lord *gives wisdom; from His mouth*
come knowledge and understanding.
Proverbs 2:6

Solomon makes this point in several places in the early chapters. Proverbs 4:1–6 gives a clear account of a godly father instructing his beloved sons in how to walk in wisdom according to the Word.

> Hear, O sons, the instruction of a father, and give attention that you may gain understanding, for I give you sound teaching; do not abandon my instruction. When I was a son to my father, tender and the only son in the sight of my mother, then he taught me and said to me, "Let your heart hold fast my words; keep my commandments and live; acquire wisdom! Acquire understanding! Do not forget nor turn away from the words of my mouth. Do not forsake her, and she will guard you; love her, and she will watch over you."

(For more of the same father-to-son teaching, read Proverbs 1:7–10, 2:1–8, and 3:1–4.)

When Solomon was a boy, he was schooled by his father, King David, in the commandments of God given through His servant Moses. For example, Solomon was raised with Deuteronomy 6:4–7, Israel's "pledge of allegiance," firmly planted in the depths of his being:

> Hear, O Israel! The LORD is our God; the LORD is one! You shall love the LORD your God with all your heart and with all your soul and with all your might. These words, which I am commanding you today, shall be on your heart. You shall teach them diligently to your sons and shall talk of them when you sit in your house and walk by the way and when you lie down and when you rise up.

David had taught his son Solomon the commandments of the Lord. Now it was Solomon's turn to teach his sons those same commands. Even though he was the king, he was not so wrapped up in his kingly position and duties that he didn't *make time* to teach and train his sons in the ways of God. You cannot train your children in God's way if you are part-time parents and if God's Word is not imprinted on your own minds and implanted in your own hearts.

I came to Fresno, Ohio, to be the pastor of Fresno Bible Church in 1986. As a young pastor, I struggled with time stewardship—I had to learn how to best divide my time between church ministry and family. If I could go back and do one thing over, I would work hard to become more balanced in that area of my life. Despite my struggles, however, and by God's grace, I protected two things: family night and family devotions. We reserved Monday evenings as our special time—what we affectionately called family night. Mondays were when we went out for pizza, watched movies together, went bowling, or contended fiercely over board games because of our competitive natures. Our girls grew up loving family night.

The second thing I guarded was our family devotions. Each night we sat together, one girl on one side of me and the other girl on the other side, and I taught and trained them in the truth of God's Word. I did this because I had read in Deuteronomy 6 that the Word of God, applied personally, was to be on my heart as their father. Also, it was my responsibility to teach the Word diligently to them in both formal and informal settings. I took that instruction to heart and did my best to transfer the Word into the hearts of my daughters. I made a ton of mistakes in parenting, but I was diligent in this to the point that I'm sure there were times when Kerry and Lindsay thought, "Dad, give it a break!" But I didn't know how to give it a break, because I'd heard somewhere that wise parents play with their kids (family night, for example) and train them to walk in the truth (deliberate family devotion time, as well as those informal teaching moments that life offers parents—if we look for them).

The apostle John, writing to his children in the faith, wrote in 3 John 1:3–4 (NIV), "It gave me great joy when some believers came and testified about your faithfulness to the truth, telling how you continue to walk in it. I have no greater joy than to hear that my children are walking in the truth." To be clear, God's Word is the truth we should walk in (John 17:17), but note the significant statement the apostle made about his greatest joy concerning his spiritual children. Can this be said of us? Are we able to honestly say with the apostle that we have no greater joy than to see our children walking in the truth? Of course, before that can happen, we, their parents, must have teachable spirits that guarantee that we are walking humbly before them in the truth.

Be that wise father or mother (or better, father *and* mother) who has made and is making God's Word and God's way a permanent part of your inner being. Then and only then can you train your children to walk in the truth of God's Word. Is there any doubt that you will be glad and thankful to the Lord that you did? Every parent begins with no experience in raising children. But if you have a teachable spirit rooted in humility and are consistently learning to walk in the truth of God's Word yourself, then you will be a natural at passing along to your children what you have learned, and you will be glad that you did!

Parenting Principle 2
Wise Parents Train Their Children to Trust in the Lord

Trust in the L*ORD* *with all your heart and do not lean on your own understanding. In all your ways acknowledge Him,*

> *and He will make your paths straight. Do not be wise in your own eyes; fear the* Lord *and turn away from evil. It will be healing to your body and refreshment to your bones.*
>
> Proverbs 3:5–8

This passage from Proverbs contains a most fundamental lesson for believers: we must place our full trust in the Lord instead of ourselves. However, teaching this fundamental lesson to our children may be difficult, for a couple of reasons. First, so many Christian parents themselves fall short of trusting in the Lord with all their hearts; instead, they lean on their own understanding. Their natural and learned mode of operation is to be wise in their own eyes. This habit is far too common among people who proclaim faith in Jesus Christ. It is important for us to acknowledge that it is one thing to say that we *believe in* God and another to say and mean that we *trust* Him.

Sometime before Solomon was born, his father, David, allowed pride to fill his heart. Foolishness naturally followed. Instead of fearing the Lord and turning away from evil, David followed his own wisdom and turned toward it. He sinned against God with Solomon's mother, Bathsheba, when she was someone else's wife. And then, when David discovered that Bathsheba was pregnant with his child, what he did to her husband was simply unconscionable. Terrible consequences for his sins followed, as David learned the hard way that turning away from God and toward evil is deadly (see 2 Samuel 11–12). *But he did learn*, and then he wisely taught this fundamental biblical principle to his son, Solomon, who taught it to his son.

He said, "Son, trust fully in the Lord. Don't be wise in your own eyes; fear the Lord and turn away from evil—there's healing in that!" There's wholeness in it too; it's what the Bible in other places calls holiness.

The second reason it can be difficult to teach our children to fully trust in the Lord is that, according to Proverbs 22:15, foolishness (and pride along with it) is bound up in the hearts of our children; therefore, they naturally believe in themselves. When my youngest grandson was just about to turn three, I shared something with him that was true. His response was, "No, it's not." I said, "Yes, it is." He said, "No!" I'm pretty sure we ended with my "Yes, it is." I always try to win such arguments with three-year-olds. Trusting in one's self is an innate and stubborn characteristic of the sin nature. Therefore, even though it's easy for children to believe in Santa Claus and in God, it is hard for them to learn to stop leaning on their own understanding. In time, they can learn to trust God in all circumstances, but it is a process.

So, parents, you have your work cut out for you in teaching your children to mistrust themselves and, instead, to trust in the Lord fully. It can be taught, though. First, *teach this principle* to them from the Word. Second, *live it* in front of them. Third, *pray this principle* into their lives. If you desire to be a wise parent, you must teach your children this fundamental principle. Perhaps more importantly, however, you must also be a living example of what full-on trust in the Lord alone looks like. Without your example, your teaching will fall flat.

Does your life consistently declare your full trust in God? If so, then you can say with all integrity, "My son/daughter, follow my example: instead of trusting in yourself, trust fully in God." If your life does not reflect this trust, what will it take to make that happen? A humble, teachable spirit is the precondition to becoming wise enough to trust God fully. We can hardly expect our children to humble themselves before the Lord this way if we ourselves fall short of the mark. When this principle is deeply embedded in our hearts, however, it will show up in our everyday lives. We train our children to trust by taking them to the Word and speaking this truth into their hearts and minds, but we must also train them through our own living examples.

Now, how do we *pray this principle* into their lives? I suggest you pray this prayer daily:

> *Heavenly Father, help me to teach my children to become humble, pliable, and teachable in spirit so that, instead of leaning on their own understanding and being wise in their own eyes, they will trust You with all their hearts, and they will so fear You that they will turn away from evil. May it be so, in Jesus's strong name. Amen.*

Pray also that in God's amazing grace, He will use your teachings, examples, and prayers to prevent your children from having to learn the hard way, as many of us have had to do. But one way or another, pray that they will learn it. Trust is fundamental to our faith and theirs. Without it, neither we nor they will have teachable spirits.

Parenting Principle 3
Wise Parents Correct Their Children through Discipline

My son, do not reject the discipline of the Lord *or loathe His reproof, for whom the* Lord *loves He reproves, even as a father corrects the son in whom he delights.*
Proverbs 3:11–12

Take note that this is a godly father teaching his son to submit to both God's and his corrective discipline that is administered to the son in love. The word *discipline* speaks of physical correction; the word *reproof* speaks of verbal correction. God and wise parents use both in correcting the wayward bent of their children. The proverb speaks of the kind of loving father-son relationship where the following conversation can be imagined:

> "Son, do you know how I discipline you when you disobey?"
> "Yes."
> "I do that because you are the son in whom I delight. In other words, I love you far too much to allow you to live a life of disobedience. Do you understand?"
> "Yes, Dad, I understand."
> "Well, that is exactly why the Lord disciplines us, His beloved children. He verbally and physically corrects us because of His great love for us."

Have you ever wondered what God's corrective discipline looks like? Our loving Lord disciplines children in their early years through those faithful parents who follow the standards and procedures laid out in His Word. Godly parents are to love their children just the way they are, but they're also to love them too much to leave them there. Administering godly discipline allows those parents to become instruments in God's corrective plan and process. Thus, because godly parents delight both in God and in the children He gave them, they discipline their children in God's stead.

I will get more specific later in the book about physical discipline, but here in Proverbs 3, allow me to emphasize *the biblical mandate* that it is the God-given responsibility of parents to correct the course of their children through discipline. This includes both verbal and physical correction. Parents, if you want to be wise and to teach your children to be wise, then you must understand your responsibility before God in His disciplinary process.

Obedience is not natural to a child—we all know that. By their very nature, children want their own way. Some of their first words are selfish and defiant ones—words like, "No!" or "Mine!" So we shouldn't be surprised when God, in Proverbs 22:15, gives us a universal truth that encompasses all children: "Foolishness is bound up in the heart of a child"—every child; no exceptions. That means, among other things, that obedience is a learned behavior that goes against the grain of every child's sin nature. And since that is true, talking and reasoning alone will not accomplish much. In fact, I'm certain that verbal reproof without physical discipline, when necessary, is almost always ineffective. (There are a few exceptions to this rule in particularly compliant children.)

Wise parents are careful not to be overly verbal in corrective discipline. Verbal correction is biblical, so it is appropriate and necessary. However, it is easy to overuse verbal correction and underuse disciplinary consequences. Let's be honest: some of us rely on verbal correction so much that we depend on it to redirect our child's course, even though it is not working. So how do we find a proper balance between verbal and physical correction? It's important to realize that most children grow dull of hearing, especially after hearing the same thing over and over. If you catch yourself saying, "How many times have I told you..." then it's time to correct less verbally and correct more physically.

Many parents seem to think that their children will somehow grow out of their foolishness or that they can be talked or reasoned out of it. But Proverbs 22:15 also says, "The rod of discipline will remove [foolishness] far from him."

The passage, of course, infers that the person wielding the instrument of correction is a wise, loving parent. Thus, removal of this most stubborn inborn trait—foolishness—from your children requires you to take up your full responsibility as a wise remover of foolishness. That, in turn, requires you to delight in and love your children. Getting personal foolishness out and divine wisdom in also requires effort, energy, self-discipline, determination, and dependence upon God. This may not be easy, but with diligent training and corrective reproof and discipline, you can be used by God to help make your children wise.

In preparing this material, I offered this chapter as a handout for our church family. A short time later, a father of three little girls told me that he and his wife had learned from the handout that they talked too much to their four-year-old middle daughter, whom he called a strong-willed child. They immediately added physical discipline to their verbal reproofs. I then received an e-mail from his wife, this beautiful, strong-willed child's mother. Here, in part, is what she wrote:

> I just wanted to give you an update on how [our child] has been doing since we started changing the way we discipline and began using the paddle. It was difficult at first, and her will was very strong, but we have seen a turning point with her. [She] has been a different kid lately. One day she told me she was thankful for the paddle, which I wish I would have recorded, because I never thought I would hear words like that come from her mouth. And then on another occasion, she told us that she loved us. This is so huge to us, because we would tell [her] that we love her, but she would have no response. And now for her to say she loves us on her own just has blessed us so much. She is now going days at a time without needing the paddle, and she is so much easier to redirect than before. We know this is just the beginning, but she is so much more teachable now.

Is there any doubt from this little girl's statement—that she was thankful for the paddle—that she somehow knew she needed firmly held boundaries? She may not have known why she needed boundaries, but we do. She desperately needed them in order to do what she couldn't do on her own: to be settled, compliant, teachable, and happy. Because her wise parents possess teachable spirits, God instructed them from Proverbs and placed in their hands His instrument of correction, to be lovingly and consistently applied to their beloved daughter so that she, too, could have a spirit that is now teachable.

A foolish heart knows only how to crash through God's boundaries. Even if the foolish child doesn't like to do it, he or she crashes through just the same, for there is an innate compulsion within each of us to misbehave. The rod of discipline, along with loving reproof, has and is turning this beautiful little one back from the borders and into God's wonderful way of wisdom. I'm so thankful that this dad and mom had the spirit to take hold of this principle from Proverbs and to begin correcting their child through both verbal and physical discipline. What a difference it is making in their little girl's heart and life!

Wise parents are visionaries. They look down the road to the time when their children will be adults, and they picture in their mind's eye what they desire their children to become. In a word, they want their children to become wise, godly, faithful, and obedient men and women. Wise parents then set their hearts on training their children to become these men and women, knowing that correcting their course in love is critical to reaching that goal.

Kathy and I delighted in both our daughters, and we still do. When we were young parents, Proverbs 3:12 told us that wise parents correct the son or daughter in whom they delight. So, when one or both of our girls were out of alignment with God's way according to God's Word, we lovingly but firmly brought them back into alignment through corrective discipline. God commands children to "obey [their] parents in the Lord, for this is right" (Ephesians 6:1). If one of them was told to clean her room but failed to do so, then it was time for parental intervention to bring her back into alignment with what God's Word in Ephesians required of her—to obey her Christian parents in the Lord, for this is right.

Kathy and I were simply being obedient to God's Word. But since Lindsay died as a young adult—at the age of twenty-two—and since she didn't have time for a second chance to be a wise Christ-follower, by God's marvelous grace are we ever glad for our obedience to this critical principle! We were wise enough to be visionaries, knowing what we wanted our daughters to become.

I pray for you, parents, that you too will be obedient and consistent in maximizing the opportunities to reach your goal of producing wise adult children. It will require both verbal reproof and physical discipline to correct and keep them on the way, which is God's path of righteousness and eternal bliss. May it be so for their sake, now and forever.

Parenting Principle 4
Wise Parents Correct Their Children's Attitudes as Well as Their Behavior

My son, give attention to my words; incline your ear to my sayings. Do not let them depart from your sight; keep them in the midst of your heart. For they are life to those who find them and health to all their body. Watch over your heart with all diligence, for from it flow the springs of life.

Proverbs 4:20–23

Solomon is most concerned about his son's heart, so he instructs him to focus on his wise teaching. He tells his son to listen carefully to his Spirit-inspired proverbs and to keep them always in his heart. They are life, Solomon says, to those who find them; they even bring a physical wholeness to their bodies they wouldn't otherwise have.

The *heart* refers to a person's whole inner being; it is the well from which attitudes form and spring forth into actions. Jesus, in Luke 6:45 (niv), said, "A good man brings good things out of the good stored up in his heart, and an evil man brings evil things out of the evil stored up in his heart. For the mouth speaks what the heart is full of." What is in a person's heart, then, determines the direction of that person's life. An attitude, whether good or bad, reflects the makeup of the person's inner being. Therefore, since the heart is the source from which all of life springs up—thoughts, attitudes, words, choices, and conduct—Solomon instructed his son to watch over his heart with all diligence.

It is important to realize that behind every behavior is an attitude of the heart. The attitude shows most readily on children's faces, in body language, and in tone of voice. What is behind the behavior, however, is more important than the behavior itself. We could rightfully call the attitude of the heart the root of the behavior. I am convinced that correcting misbehavior alone—and not wrong attitude—is a parental trap that too many have fallen into. Be sure you understand the importance of dealing with the attitudes of the heart that manifest themselves in bad behavior.

Genesis 4 shows how harmful a bad attitude can be and how it should be strongly addressed. Cain's anger toward God and his jealousy toward his brother Abel stemmed from an attitude of the heart. Verse 5 says, "Cain became very angry and his countenance fell." This means his posture and facial expressions reflected the attitude of his heart. But God, in His marvelous grace, came to Cain to address and correct his attitude: "Then the Lord said to Cain, 'Why are you angry? And why has your countenance fallen?'" (4:6). God saw in Cain's countenance the attitude of his heart, and He made it crystal clear that Cain was not justified in his anger or jealousy. God then continued in verse 7: "If you do well, will not your countenance be lifted up? And if you do not do well, sin is crouching at the door; and its desire is for you, but you must master it."

If Cain would have done well, he would have received the counsel of God and would have made the right decision to change the attitude of his heart. But he didn't. Instead of listening to God, he rose up against his brother Abel in a fit of jealous rage and killed him. Notice that Cain's attitude came before his behavior. He first grew angry within his heart, and that became evident in his fallen countenance. The attitude then manifested itself in conduct, as he acted on his anger and killed his brother.

Where did Cain's wicked act come from? The same place all *our* foolish and wicked acts originate—from the heart, for out of it flow the springs of life, including our actions. This is why wise parents will do their best to check their children's bad attitudes before they flow into bad behaviors. Be alert to their attitudes, then verbally correct bad ones and verbally encourage good ones. In this way, we follow God's example: when Cain became angry, the Lord took notice and challenged him to take the initiative to change his attitude, which, He promised, would lift up his countenance. God said, in effect, "Cain, because sin is crouching at the door and since its desire is for you, you must master it." It was God's responsibility to challenge Cain's attitude and countenance, but it was Cain's responsibility to respond well to God by checking his anger and letting it go before it morphed into a sinful action that would result in awful consequences (see Genesis 4:10–16).

In the same way, it is a parental responsibility to catch our children's bad attitudes and challenge them to make needed corrections in heart and mind. The children are then responsible for making the needed corrections before they express that attitude in action. If the attitude doesn't change, corrective disciplinary consequences will be necessary.

Let me say a word about attitude detection. The ability to read your children comes from knowing them well. Attitudes in some children may be detected in their facial expressions and body language. For example, it is easy to know when my two grandsons are angry, frustrated, or disappointed; you can clearly see it on their faces. When they have angry faces, my question to them is the same as God's was to Cain: "Why are you angry?" And a follow-up, "Do you have good reason to be angry?"

There is certainly a place for righteous anger, but typically, the anger of children is rooted in their view of fairness and rightness, which is usually way off base. It may also be rooted in selfishness, jealousy, defiance, and a spirit of disobedience. Anger should be questioned and challenged before it manifests itself in unwise action. Parents (and sometimes grandparents) should verbally reprove them, perhaps sending them off to their beds until they have a change of heart. Parents who do so are doing their best to prevent their children from sinning in their actions.

But attitudes in some children are not easily detected. These children naturally suppress their feelings and attitudes; they often have a hard time defining for themselves what is troubling them. Lindsay was like that; she was quiet by temperament, and so it was often difficult to know what she was thinking and feeling. With these children, attitudes may not be recognized until they show up in actions. When a child like this misbehaves, a wise parent will examine the misbehavior, determine the attitude behind it, and then correct both—verbally and, if necessary, with a disciplinary consequence.

Let me quickly add a caveat here. Too many children have had traumatic experiences—whether abuse or molestation or some other terrible circumstance, like the loss of a parent—that have shaken them to their core. These circumstances have given the child every right and reason to be angry. In that case, the child needs an abundance of love, support, understanding, and help to deal well with the aftermath of that trauma. If the answer to the question "Why are you angry?" justifies the response "Well, you should be angry!" then, of course, instead of corrective discipline—which would only further damage the child—there must be intervention and, most likely, some form of biblical, spiritual counseling. Whatever help the child needs to deal with the trauma, a wise parent will get and give. And then, once the trauma is effectively and thoroughly addressed, wise parents will return to lovingly addressing and correcting attitudes and actions that are detrimental to the health of the child, the family, the church family, and society. It is important to deal with bad attitudes and behaviors. Simply excusing them is not appropriate. If help is needed, get it; if discipline is in order, administer it.

For children who have not been traumatized, look for the attitudes that are behind their actions or that show up in other ways (like on their faces) and lovingly, skillfully, and consistently correct them through verbal reproof and, when necessary, corrective discipline. Until your children are old enough and capable enough to watch over their own hearts with all diligence, you, their wise and godly parents, must watch over them, for from the heart flow the springs of life.

May God grant wise parents with teachable spirits the privilege to pass along that same spirit to their children, for controlled, godly attitudes of the heart will translate into controlled, godly behaviors that elicit blessings rather than consequences.

Parenting Principle 5
Wise Parents Teach Their Sons to Be Faithful to Others

My son, give attention to my wisdom, incline your ear to my understanding; that you may observe discretion and your lips may reserve knowledge.
PROVERBS 5:1–2

While it's important to teach both sons and daughters to be faithful to others, Proverbs 5 specifically shows a father teaching his son about the infinite value of faithfulness. As Christian men, we need to understand how critical it is to teach our sons what it means to be faithful to others. They must be taught faithfulness, especially to those of the opposite sex, beginning with their mom and their sisters, so they will be faithful to their future wives. The best teacher of faithfulness to women is a faithful father and husband who is a living example in the presence of his family.

Before we get to Solomon's instructions to his son concerning faithfulness to the opposite sex, however, I need to add a word concerning daughters. I will remain true to the text—of a father teaching his son—but what you will read in the following instructions to boys applies just as much to girls. Girls must be taught the same truths about fidelity that boys are because they, too, are susceptible to the lies of the world. In fact, boys and girls both are so bombarded with worldly lies and deception that, without proper training and intervention by godly parents, neither gender will know how to be morally faithful to God, to themselves, or to others. In today's world, even girls who grow up in Christian homes and attend Christ-centered churches are pressured and drawn into believing that faithfulness in relationships is foolishness. Our young people, male and female alike, are living in a culture that cheapens the necessity and value of pure hearts, pure thoughts, pure bodies, holy living, and holy relationships. For girls, especially, their valuation of their appearance and their bodies has been terribly warped by a corrupt and degrading worldview. Their worth (or perceived lack of worth) is communicated to them in a thousand ways; ways that are rooted in externals rather than internals.

Today's culture promotes and glorifies sexual activity outside of marriage. It deems sexual infidelity and smut (i.e., licentious talk, writings, and pictures) as morally permissible. Our children's world is steeped in sexual sin. As you work your way through this section, be sure to relate the biblical instruction to your daughters as well as to your sons.

In Proverbs 5:15–19, Solomon instructs his son—probably long before the son's marriage—regarding his future treatment of his future wife.

> Drink water from your own cistern and fresh water from your own well. Should your springs be dispersed abroad, streams of water in the streets? Let them be yours alone and not for strangers with you. Let your fountain be blessed, and rejoice in the wife of your youth. As a loving hind and a graceful doe, let her breasts satisfy you at all times; be exhilarated always with her love.

The term in verse 19 that is translated *exhilarated* literally means *intoxicated*; thus, it could read, "Be intoxicated always with your wife's love." Sexual relations, within the context of marriage alone, were created by God for pleasure. Therefore, the only place a man should become sexually intoxicated is with his wife. The father's bold, unashamed, and metaphorical instruction is to drink waters from his own cistern—a reference to the depths and wonders of his wife's love. "Should your [sexual] springs be dispersed abroad [with other women]?" The rhetorical question has but one answer: "Absolutely not!" It is a call for the son to exercise focused self-control and to look only to his own beloved wife for sexual satisfaction: "Listen, son, let her breasts satisfy you at all times."

This is a timeless lesson that a wise and godly father teaches to his impressionable young son: look ahead to your future wife, even now, as a one-woman man. And then, when you're married, authentically and exclusively live out that faithfulness before her and to her. Wise fathers and mothers teach that same truth to their daughters, to be a one-man woman for a lifetime.

In every generation, and certainly in the one in which we now live, it is of critical importance that godly parents train their sons and daughters well in sexual fidelity. The world that surrounds our children mocks at such training. Despite the severe spiritual, moral, physical, mental, and societal consequences of infidelity that are so visible to the spiritually minded, the world stupidly continues to sow according to their worldly, fleshly passions, and they reap a whirlwind of destruction. But wise parents are deliberately and constantly countercultural in their training, teaching their children the invaluable lesson of living well within the defined boundaries God has given us—for our good and His glory.

Deuteronomy 6:17–18 and 24–25 give us a beautiful example of God setting boundaries for the good of His people. He gave these instructions to His covenant people, Israel, through His servant, Moses:

> You should diligently keep the commandments of the Lord your God, and His testimonies and His statutes which He has commanded you. You shall do what is right and good in the sight of the Lord, that it may be well with you... The Lord commanded us to observe all these statutes, to fear the Lord our God for our

> good always... It will be righteousness for us if we are careful to observe all this commandment before the Lord our God.

Our children need to know in the depths of their hearts that God's commandments were given to protect them, to make them secure, and to give them real freedom within specific boundaries. I used to draw a large square on a piece of paper as an illustration for my children. I would say, "The lines of this square represent God's boundaries for us. The large space inside the square represents all the freedom we have within God's lines. His restrictions are not meant to ruin our fun; rather, they are meant to protect us and to keep us safe and secure and free. It's within the lines that we know true freedom and we experience real fun." Then I would point to the space outside the square and say, "However, if you insist on living outside of God's well-defined borderlines, you will become a slave to sin and will run into a holy parent—me. And when you are older and on your own, if you still insist on living outside of the boundaries, you will run into a holy God. There are always consequences for being a slave to sin—always." Wise fathers teach such things to their children, both generally and specifically.

In Proverbs 5:20–23, in the specific context of sexual relations, the wise father continues to instruct his son:

> For why should you, my son, be exhilarated with an adulteress and embrace the bosom of a foreigner? For the ways of a man are before the eyes of the Lord,

> and He watches all his paths. His own iniquities will capture the wicked, and he will be held with the cords of his sin. He will die for lack of instruction, and in the greatness of his folly he will go astray.

That's quite a graphic picture of what happens to a young person who does not heed the wisdom of God concerning natural sexual desires. The Lord sees; the Lord knows. Our ways are ever before His eyes; no one gets away with living beyond God's well-defined boundaries. The worst consequence of such living is becoming a slave to sin, being captured and held with its cords. Wise fathers teach this to their children, sons and daughters alike: "My child, sexual sins will capture you; they will hold you captive, and you will die." That's wise instruction meant for all our children, but directed specifically in Proverbs to our sons.

Why sons? Several reasons, I'm sure, but a prominent one is because many sons (and I think probably all), especially as they move into their preteen and teen years, struggle with sexual lust. They must be taught to control their natural desires. The Lord can help them in their struggle to live controlled lives, and so can a wise, sensitive, engaged father. Our sons must be taught that, in Christ, they are able to wait until marriage. Further, they must be taught that the exhilaration of sexual relations within the context of marriage is worth the wait. Teach them also that careful protection of that husband-wife relationship has both temporal pleasure and eternal reward in it.

Why fathers? Because they were once boys; therefore, they understand the struggle. Fathers must step up to help their sons understand what they can expect as they get older. They should provide instruction that is as straightforward as Solomon's was to his son. They provide their sons with the support, encouragement, and accountability that is necessary in the coming battle with sexual desires. Without fatherly support, encouragement, and intervention, I fear that most sons will fall into sexual sin of one sort or another. Some think that a boy's sexual experimentation is simply a rite of passage, but that's nothing but worldly deception. That "rite of passage" may lead to a dark place of sexual addiction and may take a lifetime to overcome.

How is it that so many Christian fathers are passive when it comes to their sons as they come of age and are exposed to feelings and teachings that can easily pull them into dark entrapment? Fathers, we must be wise. With our eyes wide open, we must be proactively engaged in our sons' lives. Their future and their future families depend on us being actively involved in training them in sexual purity.

Again, the same teaching applies to our daughters. If we expect them to be sexually pure, then we must be just as proactive and engaged in their lives. But why fathers? Because God's Word lays the responsibility as primary instructors to their sons and daughters squarely upon them: "Fathers, do not provoke your children to anger, but bring them up in the discipline and instruction of the Lord" (Ephesians 6:4). Fathers and mothers should work together as a team to raise up their children in the Lord. Fathers may delegate some duties to their wives, for they are much better equipped to handle some situations—thus, it is a team concept. But while *all* the responsibility shouldn't fall upon fathers, they should lead in this instruction, and they are most accountable for it.

Especially when it comes to training their sons to be faithful, pure, and self-controlled in the realm of male sexuality, wise fathers step in and step up. The burden is upon them to train their sons, and they gladly, quickly, and faithfully man up and take over. Further, in all other parental matters, the father should be in his proper place, as the ultimate responsibility of raising his children falls on him.

When Adam and Eve sinned in the garden of Eden, God came first to the man. Calling for Adam, He said, "Where are you?" (Genesis 3:9). They were both guilty, but Adam was first responsible. If we men fail to raise up our children in the Lord, I believe God will come first to us and ask, "Where are you? What have you done?" Wise fathers take their responsibility before God seriously and are most engaged.

And this is where a wise father begins. Long before his sons ever think about marriage, he teaches them to respect and honor all women, beginning with their sisters and mother. Honor and faithfulness begins in the home, for the home is the training ground that will prepare our sons to respect their wives. While we want our homes to be full of fun, laughter, playfulness, and toleration on many points, we must be intolerant on some points. We should demonstrate faithfulness to our children's mothers by sticking up for our wives. Our children should know early that if they are going to get respect, they need to first give respect. This loving intolerance will train them to be faithful husbands one day. God honors those boys who grow up into men who honor Him by honoring their marriage covenant and by respecting, protecting, and cherishing the wives of their youth.

This is what faithfulness looks like, and this is what the faithful man teaches his beloved son. Until his son can stand on his own, he will keep before the boy the reminder that the ways of a man are before the eyes of the Lord. "So, son," he will say, "follow me in faithfulness to God and to others as I follow God. One day, He will vindicate you for walking in integrity!"

A special word about fathers and daughters: Fathers, understand the necessity of protecting your daughters from sexual infidelity by establishing and maintaining a pure but intimate relationship with them throughout their childhood. More than anything else, girls need the security that comes from healthy father-daughter relationships. I wanted my relationship with my girls to be so secure and healthy that they would say to themselves, "I want to marry a man like Dad; a man who makes me feel safe, secure, and loved." In that kind of relationship, most young women will be protected from promiscuity; they will be delighted to save themselves for marriage and will find sexual satisfaction in marriage with a godly man who loves them the same way their godly father loved their mother and them.

A word to single mothers: Dear mothers, the above instructions may bring you pain, because you know that your children don't have a faithful father in their lives. But you need to know that you have resources in Christ. I am often amazed at how God has equipped some mothers to step into the role that has been vacated by a father. By the power of the Spirit and with the knowledge of the above information, you can stand in and meet your sons' and daughters' needs for instruction and accountability. As you depend on the Lord, you will be surprised at what you can do in training your children in sexual and relational fidelity, beginning with your own authoritative, healthy, and loving relationship with them.

Second, allow the church to be the church to you and your children. Within your church family may very well be the godly man or men that God would have you call upon to be father figures in the lives of your children. If your children have a godly grandfather or uncle, request and encourage that manly influence in their lives. If Satan plants an excuse in your mind like, "I don't want to bother them," blow through the excuse and courageously make your request. Since our children's faithfulness is at stake, we should "bother" people more. When God leads you to the right person or persons, it won't be a bother to them, but a privilege and a ministry. Know that you have resources and that you are not alone.

As I said at the beginning of this chapter, no parent begins parenting with experience. Every parent on the planet begins this most difficult job with absolutely no personal experience. Thankfully, this means that God doesn't expect us to be experienced in the beginning. However, He does expect us to have what's even more important than experience—teachable spirits, rooted in humility before Him. May our attitudes be, "Father, I come to parenting with nothing to offer but a humble heart and a teachable spirit." This must be our attitude before Lord; without it, how could we ever expect our children to have teachable spirits before Him and us, their parents?

Lord, we need You now! In the name of Jesus, we pray. Amen.

CHAPTER 3

Wise Parenting Principles 6-10: The Way of Wisdom

Proverbs 6–11

LET'S IMAGINE A PARENT OF adult children. This parent looks back on how he (or she) failed to raise his children well because he was distracted with other priorities that didn't include being fully engaged in their upbringing. When he was around and engaged, it was usually negative and even verbally abusive. Because of his failures, the dysfunctional family cycle continues. He now clearly sees his failures in his adult children and in their children. Imagine further that this parent would do almost anything to be able to get those lost opportunities back and to reverse the damage of abuse. He desperately wants to see healthiness in his family, but the desire has come very late. Almost assuredly, it's too late.

"What is more valuable than the eternal souls of my children?"

In parenting, the earlier that Christian parents ask and answer this question, the better. Godly parents will answer, "Nothing! Nothing on earth is more precious or important!" They not only make this declaration, but all their actions toward their children back it up. They know that they have only one shot at seeing the souls of their children saved and then sanctified in Christ. By no means do wise parents neglect their ministry to the souls of their children.

According to the Bible, there are only two ways in life: one that leads to eternal destruction for all who do not obey the gospel of our Lord Jesus Christ, and the other that leads to glory when Jesus comes to be glorified in all who have believed (see 2 Thessalonians 1:6–10). Because there are only two ways in life, there are only two types of parents: foolish parents who do not instruct their children to obey the gospel, and wise parents who do. For those who are fully committed to Christ, only the way of wisdom is acceptable.

You are reading this book because you have a great, God-given desire to be a wise parent. You desire to do all within your power to set your children on the way that leads to salvation and glory, in line with the Spirit-inspired book of Proverbs, so that it will not be too late. In the following wise parenting principles, take careful note of how proactive wise parents are. They are never passive in their parenting; they do not spend the energy of their lives on anything that would rob them of opportunities to spend their time and energy on the best things. Rather, they invest heavily in their homes because they are ever aware that there is nothing on earth more valuable than the souls of their children. Wise parents do everything within their God-given power to set their little ones on the path that leads to a glorious life in Jesus Christ.

Parenting Principle 6
Wise Parents Teach Their Children the Blessings of Obedience

My son, observe the commandment of your father and do not forsake the teaching of your mother; bind them continually on your heart; tie them around your neck. When you walk about, they will guide you; when you sleep, they will watch over you; and when you awake, they will talk to you. For the commandment is a lamp and the teaching is light; and reproofs for discipline are the way of life to keep you from the evil woman, from the smooth tongue of the adulteress. Do not desire her beauty in your heart, nor let her capture you with her eyelids. For on account of a harlot one is reduced to a loaf of bread, and an adulteress hunts for the precious life. Can a man take fire in his bosom and his clothes not be burned? Or can a man walk on hot coals and his feet not be scorched? So is the one who goes in to his neighbor's wife; whoever touches her will not go unpunished.

Proverbs 6:20–29

Godly parents who carefully direct their children according to the Word of God are the paramount influence preventing them from falling into immorality. Both parents are responsible to teach or even command their children to walk in the way that leads to a moral life of blessing from God. Such teaching will lead them away from the immoral road that leads to destruction.

Wise parents understand their God-given authority over and responsibility to their children; consequently, they are not afraid of their children. They fear only that if they don't train them well, they will undoubtedly lose those children to their greatest enemies—the world, the flesh, and the devil. In other words, wise parents fear the forfeiture of their children's eternal souls. So, fearful of that happening but utterly fearless of anything else, they lovingly and confidently command their children in Christ.

Further, wise children who submit to parental commandments and implant the Word in their hearts will reap the following blessings of obedience:

- ***Implanted wisdom will guide them in their daily walk through life.*** The commands and instructions of the Lord (i.e., the wisdom of God), laid out by wise parents, will give obedient children clear guidance and direction as they walk through life.
- ***Implanted wisdom will watch over them as they sleep.*** Wisdom will not only give our children direction; it will give them protection. For example, when they

know they are protected by living in God's secure and blessed way, they can sleep at night. They don't have to live in fear, always worrying or looking over their shoulders.

- ***Implanted wisdom will talk to them when they awake.*** When wise instruction is needed during daily activities, the implanted wisdom of God's Word will come to mind and give them the ability to make wise decisions.

The commands of a godly father are a lamp, and the teaching of a wise mother is a light. With them, our well-trained, self-disciplined, wise children will not fall into the immorality that leads to spiritual and moral decadence and death. Instead, the wisdom of God's Word will give them direction, protection, and instruction that will effectively keep them on the right path—the way of wisdom.

On the other hand, if we do not instruct our children in the way of wisdom—or if they disregard our teaching—they will learn the hard way that there are awful consequences in store for them. For example, we teach our children that if they play with fire, they will get burned (Proverbs 6:27–28). If they reject our teaching, they won't have the wisdom of God bound up in their hearts to guide them in the way of life, to protect them from evil, and to instruct them in making wise decisions along the way. They will not possess the lamp of their father's wisdom or the light of their mother's instruction to illuminate the road ahead of them. In time, they will plunge into the darkness of sin, and many will fall over the precipice into an immoral lifestyle.

How do wise parents go about the business of commanding and instructing their children in wisdom? Where do we start? Go back to the foundational Old Testament teaching on raising children in the Lord. Deuteronomy 6:5–9 begins by commanding parents to love the Lord their God with all their heart, soul, and might. If parents are wise, their love for God will compel them to take His Word to heart. When God's Word is the central point of their hearts, they will diligently teach it to their children in both formal and informal settings. The formal setting refers to deliberate, regular teaching times with your children—what we call family devotions. The informal times are when you take careful advantage of the daily teachable moments God provides to impress wisdom on the hearts of your children; use those moments to strongly establish your children on the way.

Wise parents diligently teach their children the blessings of obedience and the consequences of forsaking God's way—if they forsake God's way, they can count on getting burned. But if they stay on God's way through careful obedience, the light of God's Word will brightly show them the way to temporal and eternal blessings.

How valuable are the souls of our children? Infinitely valuable! May our words and our actions prove it.

Parenting Principle 7
Wise Parents Teach Their Children That Wisdom Is Straightforward

Does not wisdom call, and understanding lift up her voice? On top of the heights beside the way, where the paths meet, she takes her stand; beside the gates, at the opening to the city, at the entrance of the doors, she cries out: "To you, O men, I call, and my voice is to the sons of men. O naive ones, understand prudence; and, O fools, understand wisdom. Listen, for I will speak noble things; and the opening of my lips will reveal right things. For my mouth will utter truth; and wickedness is an abomination to my lips. All the utterances of my mouth are in righteousness; there is nothing crooked or perverted in them. They are all straightforward to him who understands, and right to those who find knowledge."

Proverbs 8:1–9

Salvation is of God. It is His free gift that comes to us by grace alone, through faith in Jesus Christ (see Ephesians 2:8–9). Jesus Himself tells us, "No one can come to Me unless the Father who sent Me draws him; and I will raise him up on the last day" (John 6:44; see also 6:65). So, salvation is of God. It is as if the wisdom of the Father (personified here as a woman) called us, wooed us, and persuaded us, and by His grace, we listened and came to His Son for salvation. Wisdom took her stand on the top of the heights, so to speak; she stood by the city gates and cried out. We listened to wisdom and, for the first time in our lives, we understood and we were saved. By sheer grace, we were set on the way of wisdom.

Those who are saved by grace love the wisdom of God. To us, she is a most virtuous woman; her many virtues are wondrous to behold. She speaks nobly and reveals right things. Her mouth utters nothing but truth, and her utterances are wholly righteous—there is nothing crooked or perverted in what she says. Her words are straightforward to those who have understanding and right to those who have found knowledge. All that is true, noble, pure, and excellent are summed up in her. She is a most beautiful and virtuous woman!

Jesus Christ called Himself "the way" (John 14:6). The first Christians were referred to as those who belonged to "the Way" (Acts 9:2). All those who walk in wisdom walk in the way. The way of Christ is straightforward—true and straight. This makes it the simplified life. Conversely, the way of the world is crooked—perverted, depraved, corrupted, and warped by sin. It is the complicated life.

I was in Brazil a few years ago to speak at an evangelistic conference for college-age youths. My primary host was a young married couple. The woman, who spoke very good English, was the pastor's daughter of the church where I preached. I asked her lots of questions about the country and the culture, and her responses often began with the phrase "It's complicated." Throughout the week, I heard that line from her over and over: "It's complicated."

A missionary friend of mine had told me that the dominant religion of Brazil is not just Catholicism, but "Catholicism on steroids." Theirs is a faith that is heavily injected with the world and is, for the most part, a corrupt and crooked way.

I came away from that visit reminded of just how complicated sin makes life. People who are injected with heavy doses of the world may be very religious but know nothing but corruption and complication. The webs of sin entangle, ensnare, and enslave. Everything in the wayward life of the worldly is crooked and, therefore, complicated.

On the other hand, wise people who have found freedom in Christ find simplicity in life. Their way is straightforward and far less complicated by sin. It is life in Christ, who indeed is "the way, and the truth, and the life" (John 14:6). So, of course, wise parents want to pass wisdom along to their children. They want to spare them from getting caught in the crooked and complicated life of worldliness; instead, they want their children to experience the straightforward and simplistic virtues of the way of wisdom.

The Lord gave me a ministry to inmates in two Ohio prisons that lasted for several years. I became close with James Fobel, who was released in 2013 from Richland Correctional Institute (RCI) in Mansfield, Ohio. God has used the Fellowship of Christian Athletes to bring remarkable spiritual reformation to a large number of inmates at that institution. I would go so far as to say that RCI has experienced a spiritual revival in its recent past, and the fruit in the godly men who reside there is still obvious. James, a formerly wayward, worldly, crooked felon, was totally redeemed and rapidly and continually grew in his faith in Jesus. He is now free in Cleveland, but because of his own spiritual reformation, even while he was in prison, he was a free man in Christ.

A few weeks after his release, he wrote me a letter saying, "I had to go with my dad down to my brother's house; his parole officer was there with four cops, wanting him for failing to report and go to treatment programs. It is hard to watch him self-destruct like he's doing. I thank the Lord for showing me the truth, freeing me from the bondage of sin, and making me a slave of righteousness. Praise Jesus!" When I read those words, I thought, "Wow, what a contrast between brothers!" And yet James was, at one time, just as foolish and enslaved to sin as his brother. Now he has a good job, is involved in a solid church, and he evangelizes at every opportunity. What a contrast—one man's life is ever more crooked and complicated by sin; the other man's life is straightforward, simple, and powerful.

What wise parents desperately want for their children, and what they hotly pursue, are lives that walk straight forward in and by wisdom and are, therefore, much less complicated. Life in this fallen world is hard, but it doesn't have to be crooked or complicated by the wayward world of sin.

Wise parents teach their children that the wisdom of God is the straight way in Christ that leads to a life well lived.

Let us pray for our children our Lord's high priestly prayer for us, recorded in John 17:15–17:

> I do not ask You, Father, to take them out of the world, but to keep them from the evil one. They are not of the

> world, even as I am not of the world. Sanctify them [set them apart] in the truth; Your word is truth.

Jesus is the truth. And truth is the high virtue of wisdom. Seek this with all that is within you, for yourself and for your children. My friend, James Fobel, wasn't raised in a godly home. Instead, he learned the hard way—but he did learn. May our children learn now, in our homes, that the way of wisdom should be their goal.

Parenting Principle 8
Wise Parents Are Aware That Children Are Easily Enticed by Immorality

The woman of folly is boisterous; she is naive and knows nothing. She sits at the doorway of her house, on a seat by the high places of the city, calling to those who pass by, who are making their paths straight: "Whoever is naive, let him turn in here," and to him who lacks understanding she says, "Stolen water is sweet; and bread eaten in secret is pleasant." But he does not know that the dead are there, that her guests are in the depths of Sheol.

PROVERBS 9:13–18

Wise parents, obviously, are not naive. They do not wear blinders or think for a moment that their children could never fall into the world's trap of sexual immorality. They understand the powerful draw of the sinful, sexual world. They know that their sons and daughters will inevitably be exposed to it. They know that even moral young men and women who are committed to making their paths straight can give in to the siren call of immorality.

Temptations to become immoral are constant and can chip away at the determination of even the most straightforward-walking children. "Turn in here!" is the persistent sensual call of sexual enticement. In today's world, satanic snares of enticement and introduction into sexual immorality exist at nearly every turn in the way of life. More often than not, the introduction into sexual immorality begins with pornography.

Josh and Dottie McDowell, in their excellent book, *Straight Talk with Your Kids about Sex* (Harvest House, 2012), say that parents need to realize that it is no longer a matter of *if* their children will view pornography; it is a matter of *when*. Even the most sheltered children will be exposed to pornography at some level at some time.

Boys are vulnerable to porn because they are sexually aroused by sight. They are wired to be easily stimulated sexually by looking at pornography. Even what is classified as soft pornography can be arousing to the male's sense of sight, and pornographic addictions are formed rather quickly. But we must also understand that pornography is just as enticing and addictive for girls. Their introduction often comes through erotic literature, artwork, music, photography, and videos that are sexually stimulating and that create curiosity. Today's television and YouTube videos make female sexuality exciting, seemingly harmless, and fun. Even as early as middle school, boyfriends introduce girls to visual pornography on their phones, and girls feel obligated to sext them back in order to keep them because, after all, if you don't have a boyfriend, you're defective. Or so says the world.

A godly woman who has struggled with an addiction to pornography informed me that it is a misconception to believe that "girls don't like that stuff." Because it's commonly believed by most to be a "boy's sin," it is more difficult for women and girls to admit it is a stronghold issue with which they struggle. If they can't admit it, they can't confess it; if they can't confess it, they can't get the counseling and accountability necessary to overcome it. It frustrates this woman and others like her when they read a discussion on pornography that completely excludes and excuses girls from the issue. She told me, "As someone who has experienced it myself, I have to say that it is naive to continue this stance. Knowing that it is still common lore in the Christian world makes us who are caught in the trap feel more alone, more deviant, and more guilty because we're *girls* and this isn't a 'girl's sin.'"

Parents, beware: pornography is a snare that the devil and the world have successfully set for both boys and girls. Consequently, every Christian parent should be highly concerned about the easy accessibility to sexual perversion in today's world. The McDowells write,

> How concerned would you be if a stranger was slipping into your child's bedroom every day? What if the

> intruder was systematically teaching your child a distorted and perverted concept of sex? And what if this "sex education" your child was receiving led them down a path of immoral sex? You would no doubt be frightened and infuriated that the mind and heart of your child was being violated by this menacing intruder. (Ibid., 9.)

They go on to say that "studies have shown that the number one fear among Christian parents…is that a secular worldview and sexual immorality will somehow capture the hearts and minds of their kids." Many of these parents address their fears by enrolling their children in Christian schools or by keeping them home and schooling them themselves. They also look for churches that specifically offer a healthy spiritual community for children. But is this enough?

> The hope of these parents has been to counteract the negative influences of a destructive culture in the lives of their children. However, these positives steps have actually caused many parents…to drop their guard. It's natural to assume that kids are largely insulated from the influences of a corrupt culture if they live in a Christian home, are involved in a good church, are getting a solid Christian education, and are participating in monitored activities. (Ibid., 10.)

I applaud parents who take such steps to shelter their children as best as they can for as long as they can. However, we need to understand that sheltering is not enough. The McDowells are right: it is no longer a matter of *if* they will be exposed to sexual immorality—particularly pornography. It is *when.*

> Today, we have, by and large, lost control of the controls. That is because a perverted morality is just one click away from our children. With just one keystroke on a smartphone, iPad, or laptop, your child can open up some of the worst pornography and sexually graphic content you can imagine. … As a concerned parent, you no doubt warn your children and teens to stay away from "sex sites." As a responsible and proactive parent, you may even install Internet filtering and monitoring software on your computers, as you should. Yet what happens when your children visit friends and turn on their cell phones? Do the parents of their friends have sexually explicit material blocked from all of their electronic devices? The problem is that sexual oriented and perverted material through cyberspace is everywhere, and it is difficult to avoid, even when you try to block it. (Ibid., 13–14.)

The McDowells provide statistics about peer-to-peer downloads and other forms of easy access to pornography that are downright frightening. I highly recommend their book as a valuable resource. It lays out practical strategies for concerned parents to prepare their children to face the secular worldview, both by establishing boundaries (chapter 3) and building strong relationships with them (chapter 4).

Though written long ago, the book of Proverbs is startlingly current. In fact, Proverbs 13 may be more contemporary now than when it was first written! The woman of sexual folly is more boisterous in our American culture today than in any other period in the history of our nation. Those who turn in to her are terribly naive, not knowing that death awaits her and them. Both boys and girls, left to themselves, are clueless about the awful dangers and consequences of sexual sins.

There are several key elements to protecting our children, boys and girls alike.

1. Shelter Them as Best You Can for as Long as You Can

Personally, I am a strong advocate of sheltering. I prefer to train our children in righteousness and holiness for as long as possible in a sheltered, protective environment. Of course, sheltering alone is not enough; training in righteousness while sheltering is the key. Too many parents think if they just keep their children sheltered from the world, they'll be okay. That leaves them wide open at first exposure, though, because they will have no idea what to do with what they've just seen. So be sure to train while sheltering. Then, when they are eventually and inevitably exposed to the secular worldview of sexual immorality, they will be prepared to turn away from it. My wife and I sheltered our daughters as best we could for as long as we could, and we don't believe they missed out on anything—at least, not on anything good. We are happy to say that they *did* miss out on exposure to secular, sexual trash early in life. Further, a most pleasant reality to us is that our thirty-something daughter, Kerry, is not sorry for her sheltered life. She is, of course, aware of the world around her now, but she was much more prepared to handle that awareness than she would have been if she'd been exposed to it early in life. Start them on the way of wisdom earlier and keep them there, for there's life in the way.

2. Teach Them the Difference between Wisdom and Foolishness

In a sheltered family relationship, parents earn their children's respect for their God-given authority. Further, children who respect their parents and their authority will listen to their counsel. Included in that counsel must be a clear contrast from the Word between what's foolish, dangerous, harmful, and even deadly, and what's wise, safe, healthy, and life-giving. Therefore, it is important to school our children in the wisdom literature of God's Word—including Proverbs—that clearly contrasts the foolish with the wise. For example, Proverbs 12:15 makes this contrast: "The way of a fool is right in his own eyes, but a wise man is he who listens to counsel." The goal of this teaching is to raise children who, when they face that inevitable opportunity to be foolish, will be so enamored with and committed to the way of wisdom—and so aware of the awful pitfalls of foolishness—that they will make the right call.

3. Demonstrate to Them That It's All about Relationships

Healthy, protective, and safe relationships between husband and wife and between parents and children must be deliberately and carefully cultivated with the Lord in the center. Powerful family relationships do not just happen. They are formed when parents not only *talk* to their children but also *listen* to their hearts. Children who are listened to learn to trust their wise parents. They know they can share their innermost thoughts and feelings without being scorned or squashed or laughed at. Their thoughts are welcomed and their emotions are protected. In these homes, conversations freely take place. Children are encouraged to confide in their parents, trusting them to help them navigate through treacherous moral waters and dangerous sexual thoughts and emotions. Nothing protects the hearts, minds, and emotions of children better than God, through the wise and loving care of godly parents.

With these elements in place, we can reasonably hope for successful parent/child relationships. Parents and children will be free to talk and listen to one another. Parents will counsel, encourage, and support their children; they will pray for and with their children; they will listen and hear their concerns. Their children, in turn, will listen to their wise parental counsel. In this relationship, when the children are exposed to a secular worldview of sexual morality or are tempted to turn aside or are somehow exposed to pornography, they know they can turn to their loving and wise parents who will help them keep their paths straight.

What, specifically, are mothers to do? Mothers should talk to their daughters about sexual dangers and concerns from their personal experience. They should teach their girls to dress modestly to avoid attracting unwanted attention from the opposite sex. It's amazing how naive girls and young ladies are today. They need to know that, for their male counterparts, sight excites. Wise mothers, instruct your girls that in this world of overexposure, modesty is the best policy.

Also, mothers should talk to their sons about protecting the purity of girls and about how godly girls and women highly esteem godly boys and men who are more concerned about protecting the opposite sex than they are about exploiting them or using them for temporary sexual pleasures that may bring a lifetime of pain and regret. They teach their sons what a healthy, holy worldview of sexual morality looks like.

Further, mothers need to talk to their daughters about protecting themselves from falling into sexual sin. In the world in which we now live, it is just as easy for girls to believe the worldly lies about sexuality and to fall headlong into immoral temptations. Our daughters need to understand that soft pornography and initial experimentation are the gateways to an immoral vortex. We must teach them that what is the world's norm is also deadly. Mothers and fathers, please understand that sexual immorality is not a boy's sin—it is a human sin, and girls are just as susceptible as boys.

What, specifically, are fathers to do? Fathers should teach their sons how to handle the specific challenges that they will face, or are facing, as males. Boys need to hear from their fathers how easy it is to get caught in the snare of sexual immorality. Fathers need to train them in the power of Christ to resist temptation. Tell your sons they don't *have* to look at a girl lustfully just because they're "wired that way." Too many times, this becomes an easy out—an excuse for inappropriate thinking and behavior. Yes, a girl should be modest, but even if she isn't, that doesn't give boys the right to lust for her. Too often, girls are blamed for not protecting guys with their attire. However, wise fathers know better and teach their sons that if they look at a girl lustfully—no matter how she's dressed—it's not the girl's fault, but theirs. Fathers, be sure to model this behavior in how you respond to women because your sons will learn from your actions just as much (or more) than they do from your words. No doubt, *every boy* will struggle with sexual temptation and sin. But, fathers, know that it may be *every girl's* struggle as well. Prepare your children to be victorious in the battle to come.

Fathers should also talk to their daughters about boys and men. Reinforce the teachings of their mothers about the dangers of showing the opposite sex too much skin; teach them to protect themselves through modest dress and behavior. Further, fathers should establish such a manly, fatherly, godly security in their daughters' lives that they won't feel the need or desire to attract sexual attention from the opposite sex or to fall into sensual and/or sexual immorality themselves. When they come of age, they will look for the same kind of godly manliness in the man they will one day marry.

What are fathers and mothers to do together? Together, they should help both their sons and daughters commit to memory, and to life, the truth given in 1 Corinthians 10:13:

> No temptation has overtaken you but such as is common to man [and woman]; and God is faithful, who will not allow you to be tempted beyond what you are able, but with the temptation will provide the way of escape also, so that you will be able to endure it.

Further, they must teach their children that "the way of escape," more often than not, is to be like Joseph of old who, when latched onto by Potiphar's wife and enticed to have sexual relations with her, left his cloak behind in her hand and ran out of the house. (See Genesis 39:1–18.) In 2 Timothy 2:22, Paul gave this same counsel to Timothy, his son in the faith:

Now flee from youthful lusts and pursue righteousness, faith, love, and peace, with those who call on the Lord from a pure heart.

Children need to hear these messages from their parents. The power of closeness and openness between parents and children and the freedom and fearlessness of open and honest conversation within the home cannot be measured. With God's grace and power, along with our determination in Christ, we can protect our children from turning away into the paths that lead to moral depravity and spiritual death.

Parents, as we live in utter dependence upon God, may He protect our children from turning away, and may He empower us to be His primary instruments of righteousness in His protection system. May it be so in Jesus's awesome name. Amen.

Parenting Principle 9
Wise Parents Pass On to Their Children the Gift of Integrity

He who walks in integrity walks securely,
but he who perverts his ways will be found out.
Proverbs 10:9

A person who walks in integrity lives a life that is honest, honorable, transparent, faithful, loyal, and righteous in the sight of God and people. Such a person is transparently honest in all facets of life: spiritual, personal, private, interpersonal, professional, and at home. This is a life well lived, for he who walks in integrity walks securely before God and others.

To "walk securely" means to walk through life without fear of being discovered or found out. It doesn't mean that the person doesn't have some shameful things in his past. It does, however, mean that he no longer has anything to hide because of personal repentance, forgiveness from God, forgiveness from others when necessary, and because of his present and ongoing condition of transparent honesty.

On the other hand, a person who lacks integrity and perverts his way but still desires to be seen as an honest person does not walk securely in life. He (or she) lives a secretly corrupt and crooked life, with much to fear. He must work to distort his image in order to make himself look better than he truly is. Proverbs promises that this person will be found out. It's a biblical truth that's consistent with other passages, such as Numbers 32:23: "Behold, you have sinned against the Lord, and be sure your sin will find you out."

Proverbs continues on the line of integrity. Verses 1 and 3 of Proverbs 11 say,

> A false balance is an abomination to the Lord, but a just weight is His delight. ... The integrity of the upright will guide them, but the crookedness of the treacherous will destroy them.

A person of integrity does not cheat in life to get ahead; he doesn't rig the scale to rob the unsuspecting. A man or woman of integrity would rather please the Lord than pad his or her own pockets. Further, his or her driving passion to please the Lord is stronger than all other passions; it guards him from dishonesty, dishonest gain, and dishonor.

Back in my Bible college days, as a twenty-something family man with a wife and two young daughters, I was encouraged by the example of others to claim for myself a life verse, a verse that would give me personal definition and direction in my walk with God. I chose 2 Corinthians 5:9, and to this day I still consider it to be my life verse:

> Therefore we also have as our ambition, whether at home [in the body] or absent [from the body and home with the Lord], to be pleasing to Him.

Is it right to be ambitious? Yes, absolutely—if our ambitions are centered on Jesus Christ's glory and good pleasure! Certainly, to be pleasing to God, it is essential to walk in integrity, for a just weight is His delight. Personally, I love living in the light of the truth that, when I walk in my integrity, God is delighted both with my person as His beloved child (who I am) and with my practice (what I do).

Our lives are built upon the choices we make daily. We must make them wisely. Sometimes we face big decisions, but far more often, we make many little choices throughout each day. Thus, in big ways and small, we constantly choose whether we will walk faithfully before the Lord or turn down a crooked road, where we will lie or cheat for personal but temporal profit and then cover our tracks. For a person of integrity, the choice is easy: the integrity of the upright will guide them in every choice they are faced with throughout their lives.

Wise parents love integrity with all that is within them, and their parental ambition is to pass that along to their children. To that end, they train their children to walk in integrity before the Lord, before their family, before their friends, before the church, and before the world.

Here's how wise parents pass integrity along to their children.

1. They Teach Integrity by the Lives They Live before Their Children

They work hard to become known as men and women of integrity—people who can be trusted by God and others. Our children need models of personal, transparent honesty and truth lived out before them in daily life. The best and most influential models are parents who can honestly say, "Children, follow me, for I have walked before God and you in integrity." It must be modeled!

2. They Teach Integrity through Biblical Instruction

They take their children to verses like Proverbs 10:9 and 11:1–3 to teach them precepts from God's Word about the absolute necessity of living transparent and honest lives to the delight of the Lord and of the righteous. They also take them to the many scriptural narratives that give both good and bad examples of integrity. Good examples include Joseph, Job, Ruth, Esther, David (whose examples were both good and bad at different stages in his life), Barnabas, and Paul. Bad examples include Jacob, Saul, Judas, Ananias, Sapphira, and Demas.

Of course, the best example of a life of integrity is found in the Lord Jesus Himself, even as a child. The last word in the Bible about Jesus's childhood tells us that the twelve-year-old Christ "continued in subjection to [his parents]. … And Jesus kept increasing in wisdom and stature, and in favor with

God and men" (Luke 2:51–52). Wise parents begin with this statement, then take their children further into the narratives where Jesus clearly continues to walk in His integrity. They train their children to be Christlike by teaching them to follow His example. In this way, they build within them, at an early age, a biblical model of integrity.

3. They Pass Integrity to Their Children through Corrective Discipline

When a child steps off the path of integrity by lying, cheating, or selfishly trampling on others in order to achieve what he or she perceives to be personal gain, his or her wise parents will lovingly but effectively realign the course of the child through corrective discipline. One of the rules in our home was honesty; we did not tolerate lying. If one of our children got caught in a lie, we extended very little grace. We wanted to establish early that it doesn't ever pay to lie, but it always pays to be honest and to walk in one's integrity, even if it hurts.

All children are prone to lie, cheat, or even steal to get what they want or think they need. It is in their nature to selfishly seek their own desires without much concern for others. In fact, everything in our fallen world strongly promotes and encourages this self-seeking attitude. The world is all about individuals winning, succeeding, and doing just about anything to accomplish personal, self-centered goals. Our children get dishonesty naturally, both from within and from the world around them. Honesty, on the other hand, comes supernaturally from God and from godly parents and churches.

Making that transfer from dishonesty to honesty is a tough passage. Wise parents understand what they are up against in passing along integrity to their children. They also understand what their children are up against in receiving this great and gracious gift. They begin early to establish within their children lives that are built on integrity, because they know that without integrity, there is no trust; without trust, there is no trustworthiness; without trustworthiness, there is no loyalty; and without loyalty, there is no pleasing God and other people.

I have found it helpful throughout my parenting career to keep my eyes on the ultimate goal for my children: that the way they live will bring glory to God, not only in their lives, but in their deaths, as well. I have practiced looking down the road to their eventual homegoing to be with the Lord. I asked myself, "When they die, will they be ready? Am I doing everything within my God-given ability to prepare them to be ready?" A life of integrity is one that is ready to be lived well for the glory of God on Earth. It is also a life that is equally ready to pass from this life to life indeed—in His glorious presence for His everlasting glory. That is what I desired and aimed at for my children, and it is what every other wise parent aims at for their children.

Imagine: Your child is standing before the Lord in all of His glory, and He says to him or her, "My child, I know it wasn't always easy. There were many times in your life where you could have lied, cheated, and deceived. But by depending upon My grace, you have faithfully walked in your integrity.

Welcome to your reward!" And I say, what a way to go! Isn't this what we want for our children?

Wise parents begin early and teach integrity often because their children's lives and eternity depend on it. For God's sake and theirs, may it be so!

Parenting Principle 10
Wise Parents Teach Their Daughters That Real Beauty Is Inward

As a ring of gold in a swine's snout so is a beautiful woman who lacks discretion.
PROVERBS 11:22

Posed as a rhetorical question, does a gold snout ring make a pig beautiful? No. Neither does physical beauty make a woman who lacks good and godly sense beautiful! Sadly, in God's sight and in the eyes of the righteous, her beauty is merely ornamental. Let me hasten to say that there's nothing wrong with ladies wanting to look their best. The gift of physical beauty (or curse, depending on how it is handled by the person who has it) is certainly not sinful; in fact, outward beauty is even to be admired.

For example, in the Song of Solomon, the bridegroom sings long and loud about the striking physical features of his beloved bride. Physical beauty is a marvelous thing to behold—unless it is worn by a woman with no moral discretion. Her beauty is grotesquely marred by her sinful, impure, unworthy lack of biblical, spiritual morality.

The Bible teaches that true beauty is of the heart and that the inward beauty of a godly woman surpasses all other womanly beauties. For example, the apostle Peter writes under the inspiration of the Holy Spirit to Christian women, saying, "Your adornment must not be merely external...but let it be the hidden person of the heart, with the imperishable quality of a gentle and quiet spirit, which is precious in the sight of God" (1 Peter 3:3–4). The Bible is crystal clear: real beauty is of the heart!

But what a difficult principle this is to teach our daughters in a wicked world that screams at them from every direction that beauty is only a thing of the surface. Really? It's only skin deep? How shallow! But nonetheless, those the world considers most beautiful are those who have nothing but outward beauty. There is no consideration of the character of the heart. Yet the wisdom of Proverbs teaches us that when we see an absence of character and a total lack of sense and sensibility in the so-called beautiful people of the world, we are to understand that their physical beauty is like a ring of gold in a swine's snout. Outward beauty doesn't nullify the ugliness within, and it in no way tips the scale to qualify a person as truly beautiful. It only means that the world is using the wrong scale to measure out real beauty. But someday, God will set the record straight.

Both wise mothers and wise fathers have the power to teach their daughters the truth about beauty.

1. Wise Mothers

Teach your daughters the difference between surface beauty and the real beauty of the heart. Teach this foundational truth to every girl—to those particularly beautiful creatures, to those who do not quite measure up to our worldly culture's standard of beauty, and to all the other girls in between. A pretty girl needs to hear from her wise mother that her good looks do not define her true beauty, and a not-so-pretty girl needs to hear from her mother that real beauty is found within.

When we carefully read through the book of Ruth, we are given the impression that Ruth was a physically attractive young Moabite woman. When Boaz saw her gleaning barley in his fields, he was immediately drawn to her. No doubt, she was a lovely young lady. However, the wondrously beautiful portrait that is painted of her in the narrative displays the outstanding features of her inner character. In the third chapter, after Ruth proposed to an older and probably less attractive Boaz, he said to her, "Now, my daughter, do not fear. I will do for you whatever you ask, for all my people...know that you are a woman of excellence" (Ruth 3:11). And in the final verses of the book, the women of the city say to Naomi, who lost her husband and two sons in Moab but who was given a grandson by Ruth and Boaz, "Your daughter-in-law, who loves you...is better to you than seven sons" (4:15). How physically beautiful was she? We cannot know, and it doesn't really matter; what we do know and what eternally matters is that she was one of the most truly beautiful women who have graced this planet.

Mothers, your daughters need to know from you that women like Ruth—women who love the Lord with all their hearts and who are adorned from within with imperishable qualities like spiritual and moral excellence—are the truly beautiful women in the world. Model for your daughters what real beauty looks like: the inner Christlike qualities of the heart that are precious in the sight of God. Teach them that outward beauty is fleeting, but beauty within is eternal!

2. Wise Fathers

Fathers, you are instrumental in teaching your daughters that real beauty is inward. Teach them that the Christlike qualities of the heart are not only precious in God's sight, but they are also precious in the sight of their daddy, and someday, they will be precious in the sight of godly young men. This teaching comes through careful instruction and from the way you, as a godly father, treat your daughters. Your unconditional love for them, your deep respect for them as females, and all the quality time you spend with them in the context of a pure and intimate father-daughter relationship will create within them the sense of their real value and beauty.

There is nothing quite as powerful as the security of a father's love. Whether it's our heavenly Father's love or the earthly, godly love of a father, there's nothing quite as secure in a little girl's (or a little guy's) life. I learned this formula from a pastor friend a long time ago:

Time + Attention + God = Love

I will speak of this formula again, but for now let me only say that this kind of love is absolutely securing. It creates a sense of value within a child that frees her to grow in inward beauty in the Lord Jesus Christ.

My daughters grew up as my sweeties. I called them such names as *sweetheart*, *sweetie*, *honey*, and *babe*. They were (and still are) infinitely precious and beautiful to me, and I treated them that way. I watched what that kind of intimate, tender, and true love accomplished in the hearts of those two girls—they grew up to become two beautiful women from the inside out. As a counseling pastor, however, I have seen women who, as little girls, were devastated from the inside out by neglectful, harsh, and unloving treatment consistently brought upon them by their unloving fathers.

In October 2006, two years and two months after Lindsay and Jason were murdered, *Our Daily Bread*, a daily devotional published by Radio Bible Class, ran a lesson sharing how we, Jason's and Lindsay's parents, were handling our great losses and how God was bringing much good to the lives of others out of our tragedy. We could not have known that in South America, a twenty-two-year-old Brazilian woman would pick up a copy of that devotional—translated into her native Portuguese—and proceed to read about us. That reading would change her life, and ours. A void in her searching heart compelled her to Google our names, and it wasn't long before we (both the Cutshalls and the Allens) connected with her via e-mail. From that point, Kathy and I developed a long and lasting relationship with this beautiful young lady. Her name is Noadia. In time, Noadia began calling us Mom and Dad—*Mamãe* and *Papai* in Portuguese.

We have walked with her since 2006 and have been used by God to facilitate much healing within her heart and mind. She is a lifelong church woman, and her mother was a beautiful, committed Christian lady. However, an early molestation by a seminary student who was interning in her church did a number on Noadia's sensitive soul. Further, her father wasn't the encouraging and edifying type; he had a propensity for tearing down the family rather than building it up. Consequently, while she wanted to believe that she was valuable and precious to God and to His people, she found it a difficult concept to accept. We told her thousands of times the truth—that she is infinitely valuable to God and to us—but such damage is not easy to overcome.

Kathy and I visited her a few years ago, and we were privileged to lead her to a saving faith in Jesus Christ and to strongly establish our love and commitment to her. Our visit, along with the intervention of a missionary couple who were members of her church, facilitated her coming forward to disclose her secret molestation to her church family. No one in the church except her mother and the missionary couple had had any idea. When the church heard her story, they were outraged. That set into motion a confrontation by church leadership with the perpetrator, who was pastoring in a church that belonged to their association in another city. Nothing came from the confrontation at the time, but within a year or so, the man was arrested, convicted, and imprisoned for other crimes, including being an accomplice to a murder. Indeed, be sure your sins will find you out!

More recently, I returned to Brazil to speak at a conference held in her church. I found that she is now surrounded by people who love and value her. I'm happy to report that she has made significant progress since the Lord introduced her to us. We have watched God invest heavily in her life through loving Christians. It's been a slow but sure progression.

She told me in an Internet chat that she longs to be married to a godly man, but she knows she's not quite ready. I believe she will be ready someday soon, but it has been hard to overcome a foundation of destruction within the heart of a lovely young woman who has believed, for most of her life, that she is dirty and worthless because of an abusive criminal who crept into the church. And her father, who didn't know how to love his daughter, helped solidify her feelings of inner ugliness.

What a contrast between how loved and secure, *protected* girls grow up and how unloved and insecure, *unprotected* girls grow up. Fathers, you are a powerful force in your daughters' lives. Use your power well. Wise fathers certainly will, because they understand that they possess infinite, God-given power to help establish in the innermost beings of their little girls the confidence that they are precious and lovely beyond compare. They establish such confidence, security, and value through godly and intimate father-daughter relationships that are holy and pure in the sight of our heavenly Father, who watches on in delight.

Bad things will certainly happen to our children. We can't always prevent that from happening. We can't always protect our girls from awful circumstances and potentially destructive events. But wise parents, both mothers and fathers, can so establish a foundation of inner beauty in their girls that the world, the flesh, and devil can't destroy them.

The Bible teaches there are two ways in life: one that leads to eternal destruction for all who do not obey the gospel of our Lord Jesus Christ, and the other that leads to glory when Jesus comes to be glorified in all who have believed. For the families of wise and godly parents, however, there is only one way. They do their utmost to remove the other option from the family table by persistently teaching their children that Jesus Christ is the only way. He is the way of wisdom.

What is more precious than the souls of our children? Nothing. If you are successful in this endeavor, then your life is a huge success. So, wise parents, get started early in teaching your beautiful little girls that real beauty is of the heart.

CHAPTER 4

Wise Parenting Principles 11-15: Arrows in the Hand

Proverbs 12–13

In Psalm 127:3–4, we're told that "children are a gift of the Lord, the fruit of the womb is a reward. Like arrows in the hand of a warrior, so are the children of one's youth." What does a warrior do with his arrows? To begin with, long before the arrows even reach his bow, he is particularly careful to see that they are crafted out of the finest arrow-making wood available. In ancient Israel, that would likely have been cedar. The warrior would want arrows made by a craftsman who is committed to precision. Arrows must be perfectly straight and balanced. I can envision an expert archer examining his newly crafted arrows—picking them up one at a time, sighting down each shaft, rolling it in his hands, balancing it on an outstretched finger—making sure that every arrow was perfectly true.

Once those preparations are complete, what does the warrior do with the arrow in his hand? Whether he is training for war or in the heat of the battle, the warrior nocks the arrow on the bow, locates his target, takes careful aim, and releases the arrow. When the arrow is true and the warrior is skilled, he hits his target nearly every time.

I love the imagery here: "Like arrows in the hand of a warrior, so are the children of one's youth." Wise parents may be inexperienced, but that doesn't mean they can't grow quickly in the skill of parenting if they are trained in the wisdom of God's Word. Wise parents understand the necessity of crafting their little arrows with precision and purpose. They also know they must deliberately aim at a target with the developed skill to hit it. What is the target at which wise parents should aim? In a word, heaven—but not just that their children will make it, but that they will live with heavenly desires, purposes, and perspectives. We want our children to store up their treasures in heaven, with the ultimate purpose of pleasing the God of heaven.

However, I fear that Christians today are setting our sights too low. The adage, "if you aim at nothing, you'll hit it every time," comes into play here. An expert archer never releases an arrow without a target in sight. We must do the same. It is too easy for us to get caught up in the scramble for earthly treasures. I fear that Christ's imminent return for His church, our eternal residence in heaven, and the Lord's ultimate glory are more of an afterthought for us than forethought. We have lost our anticipation of heaven and our determination to send up our treasures before us, ultimately for the everlasting glory of Jesus Christ. Without that goal in mind, we certainly won't train our children to be similarly determined. We will set our sights—and theirs—way too low: on the horizontal rather than on the heavenly. Even the best arrows will fail if released with no clear target or purpose in mind.

Wise parents never lose sight of the ultimate goal for themselves and for their children: the glorification of Christ in us and in them, now and in heaven. To help you hone your little arrows for ultimate glory, here are five additional wise parenting principles from Proverbs for shaping and crafting our children.

Parenting Principle 11
Wise Parents Raise Their Children to Love Discipline

Whoever loves discipline loves knowledge, but he who hates reproof is stupid.
PROVERBS 12:1

As is often the case in the book of Proverbs, this verse communicates truth in a parallelism of opposites. Those who love corrective discipline are defined as wise people. They will grow in the knowledge of Christ. At the opposite spectrum, those who hate corrective discipline are defined here as stupid people. They hate to be called into account for their actions. Hebrews 12:11 says, "All discipline for the moment seems not to be joyful, but sorrowful; yet to those who have been trained by it, afterward it yields the peaceful fruit of righteousness."

Wise parents understand that to love discipline themselves and to teach their children to love it yields eternal fruit.

When our daughters were teenagers, we were exposed for a time to a family with younger children. During that exposure, we found that one child was terribly whiny and could have benefited from regular, consistent, loving, corrective discipline. The child's whining would occasionally break into a cry if more pressure was needed to get what was wanted. After the exposure was over and our family was alone, the *silence* was truly golden! Eventually Lindsay broke the silence, giving me my first verbal vindication from one of my children for being a father who loves corrective discipline in the home. She said, "Dad, thanks for disciplining us!" Kerry and Lindsay didn't enjoy being correctively disciplined, but there came a time when they loved "the *peaceful* fruit of righteousness" it yielded in their lives.

The retelling of that story is bittersweet. It is sweet to reflect on the time my teenage daughter declared her love for discipline; that meant she also loved knowledge. So when Lindsay died at twenty-two, I knew she was ready! She was suddenly and unexpectedly ushered into the presence of her Lord and her God as a wise young lady, not a stupid one. Her mother and I take immeasurable comfort in that knowledge.

There's much sweetness to the truth of Hebrews 12:11. We testify of that wonderful reality, and we have a passion to see other families experience the same.

The bitterness of the story is that it reminds me of the sad reality that there is much stupidity in far too many families who claim to be followers of Christ. Now, we would expect spiritual blindness in unbelieving homes. But there's an utter despising of corrective discipline in our culture that has led to a modern-day epidemic of stupidity, even within the church. Far too many Christian parents hate to discipline effectively, consistently, and biblically. They're somehow afraid of hurting their children's psyches when they should be *terrified* of failing to correct the course of those wayward children. As a result, their children hate to receive correction, and stupidity is quick to follow.

It is an epidemic of no small proportion, and we see it in every corner of Christianity. Accordingly, it is imperative that each of us evaluate our homes. We must ask ourselves the following penetrating and important parallel questions:

- Is my home a place where discipline and reproof are hated—a place where they are either rarely or never implemented? Is stupidity, as a consequence, evident in the members of my household?
- Is my home a place where discipline is loved—a place where it is applied as often as necessary? Does spiritual enlightenment and knowledge abound in our home as evidence of that love?

Make it personal: which side of the parallelism best describes your home? Below, we'll examine the opposites of Proverbs 12:1 and then apply them to a test based on Hebrews 12. This can help you determine which line best describes you and your home. These are the opposites of the proverb:

#1 Whoever loves discipline loves knowledge.
#2 But he who hates reproof is stupid.

- ***"For those whom the Lord loves He disciplines"*** (Hebrews 12:6). Can you honestly say that you are committed to consistently and diligently correcting your children through discipline because, like God and according to God's standard of love, you truly love your children? If you can answer yes to that question, then you belong to #1. If you have to answer no, then you belong to #2.
- ***"Furthermore, we had earthly fathers to discipline us, and we respected them"*** (12:9). Do your children respect you because you fairly, appropriately, and consistently correct their bad attitudes and misbehaviors through physical discipline? Most children who have been disciplined in love highly respect their parents. If you can answer yes to the question, you are #1. If no, you are #2.
- ***"[God] disciplines us for our good, so that we may share His holiness"*** (12:10). Like our heavenly Father, do you discipline your children with a high and holy

purpose, so that your children will share God's holiness? Are you out to make your children holy by training them up in an environment that necessarily includes corrective discipline? If yes, #1. If no, #2.

- ***"All discipline for the moment seems not to be joyful, but sorrowful; yet to those who have been trained by it, afterward it yields the peaceful fruit of righteousness"*** (12:11). Have your children been so trained by loving discipline that your home is yielding the peaceful fruit of righteousness? If so, then all things are typically right in your home and the peace of God is standing guard over it. Your home is place of serene peace and Christlike righteousness. If yes, #1. If no, #2.

If you could answer yes to each of those test questions, you should praise the Lord for the wonder of His grace in your life, for you belong to a blessed group. Since belonging to this group is so eternally precious and God glorifying, continue to grow in becoming Father-like in your extreme love for your children.

If you had to answer no to those questions, fall before the throne of grace in absolute humility. Ask the Lord to forgive you for missing His revealed will for you as a parent. And then, make every effort—in full cooperation with the Holy Spirit—to change the culture of your home from one that displays chaos and stupidity to one that displays the peace of God and wisdom from above.

The book of Proverbs provides clear pictures of what loving, corrective discipline will produce in our children when they grow into adulthood. It also depicts their opposites. Proverbs 12:4 (NIV) says, "A wife of noble character is her husband's crown, but a disgraceful wife is like decay in his bones." Verse 15 goes on to say, "The way of fools seems right to them, but the wise listen to advice."

Do you remember the little girl I mentioned earlier who is now thankful for the paddle? I am confident that her wise parents will attain their heavenly goal with her. May it be true for your children as well.

Wise parents raise their children with careful purpose and in loving discipline.

Parenting Principle 12
Wise Parents Bring Health to Their Children with Their Words

There is one who speaks rashly like the thrusts of a sword,
but the tongue of the wise brings healing.
Proverbs 12:18

In this parallelism of opposites, the tremendous power of words is on full display. In the first statement, words used like a weapon are deadly. In the second, words spoken in wisdom promote health. For similar verses that also communicate this truth, check out Proverbs 15:4, 18:21, and James 3:6. The point of these passages is that our words have remarkable power, both for healing and for destruction.

In this principle, I will focus on fathers because typically (though not always), fathers are not as aware as mothers of the importance and power of their words. I wonder how many children have grown up with sharp-tongued fathers whose heart-piercing, sarcastic, negative, and destructive words hurt them deeply. Even as adults, the children of such fathers continue to hurt. They struggle, still wanting, and even needing, what they could never get—the approval of their fathers. Words are incredibly powerful, and fathers are immeasurably important. Therefore, their words carry for their children life or death, and that is no exaggeration.

When I was a young husband and father, my dad and I attended a men's weekend retreat that was sponsored by his denomination. The keynote speaker, a Christian psychologist, spoke eloquently about the power of a father's tongue—both of its power to give life and health to his children and its deadly power to bring ruin to their souls. I remember watching deep conviction come over some of the fathers who were in attendance. On the final evening, we sat around an outdoor fire ring and shared testimonies of what God had done within us during the retreat.

I will never forget one man from my dad's church who confessed that he had raised up two "knuckleheads"—the label he'd most often applied to his two sons. For the first time, he was terribly aware of the damage he had done with that one word, spoken so many times over his sons. With great sorrow, he told us that he had to go home to confess his sin to his sons and ask their forgiveness. I walked away from that retreat thanking the Lord for communicating to me early that the words I spoke to my little girls had tremendous power in them—the power of life and health, or death and destruction.

Fathers must understand that they are powerful men. They need to be acutely aware of the impact that they and their words have on their homes, whether with a terrible, negative fallout or a glorious, positive outcome.

God's infallible Word says the tongue of the wise has the power to build up. As you read Paul's exhortation in Ephesians 4:29, take note of those most restrictive of words, *no* and *only*: "Let *no* unwholesome word proceed from your mouth, but *only* such a word as is good for edification according to the need of the moment, so that it will give grace to those who hear" (emphasis added). Unwholesome words bring unhealthiness and dysfunction to the hearer and tear him or her down, while good words seasoned with grace bring health and vitality to the listener and build the person up.

In Ephesians 6:4, the apostle admonishes, "Fathers, do not provoke your children to anger, but bring them up in the discipline and instruction of the Lord." There is no more effective way for fathers to provoke their children to anger than by their hurtful, destructive words. Proverbs 16:24 rightly says, "Pleasant words are a honeycomb, sweet to the soul and healing to the bones." The untamed tongue, however, "is a restless evil and full of deadly poison" (James 3:8). Wise fathers and mothers are aware of the power they possess in their tongues; they strategically build up their children with carefully chosen words and do not take them down through verbal provocation.

How is this done? Here are some suggestions to help you build a biblical framework for bringing heath to your children through your spoken words.

- ***Develop a biblical perspective.*** A biblical perspective includes being constantly mindful of the supreme value of the souls of your children, while at the same time being acutely aware of the power of your words. We learned earlier that nothing is more valuable than the souls of our sons and daughters. Now we are learning that nothing builds up or tears down quite like the power of the tongue.
- ***Choose your words carefully.*** In fact, make every effort to consciously choose your words. Train your mind to think before you speak by asking yourself, "Is what I'm about to say going to help, or is it going to be unhelpful—or even painful?" (More will be said of this in Principle 31.)
- ***Depend on God's grace.*** Learn to depend on God's grace to control your emotions so that you don't go off on your children when they cop an attitude or misbehave. It's imperative that you deliberately do not provoke your children to anger. It's also important that, through dependence on God and His grace, you do

not give your children the power to provoke *you* to anger.

- ***Consistently discipline in love.*** Consistently discipline your children in an atmosphere of love. Getting emotional and yelling at your children is not an option. Train your mind and emotions through prayer to God and meditation on His Word to speak the truth in love with your children (Ephesians 4:15). Of course, there are times that demand rebuke and reproof, but even then—*especially* then—speak to them in love.
- ***Catch your children being good.*** This is much more than a tired cliché. It is an essential strategy point to facilitate health in your children. It's safe to say that we've all found our children doing or saying something wrong. But with hard work and concentration, we can develop the ability to see them do good things. When we do, then we can wisely take a moment to reinforce the goodness in them through encouraging and uplifting praise.

Wise parents bring health to their children with their words, knowing perfectly well that the tongue of the wise brings healing. Look ahead of you. What will become of your children? Aim straight and true, knowing that your words are a most important element in raising them to become healthy adults.

Parenting Principle 13
Wise Parents Do Not Tolerate Lying

Truthful lips will be established forever, but a lying tongue is only for a moment.
PROVERBS 12:19

A person who walks in integrity is aware of and in control of his or her tongue. Under this principle, we will focus on that aspect of shaping our children into people of integrity.

The Bible is clear: God is truth. In John's gospel, Jesus called Himself "the truth" (14:6). He referred to the Holy Spirit as "the Spirit of truth" (John 14:17, 15:26, 16:13), and He prayed to the Father of truth to "sanctify [us] in the truth." He then concluded that prayer by stating, "Your word is truth" (John 17:17). We know from the Scriptures that God's truth, His Word, "endures forever" (1 Peter 1:25). Isaiah the prophet declared, "The grass withers, the flower fades, but the word of our God stands forever" (40:8). Therefore, by its very nature, God's spoken word is eternal because it is truth that proceeds from the mouth of God Himself.

What is fascinating about the proverb above is that truthful *human* lips will also be established forever, but a person who is given to lies is stunningly temporal. How fleeting in nature and in power is the expression "only for a moment." God will stand behind and with a man or woman who speaks the truth and will establish them and their words forever; the clock is ticking, however, on a lying tongue. What a contrast—one is for eternity, the other merely for a moment.

Mark Twain said that a lie is "an ever present help in time of trouble." Notice that even in that clever but untruthful little adage, the temporal nature of a lie—if it is a help at all—is only a present help. Even if a person gets away with a lie, he or she has not gotten away with it, for "there is no creature hidden from [God's] sight, but all things are open and laid bare to the eyes of Him with whom we have to do" (Hebrews 4:13). God knows all, and every one of us will be called to give an account for what crosses our lips. No one gets away with a lie. We believers will certainly be forgiven if we humbly and sincerely seek it, but we can't get away with it.

The problem facing every Christian parent is that, when children are conceived, they do not inherit the nature of God. While they are blank slates, so to speak, they inherit from their parents a fallen sin nature, and the truth of God is not in them. I believe in the age of accountability, but I also know from God's Word that our children, like we before them, are born "dead in [their] trespasses and sins" (Ephesians 2:1) and are, therefore, "by nature children of wrath, even as the rest" (2:3). Of course, our hope is in the next line: "But God, being rich in mercy, because of His great love with which He loved us, even when we were dead in our transgressions, made us alive together with Christ (by grace you have been saved)" (2:4–5). The hope we had for ourselves is the same hope we have for our children.

Our children are not saints but sinners at conception and consequently, are born with a sin nature. We might want to believe that Jesus's harsh words in John 8 were reserved only for the Jews who tried to kill Him, but truth be told, before our salvation and freedom in Christ Jesus, all of us are spiritually related to Satan. This may be hard to accept about a newborn child, but think about who you were before you placed your faith in Jesus. The following could be said of each of us back then: "You are of your father the devil, and you want to do the desires of your father. He…does not stand in the truth because there is no truth in him. Whenever he speaks a lie, he speaks from his own nature, for he is a liar and the father of lies" (John 8:44). By our nature, we were all related to the evil one. This makes it difficult to soft-soap the biblical perspective concerning the innate sin nature of every human being. Our only hope is God in Christ Jesus, our Savior and Lord. And what a great hope He is!

So, based on what has just been said, the undeniable problem before every parent is that our children are born as members of fallen humanity; lying comes as naturally to them as breathing. How old were you when you started lying? I doubt I'm alone in saying that for me it was very early. Even in Christ, it is a hard habit to break. Paul, writing to the church in Colossae, commanded believers, "Do not lie to one another, since you laid aside the old self with its evil practices, and have put on the new self who is being renewed to a true knowledge according to the image of the One who created him" (Colossians 3:9–10). Even adult believers who consistently allow the new self to be renewed will continue to struggle in overcoming the part of the old self that reverts to lying when the moment seems to call for it. In fact, for many of us, it will be the hardest spiritual stronghold to tear down.

Wise parents know all of this, both from the Word and from personal experience; consequently, they know that the power of the lie within their children's sin nature may not be completely broken until they are saved and sufficiently sanctified. However, they also know that they are not powerless; they have within their God-given capacity the authority to create an atmosphere in their homes where truth is highly valued and lies will not be tolerated.

I remember reading a book about Jim Elliot, one of the five missionaries who were killed while participating in Operation Auca, a strategy to evangelize the Huaorani people of Ecuador. Jim grew up in an environment of honesty where truth-telling was rewarded and lying wasn't tolerated. Because of my own personal struggle with lying and a growing understanding of its awful power and God's hatred of it, I came under the deep conviction that I would no longer tolerate lying in my own life or in my home.

Out of this conviction by the Holy Spirit, Kathy and I developed two basic and unchangeable laws for our home. The first law was general and all encompassing: our children will respect us, their parents, and will obey us immediately. The second law was specific: we will not tolerate lying; it will be met with swift, corrective discipline every time. I can honestly say that we exercised much grace toward our children, but when it came to these two laws, we acted quickly, decisively, and consistently. Lying especially was almost always met with corrective discipline in the form of "the rod of discipline" (Proverbs 22:15). For us, that was a paddle.

The Bible is crystal clear: our heavenly Father occasionally spanks His beloved children, but only when necessary and only for their good. As earthly parents who belong to Him and share His values, we should do the same with our children; we physically discipline them when necessary only because we love them and we desire that they share in God's holiness (see again Hebrews 12:5–11). Children who are raised to always tell the truth will have a much easier time of breaking this sin habit of the old nature when they are eventually converted and begin growing in Christ through sanctification.

Here's the process wise parents must adopt to effectively nip lying in the bud.

1. Become Deeply Convicted about Lying

Since lying is an abomination to God (see Proverbs 12:22), make it an abomination that you share with Him. Become convicted and convinced that there is no such thing as a white lie or a little lie, but that all lying is a big deal. Be sure to apply this rule to yourself first, and then to your children.

2. Make Intolerance of Lying a Law

Make it a law of your home that you will not tolerate lying in yourself or in your children. Don't respond to lying in your children as though it's not natural, however. You needn't be shocked when they tell you a bold-faced lie; rather, you should expect lies to begin early and often.

Teach your children from God's Word why, from this point forward, the law of the home will be truth-telling and nothing but truth-telling. Make sure they understand the new law, the biblical basis for it, and the consequences for violating it. Whenever a major change is brought into the home, we must carefully and consistently inform our children about it, especially when it is going to deeply affect them, either negatively or positively.

Train them to understand that even though lying may seem like a present help in their time of trouble, it destroys trust. Further, let them know that once trust is broken, it is difficult to build it back into a relationship. This is a significant consequence of lying, since life is all about relationships—beginning with their relationship with their parents, who belong to the truth, and with their relationship with the God of truth Himself.

3. Consistently Enforce the Law

Once they fully understand everything they need to know about the new law, enforce that law every time it is violated. Make the enforcement powerful enough to deter the awful crime every time it is committed. Make your children think, "That wasn't worth it!" Personally, I highly recommend using what God recommends in correcting the course of a child's dishonest thinking that then manifests in dishonest speaking. Use the rod of discipline.

4. Afterward, Reinforce Your Love

Take time after the discipline to love on your children and explain again why you disciplined them. Make sure they fully understand that you are doing it only because you want what is best for them and because you love them with all that is within you. When the discipline was over, I made sure that my relationship with my girls was tight and free from anything negative. The sin and the discipline were over and done with, so we could get on with renewed parent-daughter intimacy.

All wise parents desire eternal freedom for themselves and for their children; consequently, they take careful aim and fight for truth in their lives and in their homes. May God empower you to strongly establish this principle and law in the lives of your beloved children, for their eternal benefit and for His everlasting honor.

Parenting Principle 14
Wise Parents Teach Their Children to Keep Good Company

He who walks with wise men will be wise,
but the companion of fools will suffer harm.
PROVERBS 13:20

When Lindsay and Jason were murdered, we were reminded that in this fallen world, we suffer from our own sins and from the sins of others; it's not either/or, but both. Our families are grateful that our children died because of another person's sin and not their own. The team of detectives from the Sonoma County Sheriff's Office that worked the case quickly came to recognize that Lindsay and Jason were innocent victims of a senseless and wicked act of brutal violence. And it wasn't long before they recognized the outstanding character of these two young adults who were in California to serve God by serving other young people. Because of the nature of the crime and the exceptional character of our children, the detectives went above and beyond their professional call of duty in an all-out attempt to solve the case and bring Jason and Lindsay's killer to justice. The case was different from most murder investigations because most, unfortunately, involve a victim who fell in with the wrong crowd and was killed because of it.

All of us will suffer harm simply because we live in a sin-sick world. We will suffer from accident, sickness, disease, foolishness of our own making, and the sinfulness of others. Much of the harm that comes to us is unavoidable. What is avoidable, however, is the self-inflected harm that comes from our own personal sins. In pastoral counseling, I often think and sometimes say that the person I'm counseling is his or her own worst enemy, for much of what we suffer is the consequence of our own sin.

How many times have we seen children fall in with the wrong company and quickly become wrong company themselves? And then we see them suffer the consequences of the choices they've made. The Bible and experience both testify that the companions of fools will suffer harm. Therefore, wise parents offer to their children at birth and beyond a home environment permeated with purity, godliness, and wisdom from above. They teach their children to keep good company—first with themselves, their wise parents. And then they introduce their children to other couples with children who share their same values.

Wise parents create this environment for their children because they fully trust God when He says that those who walk with wise people will be wise themselves. They work to ensure that when their children grow up and are exposed to worldlings and their worldliness, they will be wise adults who choose to walk with other wise adults. Wise parents grow wise children who will facilitate wisdom in others. The process of growing in wisdom, however, must include the company of other people who walk in wisdom.

Psalm 1 clearly communicates the wisdom of carefully choosing the companionship of others:

> How blessed is the man who does not walk in the counsel of the wicked, nor stand in the path of sinners, nor sit in the seat of scoffers! But his delight is in the law of the LORD, and in His law he meditates day and night. He will be like a tree firmly planted by streams of water, which yields its fruit in its season and its leaf does not wither; and in whatever he does, he prospers.
>
> The wicked are not so, but they are like chaff which the wind drives away. Therefore the wicked will not stand in the judgment, nor sinners in the assembly of the righteous. For the LORD knows the way of the righteous, but the way of the wicked will perish.

Understand, of course, that parents who walk in wisdom will suffer harm, and their children will suffer harm as well. It is unavoidable on this side of heaven. But we can avoid the self-inflicted harm brought about by being foolish and falling in with foolish companions. Imprudent people are intimately acquainted with ongoing trouble, yet they are too unwise to know or admit that the trouble upon them is their own fault. Wise people, on the other hand, are intimately acquainted with the blessings of God that they receive from His gracious hand for wise thinking, speaking, and living. They give all the glory to Him for this because they understand that if it weren't for His grace, they too would be stuck in foolishness.

Wise parents take to heart the words of the man of God who visited Eli, the priest of Israel who tolerated the wickedness of his two sons, also priests. They were bad company to each other and they kept bad company. They were so wicked that they were having sexual relations with the women who served at the doorway of the tabernacle. In 1 Samuel 2:30, the man of God brought this word to Eli: "Therefore the Lord God of Israel declares, 'I did indeed say that your house and the house of your father should walk before Me forever'; but now the Lord declares, 'Far be it from Me—for those who honor Me I will honor, and those who despise Me will be lightly esteemed.'" Toward the end of the rebuke, God promised that He would raise up "a faithful priest who will do according to what is in My heart and in My soul; and I will build him an enduring house, and he will walk before My anointed always" (2:35). The faithful priest whom God would raise up for Himself was the boy Samuel, who became an influential leader of ancient Israel. His life was not free from trouble, of course, but it was free from self-inflicted trouble. God kept His promise from verse 35, too. On the same day that the man of God made these prophecies and promises to Eli, both of his sons, Hophni and Phinehas, died as a consequence of their utter foolishness. But God raised Samuel up and honored him because he honored God.

Based on these biblical realities, wise parents set out at the beginning of their child-rearing years to teach their children to be wise people and to be the companions of the wise, so that they will grow up to be men and women who intimately know the blessings of honoring God. Let me again quote the apostle John, who spoke for all wise parents when he said of his spiritual children, "I have no greater joy than this, to hear of my children walking in the truth" (3 John 1:4). What a blessing and joy it is for us to know that our children walk in the truth. Even if they die—even if it is by the hands of a great sinner—they know, and we know with them, the joy and blessing of the Lord!

I can't tell you how many times I have been encouraged and strengthened by Peter's words in 1 Peter 3:8–14:

> To sum up, all of you be harmonious, sympathetic, brotherly, kindhearted, and humble in spirit; not returning evil for evil or insult for insult, but giving a blessing instead; for you were called for the very purpose that you might inherit a blessing. For, "the one who desires life, to love and see good days, must keep his tongue from evil and his lips from speaking deceit.

> He must turn away from evil and do good; he must seek peace and pursue it. For the eyes of the Lord are toward the righteous, and His ears attend to their prayer, but the face of the Lord is against those who do evil." Who is there to harm you if you prove zealous for what is good? But even if you should suffer for the sake of righteousness, you are blessed.

Shortly after Jason and Lindsay were murdered, I came across these inspired and inspiring words. In fact, I remember exactly when it happened. Our children had been reported missing and then subsequently found dead. Bob and Delores (Jason's parents) and Kathy and I were flying back home after that first trip to California. I was sitting with Bob, and our wives were sitting together a few seats back from us. I was reading my Bible. When I came across this passage, my heart found great comfort, and I quickly shared it with Bob and then Delores and Kathy. The passage was a timely reminder that the eyes of the Lord were toward our children, the righteous, and His ears were attentive to their prayers, but His face was against the person who had done this great evil. There is so much comfort in knowing that our wise children were walking in the righteousness of Christ and that they are now enjoying their reward, for God honors those who honor Him. But God's face is against the wicked.

There are two more important points to be made under this principle. First, the adage "birds of a feather flock together" is generally true. Peer pressure is powerful, especially for children. Consequently, wise parents will ensure that the peer pressure their children experience comes from good kids, and the pressure their children impose upon their peers is nothing but good and godly. Wise parents are careful to make sure their children *are* good and godly company and that they *keep* good and godly company.

Of course, bad company can't always be avoided. Our children are not to be *of* the world, but they are most certainly *in* it. Long before they are exposed to too much of the world and bad company, we must work hard to establish a holy trend, where our children are good company and they desire to keep good company. Then, when they are in the company of the foolish, they will be the greater influence.

Jason and Lindsay served with the Christian adventure camp Rock-N-Water, and they kept good company with the other staff members, including the senior staff. When it was time for them to serve a group of young people who came in for the week, not all the youth could be classified as being wise, but the camp staff were the leaders who influenced the youth, rather than the youth influencing them. What a huge blessing to see our children grow up to become the right crowd and to be powerful witnesses to the not-so-right ones. Sometimes birds of a feather *don't* flock together. Instead, godly birds flock with another crowd in order to share with them the gospel of Jesus Christ. Wise birds can do this without being adversely affected by that crowd—instead, they impact the crowd around them for the good.

Second, much of this biblical training on keeping good company is meant to prepare our children for every lasting and important relationship in their lives, including who they date and, eventually, who they marry. Wise parents have an insatiable desire to raise up their children to be right and righteous people who marry right and righteous people. A spiritually and emotionally healthy and holy marriage requires both the husband and wife to be spiritually and emotionally healthy and holy. I have seen my share of spiritually one-sided marriages. They are never harmonious, healthy, holy, or happy.

I have counseled far too many engaged couples to be naive about marriage. A godly marriage requires two healthy and holy people, period. A "missionary marriage," where the saved spouse believes he or she can lead his or her unsaved spouse to the Lord, is nearly always doomed to fail.

As our girls matured and became old enough to date (around sixteen), I took a walk with each of them. We talked about many things—that dating should be fun, but it wasn't a game; and that she needed to guard her emotions because falling in love with the wrong person is dangerous. Further, I told her that the most important decision that she would ever make, second only to what she chose do with Jesus Christ, would be the decision concerning who she marries. I reminded her that the dating process would eventually take her to the place of marriage, but what I stressed most was the absolute necessity of *being* the right person and *marrying* the right person.

I remember being proud of my oldest daughter early on in her dating experience when she briefly dated a boy who was fully churched but, as it turned out, was more worldly minded than Christ-centered. Shortly after they began dating, even though she liked him and enjoyed his company, she broke up with him for that reason. She eventually married a good and godly man, but that early boyfriend, as far as I know, is now unchurched and not walking with the Lord. My youngest daughter dated a couple of good and godly guys. The last one, whom she chose to marry, was one of those guys. We had been excitedly looking forward to their wedding ceremony and their marriage. They were only three and a half weeks from marriage when they died.

Wise parents, you have parental authority given to you by God Himself. You must wisely exercise that authority over when and whom your children date. You may not be able to control whom they eventually marry, but you can do much in your God-given power to aim your arrows well, preparing them as best you can to eventually keep good company in holy marriages. May it be so in Jesus's name. Amen.

Parenting Principle 15
Wise Parents Know That Diligent Discipline Is an Expression of Love

He who withholds his rod hates his son,
but he who loves him disciplines him diligently.
Proverbs 13:24

Our third wise parenting principle emphasized the God-given responsibility of godly parents to correct the course of their children through corrective discipline, both verbal and physical. While physical discipline is never a pleasant experience for godly parents or their children, we are responsible before God to apply it when necessary. Wise parents discipline, not only out of responsibility, but out of love as well. This proverb places emphasis on the spiritual motivation for consistent, diligent physical discipline, and that is love. According to God's Word, the administration of discipline that does not withhold the rod is a true expression of love.

I remember a television commercial that significantly impacted my life as a father. It was an advertisement for a car oil filter. I don't remember if it influenced me to change my oil filter more faithfully, but I do know that it did inspire me. In the commercial, a mechanic was under the hood of a car, leaning over the blown engine. He calmly informed the viewer that the repair would cost hundreds of dollars. He then held up an oil filter, looked out through the camera, and delivered a punch line that went like this: "You can pay me now [for an inexpensive oil filter], or you can pay me later [for an expensive engine overhaul]." I immediately related that to how we raise our children: We can pay the price of disciplining them in love now, or we can pay a far greater price later in our children's undisciplined lives. Because I love my children deeply, I chose to pay the price early. Am I ever glad I did.

Proverbs 13:24 is an attention grabber. Using the powerful verbs *hate* and *love*, the inspired writing shows us what our parental attitudes toward our children look like. Take the time to read the verse again and allow the point of the proverb to sink in.

I'm sure that most parents who spare the rod would take strong exception to the statement that they hate their children. However, in God's economy and according to His perfect wisdom, withholding physical discipline in the form of spanking is equal to withholding love and is, in fact, a form of neglectful hatred. In other words, for a father to spare the rod when it is needed to correct the path of his child is to act as though he hates him or her.

The New Testament teaches the same biblical truth in Hebrews 12:7–8: "God deals with you as with sons; for what son is there whom his father does not discipline? But if you are without discipline, of which all have become partakers, then you are illegitimate children and not sons." God the Father is like the best godly parents in this way: He and they prove that their children are both legitimate and loved by appropriately disciplining them. Think of it like this: if withholding discipline is a form of parental hatred, then failing to administer appropriate physical, corrective discipline has the same effect as any other neglectful, unloving treatment of a child. The parent withholding discipline may not be aware that it is an unloving and neglectful act; nevertheless, it is.

On the other hand, "Those whom God loves He disciplines, and He scourges every son whom He receives" (Hebrews 12:6). Like our heavenly Father, like earthly fathers and mothers—they *diligently* discipline the child they love

(Proverbs 13:24). The Hebrew word here, *shachar*, could also be translated "promptly," "carefully," or "early." Since all those renderings are possible, and since we can't be certain which is to be preferred above the others, perhaps God had all nuances in mind: loving parents discipline their children carefully, promptly, diligently, and early—as soon as the child is old enough to know the difference between right and wrong.

The wording of the proverb places strong emphasis on the proper biblical motivation for physical discipline that begins early and continues during the formative years of a child's life; again, the motivation is love. Physical, corporal discipline, appropriately applied, is a most loving act from loving parents. The wisest and most loving parents discipline their children in love; their discipline strikes the right balance between being lenient and being severe. The right balance is firm discipline that is an effective deterrent to inappropriate behavior; it appropriately administers pain but is not in any way abusive. Wise parents know the difference.

Far too many parents use what they call love as an excuse for being too severe or too lenient. Severity does not communicate love; rather, it demonstrates a *lack* of love, tenderness, and grace. It provokes the child of such treatment to anger (Ephesians 6:4). Parents who claim to love their children but treat them harshly are self-deceived and will reap embittered adult children as the fruit of their labors.

Conversely, parents who verbally express their love but withhold loving, corrective, physical discipline when needed are simply fooling themselves. They may genuinely love their children, but they are not expressing their love appropriately. This actual lack of true love carries with it a hefty price tag: *they will pay later.*

I think it should also be said that mothers are not at all exempt from applying the rod to the seat of their children when necessary. I couldn't be more proud of my daughter, Kerry, who, along with her husband Ben, does not hesitate to spank her boys when they need it. She hates to do it, but she loves them too much to withhold correction from them. Further, mothers who are raising their children alone have no choice but to love their children through appropriate discipline.

If there is a godly father in the home, however, the Bible consistently places emphasis on him leading the way in discipline. It is not exclusively his responsibility, but he is meant to lead. Ephesians 6:4 exhorts, "Fathers...bring [your children] up in the discipline and instruction of the Lord." Wise fathers lead and are diligent, consistent, and careful in corrective discipline, knowing that it is an essential expression of love; wise mothers are in full agreement.

Back in my Bible college days in Phoenix, Arizona, our senior pastor, Tim Smith, shared from the pulpit what he called "the three father types." I wrote them down and have not forgotten them. They are the *permissive* father, the *authoritarian* father, and the *authoritative* father. The permissive father is high in love but low in discipline or low in both, which is a form of abuse. The authoritarian father is high in discipline but low in love, which is also a form of abuse. The authoritative father is high in love and high in discipline. He is well balanced in his love; he knows that tender love and tough love are both necessary elements in raising well-balanced, stable, and secure children who will walk with the Lord when they come of age. I don't know where I came up with it, perhaps from Pastor Tim, but I often refer to tough love and tender love as opposite sides of the same "love coin." They are both essential elements of a single coin. Neglect of either side results in love that is not true or complete.

How can godly parents strike that proper balance of being high in love at all times and high in discipline when necessary?

1. Study the Bible

Study the Bible to determine what God says about physical discipline. The principles laid out in this book about corrective discipline closely follow Scripture and can be used as a guide in this study. When both parents are involved, they must be on the same disciplinary page with each other and with God. By God's grace, Kathy and I were in full agreement when it came to disciplining our children. We were never at odds with each other as to the offenses for which we would discipline and the methods we would use in the correcting process. I, more than she, did not hesitate to use the paddle if an attitude or behavior in one of our girls needed correction, but I always had her full support. I cannot overstate the importance of this.

2. Seek Counseling if Necessary

If, as a couple, you can't agree on appropriate forms of discipline, then I highly recommend counseling. Choose a godly older couple whom you respect for having successfully raised their children in the Lord. It may be important that they have children with differing personalities. I know a couple whose only child had a sweet and compliant temperament. This couple was often critical of other couples whose children weren't as compliant as their daughter; they even judged others as being poor parents. Then they had another daughter later in life—a daughter who was the exact opposite of their first one. She was strong willed and anything but easy to raise. The second child is growing up well, but her parents' perspective and judgment have radically changed. Find a couple whom you trust to be excellent parents, then humbly submit to their counsel.

3. Allow Yourself to Be Held Accountable

Allow yourself to be held accountable by your spouse. If you are a single parent, allow someone close to your family to hold you accountable. Accountability is a valuable tool in striking an appropriate balance between the extremes of leniency and severity. My tendency was to lean toward severity on occasion; I wanted to nip the behavior in the bud. My wife, on the other hand, would sometimes lean toward leniency. We respected each other's opinions and would often submit to the other's counsel. That helped us both remain well balanced in our love. Our mutual desire was to be tender at all times and tough only when necessary.

4. Seek Accountability Outside of the Home

Accountability with another couple may be equally important. If you have a relationship with a wise, older couple, add accountability to that relationship. Regularly meet with them, perhaps once a month, maybe once a quarter, and share some real-life experiences with them to discover what they think about how you and your spouse handled the situations. Ben and Kerry and Kathy and I have that kind of relationship. We may not always agree with each other on how a disciplinary event was or should be handled, but our adult children welcome our advice and are often influenced by it.

Allow God and His Word to convince you of the truth about how best to love your children, which will include disciplining them diligently. In their quest to bring up their children in the Lord, wise parents are mindful to "not be conformed to this world," for the world is foolish and darkened in its understanding. Instead, they strive to "be transformed by the renewing of [their minds], so that [they] may prove what the will of God is, that which is good and acceptable and perfect" (Romans 12:2). Allow God and the godly to conform your mind to the truths of the Bible. Resist conformity to the world's false ways.

If our chief aim is to raise our children to be successful, wealthy, popular, healthy, happy, or beautiful in this life, what affect will those values have fifty years from now? A hundred years from now? The truth is that these are only temporal qualities that will mean little, if anything, in the long run. If, however, our chief aim is to raise our children to fear the Lord, to grow in Christlike character, to lay up treasures in heaven rather than on earth, to have a heavenly perspective, and to ultimately bring glory to Jesus Christ, then we can rest in the knowledge that these values will be infinitely priceless, even hundreds of years from now. How valuable is a child's temporal success in the world when compared to an eternal soul that delights the Lord now and forever?

If we claim that the Word of God is the God-inspired truth, then we must take the time to think about how the way we are raising our children will affect their eternity. Several of Lindsay's diary entries, written just prior to her leaving for California in 2004, are a good reminder of the immense value of aiming your little arrows at the ultimate target of heaven. These are the words of a twenty-two-year-old pilgrim:

> *I greatly desire to have many crowns to give my God when I get to heaven.*
>
> *Nothing on earth matters in light of eternity. It is so easy to get caught up in the things of the world and forget what really matters.*
>
> *The more we worship and spend our lives for Christ on earth, the better we can serve Him in heaven.*
>
> *I sometimes think of myself as a pilgrim in a foreign land, traveling through life. We are here temporarily. I should be less materialistic and give more to God. Don't waste time.*

Psalm 127:3–4 says, "Children are a gift of the Lord, the fruit of the womb is a reward. Like arrows in the hand of a warrior, so are the children of one's youth." Aim well, my brothers and sisters in Christ. May God bless you and those most precious arrows in your hand.

CHAPTER 5

Wise Parenting Principles 16-20: Strong Parent-Leaders

Proverbs 14–17

One of my favorite Old Testament stories is of Joshua and Caleb when they were chosen to be two of the twelve spies for Israel's twelve tribes. God's people had arrived on the border of Canaan, the Promised Land. The spies were representative leaders of the twelve tribes. Their assignment to survey the land was important for reconnaissance purposes. Primarily, however, it was a test of their character, a test to determine how faithful they would be in serving God by leading the people they represented.

The twelve are named in Numbers 13. We all know Joshua and Caleb, but can you name the other ten? I can't either! Only two of the twelve are readily recognized today. The other ten failed to trust in the Lord and His Word when He promised to give Canaan to Israel. By failing to trust God, they proved to be incompetent in leading God's people.

All twelve spies set out on a forty-day exploration of the land. Upon their return, they came before the nation and all testified of the richness of the land. However, ten of the twelve alarmed the people by reporting that there were giants in the land, and that in comparison, they were "like grasshoppers." Their report caused the entire nation to weep, to grumble against Moses and Aaron, and even to cry out against God, accusing Him of bringing them all the way from Egypt to this unconquerable land where they would die by the sword.

A mutinous rebellion rushed over the people until it reached its climax with the unified decision to appoint a leader to take them back to Egypt. With that, Moses and Aaron prostrated themselves on the ground, and Joshua and Caleb tore their clothes in extreme consternation. The two faithful spies implored the people of God to end their rebellion against the Lord. They urged them to not be afraid, because God would surely give them the land just as He had promised. However, their pleas only enraged the people, and they set about to stone the two to death. But then the glory of the Lord appeared in blinding brilliance and brought the rebellious nonsense to an abrupt end.

Only two of the twelve proved to be faithful and, therefore, competent leaders in Israel. The thing that separated them from the other ten was their well-placed fear of God, who had consistently proved Himself faithful before the nation throughout the long journey to the edge of the Promised Land. The fear the other ten demonstrated was misplaced, for it was the fear of men rather than of God. When their faith in God was tested, there was none to be found, and they led God's people away from the fear of the Lord. The ten had no confidence in God, and the legacy they could have had melted away. The two maintained complete confidence in God and thus became immortal, known for all eternity as leaders whom God could trust.

Parents, like it or not, are leaders in their homes. They may be good ones or bad ones or somewhere-in-between ones, but they are leaders just the same. As parent-leaders in the home, we have a choice: we may become leaders who possess and convey little to no confidence in God, or we may become leaders who exude confidence in Him so that, when faced with giants in the land, we will pass the test. Our children need leaders who will be faithful to God; leaders who fear the only One who can empower us to withstand all the forces of this world, including the satanic ones until, finally and confidently, we enter the Promised Land.

Our study of Proverbs began with the foundational fear of the Lord. That fear must stay with us all along the way. As we continue our study of wise parenting principles from Proverbs, let us keep before us the necessity of being strong parent-leaders who will remain faithful to God until our successfully completed God-given assignment is celebrated to His everlasting glory.

Parenting Principle 16
Wise Parents Make Their Home Secure

In the fear of the Lord *there is strong confidence,*
and his children will have refuge.
Proverbs 14:26

Joshua and Caleb feared God alone, and in that fear, there is incredibly strong confidence. Our children do not need grasshoppers for parents, who can't lead when the family must pass through the valley of the shadow of darkness or even death. They don't need parents who wilt under pressure. Faithless leadership leaves children with a profound sense of insecurity that will eventually force them to look elsewhere for security, safety, and refuge. If these parents claim to be Christians, their children will likely surmise that Christianity doesn't work and that trusting God is an awful way to live. As a result, they will seek security and refuge in themselves, the world, or both. Weak leadership leads to disaster in the home.

I once worked with a couple who had young children in the home, who professed faith in Jesus Christ, and who were members of our church. They came to me for help with a truckload of baggage from their individual pasts. Both had grown up in faithful, churchgoing homes, but neither home had exemplified confidence in God—just the opposite, in fact. They came from fearful and angry homes (one of the parents in each home was fearful, while the other was angry).

This couple met with me weekly; we were working hard together in the power of the Spirit to move them from the insecurities of the past to the fear of the Lord that brings confidence in Him. We were making steady progress toward a safe and lasting refuge. Then, a series of stressful circumstances brought a time when any faith in God that they may have possessed seemed to collapse. In short order, they turned away from me, our church family, and (presumably from) God. Not long after they left our church, their marriage and their home fell apart.

Parents often end up perpetuating the instability of the homes from which they came. Perhaps they would be well on their way to being God-confident when unexpected circumstances cause them to turn away and return to being grasshoppers. This sets their family on a hopeless course that leads to dysfunction and destruction, and the cycle of insecurity continues. And that breaks this pastor's heart!

Our families need fathers and mothers who have found strong confidence in the fear of the Lord. Our homes need true parent-leaders who will acknowledge the obstacles of trials and troubles in the world, but because their confidence is in the overwhelming power and glory of God, will not see those obstacles as insurmountable. The reward for parents who have well-placed fear is an unshakable confidence that creates a safe, secure refuge for their children. The benefit of this cannot be overstated.

Another young couple in our church requested my counsel in dealing with some hard issues that had popped up in their family life. The husband sought me out as a mentor, desiring to know God's Word, will, and way for himself and his family. We met weekly for several months. I watched him as we worked through a study on systematic theology. This young man grew, not only in his understanding of what the Bible says about a doctrinal truth (for example, the sovereignty of God and our appropriate response of faith to His gracious plans and purpose), but also in understanding how it worked in daily life. He then took the truth home and shared it with his wife, and she quickly and faithfully followed his lead. He even spoke it as best he could into his oldest son's life.

Like everyone else in the kingdom of God, that young family is not exempt from trial and trouble. In fact, it seems like one trial after another has come their way over the course of their marriage. However, their steadfast fear of the Lord has led them to a firm confidence in Him, and they have faithfully persevered through every difficulty.

This couple reminds me of Joshua and Caleb as they live out these godly men's words: "The Lord is with us; do not fear" (Numbers 14:9). I am confident that, if the Lord leads this young man in that direction, he will one day be a servant-leader (an elder) in our church family because he is first a godly leader to his wife, and together, they are strong parent-leaders in their home. Furthermore, their children have a refuge in their strong confidence in God. I couldn't be prouder of this couple and other couples in our church who are like them. They make their pastor's heart glad; they compel me to esteem them highly and to thank the Lord for their faithfulness to Him, their family, and their church family.

This security and safety in the Lord is also taught in Proverbs 18:10–12.

> The name of the Lord is a strong tower; the righteous runs into it and is safe. A rich man's wealth is his strong city, and like a high wall in his own imagination. Before destruction the heart of man is haughty, but humility goes before honor.

When "the name of the Lord" is used in the Bible, it stands for the divine Person named Yahweh, but also for His character, conduct, glory, majesty, might, and everything else about Him. Verse 10 speaks of Yahweh God in all His awesome perfections as being a strong tower—a place of highest protection, safety, and security—for there is no higher or safer place than His strong name! Wise parents who have confidence in God take their families to this strong tower, knowing that nothing can touch them there that God does not allow. And if God allows it, these parents know without a doubt that whatever He allows, He means it for their good and for His glory.

The proverb also provides a contrast between a righteous person who finds safety in the Lord (10) and a rich person who is putting all his faith and security in his wealth (11). In the rich person's imagination, his wealth is like a high wall that he thinks will provide the kind of safety that no person or power can touch or take away. But this wall is only in his imagination; it is nothing more than illusion and false security.

The contrast continues in the final verse. Pride in what the wealthy person has gained on earth goes before his destruction. In his arrogance, he is sure that his wealth is a safe haven of protection, but an economic crash or some other catastrophe is on its way. Even Christians, if they place their confidence in riches gained rather than in God, will know destruction. They may lose their wealth, or worse, they might lose their eternal rewards once earned because of pride and misplaced confidence. God gave, but God can easily take away.

On the other hand, humble Christians are acutely aware that they have no strength outside of God and no safety without Christ, so they gather up their children and run into the strong tower that is our Lord. Security and safety are only found when God is our refuge. Joshua and Caleb exemplified that truth, for they knew that the only safe place on earth was in their God, and they proved it with their full confidence in Him. Wise parents know and do the same, and in so doing, they make their homes secure in Christ, who promised to honor the humble.

Of course, we live in a fallen world, and physical harm can still touch us here. I cannot remember a time as a parent when I thought our children were safe from harm. I knew they might experience injury, disease, spiritual stronghold, or even untimely death. So I was not surprised that we were visited by evil when Jason and Lindsay were murdered. I do remember, however, being shocked and almost disbelieving at just how evil this personal visitation was. I suppose that because we live a rural community in the Midwest, I didn't expect the evil of murder to find us. Personal visitations of evil can be quite shocking in their awful power, but we needn't be surprised that they come our way.

Our complete safety is not at all to be expected while living in the world. What we *are* safe from, when our confidence is in God, is living in fear of anything other than God. We are safe from wasting our lives on the trivial and temporal. We are safe from ultimately losing to pain, disease, and death. And someday, when we've finished our God-given course, we will be completely delivered, once and for all and forever, from the presence of sin and its consequences.

This is the truth of God's Word that I set out to teach my daughters, and along with my wife and the Allens, I believe that Lindsay and Jason were indeed safe all the way home. My prayer is that you will know the satisfaction and power of such safety and security. May the fear of the Lord be your strong confidence, and may His name be your strong tower. And then, as strong parent-leaders who make their homes safe in Christ, take your children by the hand and run into all that He is and be safe.

Parenting Principle 17
Wise Parents Are Concerned about Motives

All the ways of a man are clean in his own sight,
but the Lord *weighs the motives.*
Proverbs 16:2

It is innately human to justify and rationalize our behavior in an attempt to make ourselves look better (cleaner) than we are. Why do we have such a strong distaste for the transparency and honesty about ourselves that God so longs for in us?

Uriah the Hittite was one of King David's "mighty men"—those elite warriors who were so thoroughly dedicated to their king that they would die for him. During one spring military campaign, David remained behind in Jerusalem. From the roof of his palace, David saw Uriah's beautiful wife, Bathsheba, bathing. Even after discovering that she belonged to one of his loyal mighty men, he coveted her. He sent for her and committed adultery with her. When he received word that she was pregnant, he deepened his walk in sin with an awful cover-up campaign that led to his having Uriah the Hittite killed in battle.

Some months later, "the LORD sent Nathan [the prophet] to David" (2 Samuel 12:1). Nathan told the king a story about a rich man who had a large flock of sheep but who stole a poor man's one and only beloved lamb to feed to his guest. When David's anger burned against the rich man, he declared that "surely the man who has done this deserves to die." Then the prophet of God said to David, "You are the man!" Suddenly the cover-up came to an end. We find David's prayer for pardon in Psalm 51. There he confesses his sin, pleads for forgiveness, and declares of God, "Behold, You desire truth in the innermost being" (Psalm 51:6).

Human beings are naturals at downplaying, justifying, rationalizing, and even attempting to cover up their sins before God. Some people make it an art. However, the Bible clearly warns, "Be sure your sin will find you out" (Numbers 32:23), because God is truth and loves truth and knows that the truth will set us free (John 8:32). Inner honesty and transparency is His desire for us, but since it's not natural, it comes hard. We don't want to know why we do what we do; examining our motives is too painful. Instead, we pretend that all our ways are clean in our own sight…but God doesn't. He weighs every motive of the heart.

In his book, *On Being a Servant*, Warren Wiersbe made a statement that arrested my attention. It continues to disturb me because I'm sure it's true. He wrote,

> The glory of God is the most important [element involved in Christian ministry] because the glory of God is what salvation and ministry are all about. He saved us "to the praise of the glory of His grace" (Ephesians 1:6, 12, 14), and He commands us, "Whatever you do, do all to the glory of God" (1 Corinthians 10:31). If our motive for serving is anything other than the glory of God, what we do will be only religious activity and not true Christian ministry. (Baker Books, 1993, 19.)

Then, a couple pages later, he wrote the line that still makes me stop to think:

> It is doubtful that anybody ever does anything out of a purely unselfish motive; but with God's help, we can try. (Ibid., 21.)

Is that statement true? It is if "purely" means 100 percent pure, and I'm fairly confident it does. It's like the love of God that the Spirit pours out in our hearts at the point of salvation. None of us reach the pinnacle of loving as perfectly as God loves in a lifetime—we will only love perfectly when we enter perfection in heaven. We may, however, grow in it throughout our lives, ever increasing in our ability in Christ to love as He loves.

Our motives are like that, too. We will never have perfectly pure motives on this side of heaven, but we can work toward ever increasing that purity. As we allow the Lord to expose our motives, we can move forward, progressing far from those shallow and superficial evaluations of ourselves.

This exposure will occur as we honestly humble ourselves before God and allow His Spirit to open us up to the truth of His Word. It comes hard, however, because pure motives are not natural; they're supernatural. As we humbly apply God's Word to our hearts, the Holy Spirit will do His great work within, gradually conforming us and our motives to the image of Jesus Christ. It is of vital importance, then, that we as parents are growing in this process because the first instrument God desires to use in purifying our children is us—their parents.

The secret to uncovering motives is answering the vital question, *Why?* Why do we do what we do? Why do our children do what they do? When we find the answer, we will uncover the motive. And since God is most interested in what motivates us, our motivations should be especially important to us as well.

When our children are young, it's usually easy to discover their motives. Since they are born selfish, much of what they do is for selfish reasons. Knowing this, when my children behaved badly, I pointed out to them not only the bad behavior that was unacceptable, but the bad motive behind it. When discipline was necessary, I made them understand that I was disciplining them for both the bad behavior and the bad motive.

Many parenting experts think that disciplining a child for their wrong motives and bad attitudes is not appropriate. Parents, they say, should discipline only for misbehavior. To the contrary, God and godly parents are more concerned about the *root* of the bad behavior than the *fruit* of misbehaving. Therefore, it becomes imperative that we confront, challenge, and work toward correcting the motive behind the behavior.

The sooner you begin correcting your child's motives, the better. As I said, when a child is young, it is not hard to discover selfish or mean-spirited motivations. Thus, we should begin examining them early, because as children get older, their motives become more difficult to discern—unless the child is outwardly and blatantly rebellious. Most children, as they grow older, also grow in their ability to hide their motives through self-deception, justification, and lies. They learn to cover up and deceive so that no one will know. Thus, it is vitally important to start early to detect and correct the motives behind a child's words or actions.

As our girls grew up, over time I came to recognize that Kerry's greatest spiritual stronghold was selfishness, and Lindsay's was laziness. Apples don't fall far from the tree, so I wasn't surprised by these discoveries—I struggled with the same things as a child. So when Kerry did something purely selfish for selfish reasons, or when Lindsay did something purely lazy for lazy reasons, I confronted both their bad behaviors and their bad motives. Kerry and Lindsay grew up knowing what the issues of their hearts were because I took the time to show them when it was clear to be seen. I made sure to instruct and to correct—sometimes tenderly, sometimes severely—but always teaching them "the truth in love" (Ephesians 4:15).

The reason wise parents are so deeply concerned about their children's motives is because God is, and one day their motives will be disclosed. 1 Corinthians 4:5 speaks to this:

> Therefore do not go on passing judgment before the time, but wait until the Lord comes who will both bring to light the things hidden in the darkness and disclose the motives of men's hearts; and then each man's praise will come to him from God.

We and our children will only receive praise from God if our motives have grown increasingly pure. Consequently, since the Lord weighs the motives of the heart, wise parents do the same, finding out the vital *why* behind the action, so the wrong motive can be corrected.

I realize that all this requires hard work and careful attention, but investment in your children's eternity holds great reward both for you and for them. Allow me to suggest two things you can do to discover your children's motives.

1. Be a Careful Student of Your Children

First Peter 3:7 instructs husbands to "live with your wives in an understanding way...so that your prayers will not be hindered." That good counsel applies not only to the husband/wife relationship but to every family relationship, including parents living with their children in an understanding way. We can gain understanding by becoming students of our children. This requires spending quality time with them and developing intimate parent-child relationships, where they talk and we first listen and then respond, especially with questions to draw them out in conversation. I had to fight my tendency to talk more than I listened to my children, and perhaps you will have the same fight within yourself. However, if we are going to get to know their hearts, we must be good listeners first. Then, once we have listened, we may talk and then listen some more, all for the purpose of understanding and knowing their little hearts.

2. Pray and Study for Understanding

The Lord said through His prophet, Jeremiah, "The heart is more deceitful than all else and is desperately sick; who can understand it?" He then answered, "I, the Lord, search the heart, I test the mind" (Jeremiah 17:9–10). There are two truths in those verses that we cannot deny. First, the unregenerate heart is deceitful and sick. It is not just *difficult* to understand; it is *impossible* for humans to fully understand it. Second, only God fully understands the human heart. Secular psychology lacks divine revelation and insight; it can only understand so much.

Thankfully, we don't have to be psychologists to understand a good portion of our children's hearts, motives, and attitudes. We do, however, need to know what God's Word says about humanity, and we do need to pray for His assistance to better understand what only He fully knows. If we want to live with our children in an understanding way, it is necessary that we pray for God's help and become careful students of His Word.

Once our children's motives are revealed to us, we must begin the hard work of correcting them. Since the human heart is most deceitful and desperately sick, correcting our children's hearts is difficult. But it is doable in Christ. Here are some suggestions.

- ***Measure Their Motives by the Divine Standard.*** The Scriptures are our final authority for faith and life, so they are also our measuring stick for morals and motives and everything else in life.
- ***Take Your Children to the Word.*** Open the Bible with them and show them what God authoritatively says about a bad motive. For example, Philippians 2:3 addresses selfishness: "Do nothing from selfishness…but with humility of mind regard one another as more important than yourselves." The goal is for your children to see that the Bible addresses the issues of our hearts. Teach them the biblical reasons why certain actions and attitudes are not acceptable.
- ***Begin Correcting the Wrong Motive.*** Don't expect that you will be able to reason with your children in

> a way that they will immediately change their motives from impure to pure. One can't reason with a deceitful, desperately sick heart. Purity doesn't come through reasoning; it comes through teaching, training, and corrective discipline, done in obedience to God and in the power of the Holy Spirit. The Bible says that our earthly fathers "disciplined us for a short time as seemed best to them, but [God] disciplines us for our good, so that we may share His holiness" (Hebrews 12:10). Godly parents follow God's example of disciplining their children for their good, so that they will share His holiness.

A godly, courageous determination to be a strong parent-leader is required for diligent application of this wise parenting principle. Some of us are natural leaders, and some of us have been called and equipped by God to be leaders. But most of us are leaders in our homes because we choose to be. We depend on God to provide the strength and grace we need to be the gutsy, godly leaders that our children need us to be. If you don't feel called to leadership in your home, don't let that stop you. Instead, call on God to make you strong in Christ as you simply and faithfully follow Him. Then command your children to follow you as you follow Christ. You will be surprised what God can do in and through the surrendered and dependent parent who is faithfully following Jesus.

Parenting Principle 18
Wise Parents Make Their Home a Place of Peace

Better is a dry morsel [i.e., a crust of bread] and quietness with it than a house full of feasting with strife.
Proverbs 17:1

What is more desirable to you, wealth or peace? In our nation of plenty, both may belong to us, but if a choice must be made, which would you choose? The wise and the experienced among us would always choose peace. But perhaps in your past, you didn't have a choice. Many of us grew up in homes where there was constant strife. Others, as adults, have been in marriages where there was much strife. If you experienced one of those scenarios, what was that like for you and your family? If you had money and material possessions along with that strife, what would you rather have had in your home, possessions or peace?

Take a moment to examine your present home life. If *peace* does not describe your home but you strongly desire it, what do you need to do or give up in order to have sufficient time, energy, and focus to pursue and secure the peace of God, first in your own heart and then in your home? Are you willing to make the necessary changes to obtain the peace of God and His true and eternal prosperity in your home? The answer depends on what is more valuable to you—peace or material possessions.

My daughter Kerry was visiting a friend. During their conversation, the friend told her that her father had worked eighty-hour weeks while she was growing up. He had recently told her that he'd worked those long hours for the sake of the family—work had been his priority only so his family could have everything they needed and wanted. In contrast, Kerry's friend and her husband were deliberately living at a below middle-class level so they could provide their children with what they *really* needed. She thought this would speak volumes to her father. "But," she said, "Dad doesn't get it!"

I wonder if her father was trying to justify his actions because of guilt—trying to make himself feel better about the choices he'd made that had brought deep hurt to his daughter's life. Even in her midthirties, she lives with the regret that her father didn't spend the quality and quantity time that she needed from him. Instead, what she and her family got was a perpetually tired and stressed-out dad who negatively released his tensions on them. It's like, "Okay, Dad, you did it for us. But, honestly, we would've much rather have had your presence and vital involvement and barely gotten by with a forty-hour work week, minus all the stress and strife."

Some children cry, scream, and even rebel out of the pain of not being a high priority to their parents. They seem to understand—better than their parents—the desperate need they have for their parents to fulfill their physical, emotional, relational, and spiritual needs more than their "need" for more of what they already have. Wise parents do their children a favor by making their homes a place of peace through the investment of themselves, even if they sacrifice some prosperity along the way to do it.

Over the years, several families in our church have been involved in foster parenting; consequently, many of those foster children have attended our church. Something that struck me early in being around foster children is how most of them, particularly the younger ones, almost immediately call their foster parents Mommy and Daddy. Kerry and Ben fostered an eighteen-month-old girl in their home, and immediately they were Mommy and Daddy. Not long after that, Kathy and I were Grandma and Granddad. That speaks volumes to her need, doesn't it?

All our children really want or need is a bigger significant someone to love them and to give them their precious time, attention, and love. Nothing brings peace to a child's heart like the knowledge that he or she is truly loved by his or her parents. For many foster children, the damage is done early and deep. They strive all their lives to convince themselves that they are worthy of love. Unfortunately, far too often, this same damage comes to biological children who grow up with their parents but don't get from them what they need.

I have worked with many people who are caught in this family cycle of trouble and strife, generation after generation. By the time they come to me for help because they are sick and tired of continuing the cycle, breaking free from it is not easy. Only by faithfully and consistently seeking the

God of peace and the peace of God can they finally break free and end the cycle. Ask these people what they would rather have had as children, and they don't hesitate: "Give us peace of home and heart over prosperity with strife any day!"

Outward strife always begins with strife within. If you, as a parent, are not satisfied in your heart and not content in your soul, the first thing you must do is make sure you have peace with God. Peace with God is an eternal blessing of our salvation; specifically, it is the fruit of justification in Christ that comes to us by faith. The apostle Paul wrote in Romans 5:1, "Having been justified by faith, we have peace with God through our Lord Jesus Christ." The spiritual process leading up to justification by faith looks like this:

- You recognize that you are a sinner like all the rest of humanity (Romans 3:23).
- You understand that you are under the condemnation of God because of your sins.
- You recognize that Jesus Christ, God's only begotten Son, died to pay the price for your sins.
- You realize that the salvation God offers you is by grace (undeserved favor) through faith.
- You sincerely confess your sins and your need for a Savior.
- You then simply ask Jesus to save you from the penalty of your sins. This means that your sins, that were so offensive to a holy God, are now forgiven because

Jesus' sacrifice fully satisfied His holiness. Upon your request, He can and He will save you from yourself.

- You are, at that moment—among other miraculous things—justified (declared righteous) by faith.
- The added eternal blessing is having peace with God through Jesus Christ.

If you are genuinely faithful to that salvation process, the promise of God is that you have "now been justified by [Jesus's] blood," and are "saved from the wrath of God through [Christ]. For if while we were enemies [of God] we were reconciled to God through the death of His Son, much more, having been reconciled, we shall be saved by His life" (Romans 5:9–10).

Have you been justified by the blood of Christ and thus reconciled to God through the sacrificial death of His Son? If so, then the condemnation that you so terribly deserved has passed from you, and you have peace with God! "Therefore there is now no condemnation for those who are in Christ Jesus" (Romans 8:1). Hell is canceled for you, and heaven is guaranteed.

Unfortunately, I have seen people confess their sins and ask Jesus Christ to forgive them and save them, only to see them fade away from the faith quite quickly and completely. I remember when, in the late 1970s, Bob Dylan confessed faith in Jesus Christ. In 1979, he gave the world his song of faith, "Gotta Serve Somebody." It was his last hit single, and it peaked at #24. In response to Dylan's hit, John Lennon wrote and recorded the song "Serve Yourself," meant to mock Dylan's faith and his injection of it into his music. Apparently, the enemy of reconciliation to God wasn't happy with Dylan's song. In time, word about Bob Dylan's faith faded. Years later, during an Internet search, I came across an interview with Dylan where he was asked about his faith. Sadly, he denied having it.

A few years ago, a young lady started coming to our church and quickly sought counseling from me. She was distraught over some serious relationship problems, and by all appearances, she seemed to be sincerely seeking Christ. I shared the gospel with her, and she immediately lit up at the opportunity presented to her to accept Christ as her Savior and to be His follower. She bowed her head in my office and accepted Christ as her personal Savior. For the first two or three weeks, she was thrilled about her faith. But within a month or so of her decision, she fell away from church and from God completely. I still see her on occasion in the community, and she makes it clear to me with her body language and tone of voice that she is no longer interested in Christ.

Jesus addressed this spiritual phenomenon in the parable of the sower and the seed in Luke 8:4–15. The seed that the sower sows is the Word of God—specifically, the gospel of Jesus Christ. In this powerful teaching, the Lord shows us that there are four types of reception of the Word.

First are those who have heard the Word, but, like a bird, the devil swoops in and steals it away from their hearts so that they will not believe and be saved. They hear it, but they don't receive it. Second is the group who hear the Word and receive it with joy, but the Word doesn't take root in their hearts.

They believe for a while, but in times of temptation and trial, they fall away. A third group hears and receives the Word, but in time, the worries, riches, and pleasures of the world choke it out, and they bring forth no spiritual fruit to maturity. They may still say they believe, but there's no fruit to back up their profession. For each of these groups, Jesus points out that something is wrong with their hearts—the soil of their hearts cannot produce a harvest.

The fourth group are those who prove to have good heart-soil, for they "have heard the Word in an honest and good heart," and they fully receive it and prove it by holding it fast and bearing fruit with perseverance (Luke 8:15).

I believe the only way to know for sure if a person is truly saved is not through a profession of faith, but by perseverance in the faith. Time, steadfastness, and the fruits of faith are the true tests of authentic faith. So allow me to ask you again: Are you sure you have peace with God through the Lord Jesus Christ? Are you proving it by your steadfast faith? Is God your priority in life? And is your faith productive? If you can answer yes with absolute certainty, then your peace with God is sure.

However, being reconciled to God and having peace with Him is not a guarantee that you intimately know and experience the ongoing peace in your heart and mind that is the product of a vital relationship with Him. Paul wrote in Philippians 4:6–7:

> Be anxious for nothing, but in everything by prayer and supplication with thanksgiving let your requests

> be made known to God. And the peace of God, which surpasses all comprehension, will guard your hearts and your minds in Christ Jesus.

To paraphrase, Paul is saying, "Don't worry about *anything*; instead, pray about *everything*. Trust God to answer the prayers and requests you present with a genuinely thankful spirit. Then the incomprehensible peace of God will stand guard over your heart and mind in Christ Jesus." Do you see it? We're back to personal priorities. Is God at the center of your life and relationship with Him? If He is, then as you grow to fully trust and depend on Him, you will come to know His peace at the core of your being, which is where Jesus Christ resides.

Peace *with* God comes to us at the point of salvation—it is one of the great salvational perks: we are, in Christ, reconciled to God. Ah, peace with God! The peace *of* God, on the other hand, grows out of our vital relationship with God. Five times in Matthew 6:25–34, Jesus exhorts His followers to not be worried. Instead, he tells them to "seek first His kingdom and His righteousness, and all these things will be added to [them]" (33). When we put Jesus Christ at the center of our lives, what do we have to be worried about?

Homes that are places of divine peace are light-years beyond homes of prosperity with strife. Maintaining a peaceful home will take strong parent-leadership, but wise parents gladly take the lead. My home, the place where my wife and I reside and where our children and grandchildren visit regularly, is usually a quiet place. The television is a bit louder when we watch it now because our ears are not what they used to be. And our grandchildren are pretty rambunctious and loud—just the way we like it, knowing that we will get to send them home soon. But our hearts and minds and spirits and souls and emotions are typically quiet and at peace. That is an enormous gift of God's grace to us, and I hope we never take it for granted.

If you and your family don't know this kind of quietness in your home, and if your home is not typically stress and strife free, then may I lovingly suggest that you seek with all your heart the peace of God that surpasses all comprehension and that will guard your minds and hearts in Christ Jesus. You will find His peace as you faithfully seek God. If He's the center, then you and your family will know peace. For God's sake, and for your own, may it be so for you.

Parenting Principle 19
Wise Parents Prove Their Worth to Their Children

Grandchildren are the crown of old men, and
the glory of sons is their fathers.
PROVERBS 17:6

Grandchildren are the "crowning glory" of their grandparents (NLT). When godly grandparents look at their grandchildren who are either being raised up in Christ by their godly children or who have grown up in Christ and are living godly lives, they recognize this to be their crowning achievement, their joy and pride. I'm watching my daughter and son-in-law raise up our grandchildren in the Lord, and I can't tell you how pleased and overjoyed I am with both the parents and the grandchildren. It is the glorious icing on the cake for this old man.

I feel the same joy and pride when I look at all the godly younger parents in our church who are also bringing up their children in the Lord. I walk around our church like a proud and pleased father and grandfather. These parents and their children, along with my own children and grandchildren, are a crowning achievement to me as their pastor, as well as to all their godly grandparents. It doesn't get any better than this, because it means that we brought up our children well in the discipline and instruction of the Lord, and our children are doing the same with their children.

It is most satisfying to know that we spiritually minded and hearted older folks proved our worth to our children by investing heavily in their spiritual and eternal well-being. We proved our worth as godly parents in the following ways:

- We loved our children with the love of God that the Spirit of God poured into our hearts. We allowed the Spirit to pour out His love through us, like channels, into the hearts of our children. We loved them tough when necessary, and at other times, we loved them tender. Regardless of the circumstances, we loved them strong, just like Jesus loves us.

- We loved them with quantity and quality time. We spent as much time as possible with our children during their childhood years because time is fleeting and *time + attention + God = love.* We also made sure that much of the time we spent with them was quality time. We got down on the floor or out in the yard and played with our children on their level. We taught them how to play ball and other fun activities. Why, we even did things that we abhorred, like taking them bowling. I hate bowling! But I bowled with a smile and a laugh and had a wonderful time because it wasn't about me; it was about my time spent with them and on them. But time well spent is not just raw time. It's quantity and quality time.
- We brought them up in the discipline and instruction of the Lord. We were careful to correct their course when they began to stray from the way of Christ. And we took sufficient time to train them up in the knowledge of Christ and His Word—not just head knowledge so they know *about* the Lord and His Word, but heart knowledge so they personally and intimately know Him. We did our best to give them the attitude and spirit of the apostle Paul, who stated with deep conviction, "I count all things to be loss in view of the surpassing value of knowing Christ Jesus my Lord... and count them but rubbish so that I may gain Christ" (Philippians 3:8).

- We taught them social graces so they would not be awkward in interpersonal relationships. We demonstrated to them what healthy relationships *look* like as they watched their parents in a loving marital union. We showed them what healthy relationships *felt* like as we related to them in a healthy manner. Further, we showed them what it was like to experience a healthy relationship with God, their Father, and Jesus Christ, their Savior and Lord. Our prayer was that, when they looked at their earthly parents, they would see glimpses of their perfect heavenly Father. We prayed that they would easily grow to love Him with all their hearts and walk before Him in the highest reverential awe, treating His name as most holy and thus becoming comfortable in His holy presence.
- We lived before them with consistent integrity so they could clearly see what an honest, faithful, worthy life looked like. We proved our worth by walking before the Lord, our family, our church family, and the world in a manner that was worthy of our Lord, well-pleasing to Him, and beneficial to all others (Ephesians 4:1–3). And we taught our children the vital importance of following our example by walking in their own integrity.
- We prayed with our spouses, with our children, and for our children. Kathy and I even prayed for our grandchildren while our girls were still young. We realized how important it was for them to witness in

us a consistent prayer and devotional life. We taught them to pray, how to pray, and how to have a devotional life centered on God's Word and prayer. And we consistently helped our children see how God answers prayer in wonderful and unexpected ways.

- We gave them ourselves as examples of forgiveness. We had been forgiven much by God and by others; in turn, we willingly, readily, and easily forgave others for their trespasses against us. We demonstrated in ourselves lives that were transformed by the mercy and grace of God; we taught them that we are not only saved by grace but that we are dependent upon grace every step of the way and, in the end, we are translated to our heavenly home only by grace. We don't deserve anything that we get or become or that we have accomplished—it's all by grace. We are ever grateful to our Father for the sufficiency of His ongoing and eternal grace toward us. It makes us channels of that same grace to others.
- We taught them what obedience looks like. It began with helping them understand that we are people under divine and human authority. When we had authority over others, we showed them what that looked like—seasoned with patience, humility, love, and firmness. We modeled submission and obedience before them so they wouldn't be confused when we demanded and expected the same from them. We trained them in obedience and administered appropriate reproof and

correction when necessary, because we understood the utter value and necessity of a submissive and obedient life—first before God, who is worthy, and second, before those in authority over us. Even if we couldn't respect the *person* of authority, we demonstrated to our children a respect for their *position*.

- We modeled before them godly lives from godly living so that they would be without excuse when they came of age and were no longer held accountable by us, their parents. We wanted our children to see firsthand how God blesses those who bless and honor Him. When we treat God according to His worthiness, He does an amazing thing: He treats us as worthy! We wanted them to see that lived out so that they too would treat God the way He deserves, as most worthy.

We did none of this perfectly, but we did it to the best of our ability as Christ gave us strength, knowing that God was pleased with our best efforts in Christ. Then we depended on Him to make up for our shortcomings because we knew we had plenty of them. Despite ourselves, we have proved our worth to our children.

And now, when we look at our grandchildren being brought up well in the Lord by our children, our shirt buttons feel the strain of godly pride, joy, and pleasure. Our cups truly overflow! To this old man, my grandchildren are my crowning achievement and glory. All I can do is fall on my face before the Lord and give Him thanks for the things He has so graciously done in and through me.

> *I thank You, O my Father, that when I look at my godly children and grandchildren, I don't feel shame for a wasted life that failed to make heavy investments in those under my care. Thank You that, instead, I can look at them with great satisfaction, with the deepest pleasure, and as the highest crowning glory in life, on earth and in heaven. In Jesus's strong name I pray. Amen.*

The second half of Proverbs 17:6 says, "The glory of sons is their fathers." The New International Version puts it, "Parents are the pride of their children." Well, that begs the following questions: Growing up in your home, were your children proud of you? Are your adult children proud of you? If you still have children in your home, are they proud of you? Will they be proud of you as adults? Do they and will they highly esteem you and say, "My parents are amazing examples of God's grace and glory to me. I am so proud of them and blessed to call them my parents!"

Parents, are you the glory of your children? You can be, for the following reasons:

- They highly esteem you because you've proved your worth to them. Even as adults, they will treasure their childhood home life as the most foundational and important gift that God could have ever given to them.

They felt safe and secure there; they were introduced to Jesus there; and their childhood was full of holiness, fun, laughter, and pleasure. They could give you "Best Father" and "Best Mother" mugs and actually mean it.

- They are pleased and proud to introduce you as their parents. There is no shame in them toward you because you did not act shamefully in life. Conversely, if you did behave shamefully, you have since fully repented by the glorious grace of God and now bring praise from your children rather than words, attitudes, and actions of shame.
- You are proving yourself faithful to them throughout their lives. You are faithfully involved in every aspect of their lives; faithfully raising them up in Jesus Christ; faithfully presenting God the Father as a most holy, good, and gracious Father, One whose throne they can "draw near with confidence to...receive mercy and find grace to help in time of need" (Hebrews 4:16), and at all other times as well. You are also faithfully bringing them up in a healthy church environment so they grow up loving church rather than despising it.
- You are proving your worth to your children by living out the Word of God before them. You know the commandments and the promises of Scripture, and you don't hesitate to obey and trust them. You never need to say, "Do as I say, not as I do." Rather, you can say, "Follow me, children, as I follow Christ. He is

trustworthy and, since we can trust Him, we will obey Him."

- You show your worth when circumstances become difficult. You don't fall apart when the evil one brings trouble into your life or home. There's a steadiness about you, a confidence in God's sovereign care and control, so that your children look to you for strong parent-leadership through dark valleys and shadowlands. You prove to be up to the calling and task before you because of your steadfast faith in your heavenly Father. When Lindsay and Jason were murdered, I felt the eyes of my family, church family, and friends upon me, needing me to lead through the darkness and pain as I followed Jesus Christ. Wise fathers, as you grow in your trust and dependence upon God in times of peace and plenty, you will be prepared to lead when your family passes through the valley of the shadow. It is a critical time for you to stand up in Christ to prove your worth.
- You show your worth by protecting your children from deep frustration and anger. The Scriptures exhort, "Fathers, do not provoke your children to anger" (Ephesians 6:4) and "Fathers, do not exasperate your children, so that they will not lose heart" (Colossians 3:21). Why does Paul specifically address fathers here? For one thing, fathers are not mothers—that is to say, they are not motherly. We fathers tend more toward toughness than tenderness. We often expect and

demand too much, instruct too little, and relate to our children in less than an outwardly loving manner. Since that is typically true, instead of provoking our children to anger, we are to be a blessing and encouragement to them, even when the situation screams for corrective discipline. Discipline them when needed, but be sure to do it in a loving manner. Prove your worth by protecting your children from anger so they do not lose heart and/or use their anger as an excuse to walk away from you—or from faith in Christ.

- You show your worth by listening to your children, building trust as a ready listener, and learning to understand their personalities so you can instruct and encourage them in the way of Christ. Instead of listening only long enough to *fix* a problem—which is the tendency of men—you listen with the intent to understand, encourage, and embrace. Then, perhaps, you can give solutions to their problems. What your children need more than solutions is understanding, sympathy, and love. It's a hard world we have birthed them into and, oh, how they need us to help them bear their burdens triumphantly. Bearing burdens looks different than fixing them.
- You prove your worth through preventative discipline. I define preventative discipline, in part, as a heavy investment in their lives. Especially when they are young, get down on their level; interact and play with them. Further, take advantage of all the teachable moments

> that life with your children on the floor will present. Any corrective discipline should be preceded with ample preventative discipline. Give them overwhelmingly positive attention; it will go a long way in preventing them from seeking negative attention. Children who do not receive positive nurturing attention will seek any attention, because negative attention is better than none, even when it comes from them acting out.

Wise parents are the pride of their children. Are you? It is never too late to start fresh through confession of and repentance from sins. Begin with your heavenly Father, then with your spouse and children. Confess your sins to them and, with godly sorrow, ask them to forgive you. Then prove your worth in Christ to them by producing fruit in keeping with your repentance. You may live with some regret—all of us do—but you will never regret turning back to God and beginning fresh to prove your worth to your family, knowing how eternally worth it they are.

I have an ex-brother-in-law whom I loved and love still. But when he abandoned my beautiful, godly sister, he divorced all of us with her, including his sons. At a recent Fourth of July family reunion, I asked my nephew, now in his forties, if he ever hears from his dad. "Not for the last ten years," he told me. "Worse than that, he's never met my sons, his grandsons." My nephew has a hard time comprehending that, and I with him. But one thing is certain: we cannot say of my nephew's dad that his grandchildren are his crown, nor is he the pride of his son. How sad that is! On the other hand, my nephew is proving his immeasurable worth to his children, and I am supremely proud of him. But much better than that, his God is proud and pleased with him. He's proving his worth as a strong father-leader. Way to the break the mold, nephew!

Proverbs 20:6 asks, "Many a man proclaims his own loyalty, but who can find a trustworthy man? A righteous man who walks in his integrity; how blessed are his sons after him." If you find a righteous man who walks in his integrity, you have found a trustworthy man whose sons after him will be highly blessed. What a way to go in the end, godly parents—leaving behind highly blessed children and grandchildren because you proved your worth to them! Think of the awful alternative. Your worth is either an eternal value, or it is worth nothing.

Prove your worth, parents. Be the strong parent-leaders your children need you to be. May it be so in Jesus's precious name. Amen.

Parenting Principle 20
Wise Parents Train Their Children to Love Each Other

A friend loves at all times, and a brother is born for adversity.
PROVERBS 17:17

How do you teach this principle to two, three, four, or more fallen creatures who live under the same roof, who couldn't be more opposite from one another, and who are competing for the same things—namely, their parents' time and attention? Normal childhood often includes selfish competition and incompatibility between siblings. However, if parents are purposeful in training the family in the unity of the Spirit and are steadfastly consistent in nipping selfish competition in the bud, siblings will at least learn to tolerate each other and will probably become close-knit friends as adults. Personalities play a huge roll in this, but environment is also important.

Parents, it will take God's grace and dynamic power, but if you can pull it off, it's a beautiful thing when siblings love each other and prove themselves fiercely loyal to one another. And when adversity comes, who can estimate the value of such a loyal brother or sister at one's side? In true brotherhood and sisterhood, where blood is thick and kinship devotion is strong, siblings are *born* for this purpose—to face hard times and hardships together.

I am speaking primarily from Scripture, our ultimate source of authority and truth, but also from personal family experience. Both my wife Kathy and my daughter Kerry had one sibling each. Both siblings were sisters, and both were lost early to death. Joette died when Kathy was in the second grade, and Lindsay died when Kerry was twenty-five. I can tell you from my close relationship with Kathy and Kerry, living without their sisters is a difficult thing. They no longer have their sisters around to share in life together, to confide in one another, and to come to each other's side in times of trouble. They both would testify that since a brother or sister is born for adversity, not having them physically present is a huge loss and, at times, a heavy burden. Of course, they didn't realize this as children, but they are intimately acquainted with it as women.

When Kerry and Lindsay were growing up, we had a *Waltons*-like tradition. After we'd put our girls down for the night, from the living room we would call out, "Love you, Kerry," and she would respond, "Love you, Dad. Love you, Mom." We'd call, "Love you, Lindsay," and Lindsay would also reply, "Love you, Dad. Love you, Mom." But then we made them say "Love you, Lindsay" and "Love you, Kerry." I remember how ready and willing they were to express their love back to us, but they were often reluctant to express their love for each other. We could hear it in their voices, kind of monotone and flat: "Love you." "Yeah, love you, too..." *not much*. But we made them say it anyway and tirelessly worked to reinforce the immense blessing and privilege they had in having a sibling and, along with that, the strength of family unity. We knew that someday, the wonder and power of that oneness would come in handy, particularly in times of adversity.

Kerry and Lindsay didn't fully accept that as a reality until they became young adults. Then Kathy and I watched the bond grow from simply being sisters to being close family members and trusted friends. That gave us tremendous joy. But then we also watched that close and personal relationship come to an end through Lindsay's death. That ache is still in Kerry's heart to this day, more than twelve years later, and it will never fully disappear. I know, because I see and hear it, not only in her but in her mother as well, who lost her sister decades ago.

Parents, with these examples of great loss fresh in your minds, set out to do your best to teach your children while they are young the enormous value of having a sibling. Help them look ahead to believe what—for some, at least—might seem nearly impossible: that there will be a time when a faithful brother or sister will be so much more valuable than a friend. Teach them that their siblings will be with them through thick and thin and through the adversities of life. Very little is guaranteed in this harsh world, but much is promised, including great trouble and trial. Further, as we know personally, it's possible that your children may lose a sibling in an untimely manner. Train them now to understand the inestimable value of a brother or sister; warn them of the grave mistake of taking each other for granted.

A friend of mine has two sons in their forties. He's told me that they call each other on the phone nearly every day, and they have been doing so for years. For a while, one of the brothers lived on the West Coast, while the other lived in Ohio; yet every day, almost without fail, they interacted on the phone. I know my friend's two sons; they are anything but codependent on each other. What they share is a healthy interdependence that will continue to be invaluable when the storms of life threaten.

Think about the kind of friends your children can be to one another, particularly in their adult years: true friends and siblings that love at all times. Think of that and set out to create a home environment that will facilitate a brotherly/sisterly devotion that is saturated with the power and grace of heaven. Life for your children in their adult years will be all the richer and fuller for it.

As we close this wise principle and chapter, ask yourself what your children desperately need from you. They need strong parent-leaders who fear nothing and no one because of their fear of the Lord. Such parents will champion the Lord's cause in their homes by raising children who are not afraid to follow their parents' lead.

For this to become the reality of our homes, we must be like Joshua and Caleb, who depended on and trusted in the Lord with all that was within them. That unfaltering God-confidence consequently made their enemies seem as grasshoppers in their sight. Likewise, our God-confidence will make the enemies of our homes—the flesh, the world, and the devil—mere grasshoppers to us. Sounds wonderful, doesn't it? Listen, my brothers and sisters. In Christ, you can do this!

CHAPTER 6

Wise Parenting Principles 21-25: The Small Window

Proverbs 19–22

I Took a Piece of Plastic Clay
Author Unknown

I took a piece of plastic clay,
And idly fashioned it one day.
And as my fingers pressed it still,
It moved and yielded to my will.
I came again when the days were passed,
And the bit of clay was hard at last.
The form I gave it still it bore,
But I could change that form no more.
I took a piece of living clay,
And gently formed it day by day;
And molded with my power and art,
A young child's soft and yielding heart.
I came again when the days were gone,

It was a man I looked upon.
He still that early impress wore,
But I could change that form no more.

Wise parents may be likened to potters who shape the human clay God has gifted to us. Just as the Holy Spirit molds and shapes us as Christians who bring glory to our Father and blessings to others, so we are to mold and shape our children for God's glory, for their own eternal benefit, and for blessings upon those with whom their lives intersect. Think of your children as living clay with eternal souls and yourselves as their primary human potters. Be constantly mindful that you have only a small window of time in which to raise them up in Christ before that living clay hardens, and they leave the home to strike out on their own.

Knowing then the short time you have for the molding process, determine to allow God to empower you to shape them with supernatural skill into the likeness of Jesus Christ. In this chapter, the book of Proverbs gives us wise counsel in allowing this to happen.

Parenting Principle 21
Wise Parents Take Advantage of Their Window of Opportunity

Discipline your son while there is hope, and do not desire his death.
Proverbs 19:18

Allow me to paraphrase Galatians 6:7–9, in order to apply the passage directly to parents:

> Do not be deceived: God cannot be mocked. Whatever a parent sows, he will also reap. Parents who sow to please their own sinful nature, from that nature will reap destruction; but parents who sow to please the Spirit, from the Spirit will reap eternal life. Parents, let us not become weary in doing good; for at the proper time we will reap a harvest if we do not give up.

These verses, applied to parents, provide a convicting, convincing, and encouraging word for us to wholly invest in the righteousness of God in our homes and to sow in the soil of our children's hearts seeds that will please the Holy Spirit. These verses use farming terminology to demonstrate that there is only a small window of opportunity to sow our seeds in hopes of a good harvest.

Our proverb exhorts parents to discipline their children while there is still hope. *The Living Clay* poem, reprinted above, reminds us that, once clay is removed from its wrapper and exposed to the elements of the world, only a short time is open to the sculptor to mold and form it into something useful. Likewise, parents have just as short an amount of time to shape their young children's soft and yielding hearts. Wise parents, then, keep ever before them the understanding that the window of their life-shaping influence in their children's lives is indeed small.

Of course, like in farming, there are other influencing factors beyond our parental control. Just as harsh weather affects a harvest for the farmer, difficult personalities and strong self-wills in our children, along with outside influences from other people, can adversely affect our children's molding process. Regardless, to the best of our ability in Christ and as far as it depends upon us as parents, we must intentionally sow now, and weed and nurture all along the way of their formable years. Beyond that, we pray for Providence to provide what we cannot control in order to assure a bountiful harvest.

John Rosemond wrote in *The Well-Behaved Child*,

> It is important to note that I've focused most of my strategies in this book on disciplining children between the ages of three and thirteen, what I refer to as the "Decade of Discipline" … [However,] parents can lay good disciplinary foundations prior to age two and can begin making significant inroads between the second and third birthdays. (Thomas Nelson, 2009, xvii.)

Whether you fully accept Rosemond's "Decade of Discipline" proposal or not, we will all agree that a decade is a shockingly short time available in which to influence our children. Wise parents will make the best of the time God gives us, for the consequences of not making the best of it are too terrible to consider.

To discipline your children while there is hope, you must be diligent in both kinds of discipline—corrective and preventative. As we've already studied, corrective discipline involves diligently and effectively correcting the course of your child from going his way to walking in obedience on God's way. Preventative discipline requires an investment of time, energy, and affection in your children. In preventative discipline, you take the necessary time to train them, teach them, enjoy them, and interact with them in a meaningful and purposeful manner. This includes making plenty of time to play with them. I believe that parents who spank their children should also be those who play with them.

This is the second time I have mentioned preventative discipline. Since the window of shaping our children through discipline is so small, the following is an acrostic that will help illustrate this necessary type of discipline.

P **Play.** An old adage says that people don't care how much you know until they know how much you care. Young children don't care how much you know or how important you are in the church or in the world; they only care about how much you care for them. That care is often best expressed and received by them through playtime. Every night before I put my girls to bed, I gave them rides—I put them on my shoulders (one at a time!) and ran the length of our house like a runaway horse, with them laughing all the way. Sometimes I gave them bucking bull rides on my back while on all fours. Sometimes I walked through the house with the girls sitting on my feet and hanging onto my legs. They loved it! This has carried over to our grandsons.

When they spend the night at our house, we have a few traditions that they are sure to enforce. One is having their grandmother read from the conch book that describes the shell fish in detail (our grandsons never tire of her reading about them!), and the other is their granddad playing what they call bedtime games. This isn't the only time I played with my children and grandchildren, but they will never forget our special time before bed. Preventative discipline must include play. That way, when you must correct them, they will know that you are correcting them in love.

R **Relate.** Central to life should be relationship. We sometimes say that Christianity is much more than a religion—it's a relationship between human persons and divine persons, between us and our triune God. For our relationship with the Lord to be true and vital, we must relate to Him in personal and intimate ways. More than anything else, we need God's love in our lives. More than anything else, God wants us to love Him in return. If our relationship with God is critically vital to our health and well-being, then how important are our other relationships, including those with our spouses and our children? Wise parents understand that they must intimately and powerfully relate to their children. They can't be distant, disengaged, aloof, indifferent, detached, unfriendly, or cold. Instead, they must be consistently up close and personal, constantly engaged, attached, enjoyable, fun, and funny. There are times for serious relating, but set up that seriousness with preventative relating that communicates our keen understanding of the eternal value of the eternal souls of our beloved children.

E **Events.** Parents should plan events that bond the family together in an environment of fun and laughter. I mentioned earlier that Monday evenings were family nights for us. These were special nights where we went out to eat and then had fun doing something together, like miniature golf. We planned other events, too—Saturday morning fishing outings, weekend trips away, fun-filled vacations together. Family passes to the local pool or the closest city zoo allow for wonderful bonding times for families. Be creative and proactive. Very little happens unless it is planned, but spontaneous little events like a short trip together to get ice cream or a walk in the park are always big hits with children.

V **Venture.** Be adventurous in your family ventures. My family did not hunt animals, but there's one thing that we did and still do hunt: morel mushrooms. In the spring in Ohio, wild morels pop up in wooded areas and old apple orchards and the like. It is still a challenging and enjoyable venture for our family (challenging in that morels are not always easy to find; sometimes you must walk long distances over difficult terrain to find them). Our family goes together out into the woods, and if we are fortunate enough to find a batch, I clean them, my wife fries them, and together we all eat them. Kerry makes sure we go out early in the season, usually two or three weeks before they can be found, and we go out often, sometimes two or three times a week, until the season is over. "Dad, are we going mushroom hunting later today?" Wise parents plan ventures together and are adventurous because ventures are investments that create togetherness and memories that will last a lifetime. I will never forget going mushroom hunting with my dad, and Kerry will never forget going with me. And she's passing that tradition down to her children as well. We are mushroom hunters!

E **Enjoy.** Greatly enjoy your relationships. First, enjoy your relationship with your God. Then enjoy your relationships with your spouse, your church family and friends, the unbelieving folks that you are trying to reach for Christ—and enjoy your relationship with your children. Actively enjoy each stage of their childhood, including the difficult ones. Purposefully enjoy your children and prove it by telling them and showing them that they are a joy to you. Tell them things like, "You know what? You are the apple of my eye!" and then demonstrate just how special they truly are. It is heartbreaking to see parents who delight in hobbies and friends, spending way too much of their leisure time pursuing both, but who delight very little in their children. I'm convinced that if you delight in God, you will delight in your children, and you will purposefully spend much time in their presence delighting in them, over them, and with them, to their everlasting joy.

N **Nurture.** Ephesians 5:29–30 exhorts husbands to *nourish* and *cherish* their wives "just as Christ…does the church, because we are members of His body." Husband, do you nurture your wife because you highly cherish her? I was once working with a couple who were having marriage problems. During this process, I asked the woman after a worship service how she was doing. She responded quietly so only I could hear her: "I just want my husband to cherish me." If adult married women need that from their husbands, how much more do our children need that from their parents? *Cherish*—treasure, value, prize, esteem as of great worth. Do you treasure your children the way your heavenly Father treasures you? *Nurture*—carefully and caringly raise, develop, cultivate, support, and encourage growth. Nurturing takes much time, attention, and love. But for wise parents, that's not a problem, "for what does it profit a man to gain the whole world, and forfeit his [child's] soul?" (Mark 8:36).

T **Time.** Remember, time is of the essence. Proverbs instructs us to discipline our children while there is hope. The window of opportunity is small. Living clay does not stay soft and pliable for long. Think about it—doesn't time fly? We often marvel over how quickly our children grow up. When it comes to raising your children up in the Lord, take my youngest daughter's counsel to heart: "We are here temporarily…Don't waste time." Instead of wasting time, *spend* the time God has given to you on those who need you most—namely, your spouse and your children. Wise parents will apply the counsel Paul gives in Ephesians 5:15–17 to their family time:

> Therefore be careful how you walk, not as unwise men but as wise, making the most of your time, because the days are evil. So then do not be foolish, but understand what the will of the Lord is.

He further warns us not to spend our time wastefully, but to come completely under the Spirit's influence and control…because time is so short.

A **Attention.** *Time + attention + God = love.* Never forget that formula. I remember once watching a mother with her young daughter in our church. The daughter came to church often with her aunt; the mother had made a rare visit that day. Some of us were in the worship auditorium, visiting. The little girl was sitting in a pew right beside her mother, trying her best to get her attention. The child must have said, "Mommy," at least ten times, to no avail. I was sickened by what I watched because *no time + no attention + no God = no love* is also an accurate equation. The situation made me think. I trust it will make you think as well.

T **Train.** Proverbs 22:6: "Train up a child in the way he should go, even when he is old he will not depart from it." Ephesians 6:4 (NIV): "Fathers, do not exasperate your children; instead, bring them up in the training and instruction of the Lord." I know a man who trained his children to be extremely successful in the business world. He made sure they were also brought up in the church, but his emphasis seemed to be much more on their success in the world than their success in Christ. I have no doubt these adult children are saved; as far as I know, they are churched, but their spiritual training was not the priority. While teaching a solid work ethic is important and even biblical, training up our children in the Lord and for the Lord's glory is our primary parental responsibility. Am I being too critical of some Christian parents? I don't think so. But I am passionate about the eternal perspective of parenting; so much so that I get a bit melancholy at times over the fact that eternal values have become less—sometimes far less—than our first priority. I have a pastoral, fatherly, and grandfatherly passion within me that desperately wants to see our children trained to prosper in all areas of their lives, yes—but far more importantly, to spiritually prosper now and forever.

I **Invest.** Investing heavily in the spiritual, emotional, mental, social, and physical well-being of our children is certainly an important aspect of preventative discipline. When Lindsay was a senior in high school, we were using Oswald Chambers's classic, *My Utmost for His Highest*, during our family nighttime devotions. I still remember February 24 of that year. The verse of the day was 2 Corinthians 12:15 (NKJV): "I will very gladly spend and be spent for your souls." When Lindsay and I read that verse, it resonated within us. Together, we got excited about the prospect of *spending* and *being spent* for the souls of others. Some of the best time and attention I spent on my daughters came in those moments we shared focused attention together on the Word of God. I strongly encourage you to claim the verse as your own and apply it to your relationship with your children: "Sons and daughters, I will very gladly spend and be spent for your souls." What better way to spend your limited time and expend your short life! Since the window is so small and time is so short, invest heavily in those eternal souls.

V **eVangelism.** Wise parents set out to evangelize their children while they are young and aren't yet know-it-alls. There has been a lot of debate over the years about whether young children—let's say four to seven—can fully understand the gospel, especially the bad news portion of the gospel—the truth that they are wretched sinners in desperate need of a Savior. Many books have been written on the subject, some saying they can be saved and some saying they can't. Personally, I think the salvation of a soul is a process, and many children who come to faith early may need to complete the deal when they are a bit older, and I'm all right with that. Children who are raised in a Christian home with wise parents and in a wise church with purposeful outreach ministries to children are exposed often to the gospel, and consequently, many of them come to faith early; we wouldn't want it any other way. What we typically see is that those same children make a deeper, later commitment when they better understand the decision they made early in life. In fact, how many of us fully understand grace and our desperate need for it, even as adults? Salvation is of God, but He has given us the privilege of facilitating the salvation process early in many of our children. Wise parents won't stand in the way of that process but will do all that they can to lead their children to a childlike faith in Christ.

E **Evaluate.** In both preventative and corrective discipline, it is good for a godly couple (or a godly single parent) to regularly set aside time to evaluate their effectiveness in taking advantage of the window of opportunity God has given them. I suggest you develop mutual accountability questions, using this acrostic as a guide, to see how well you are doing in bringing up your children in the training, preventative discipline, and instruction of the Lord. Be humble and honest in your evaluations; be willing to accept constructive criticism from your spouse (or from a godly friend) that will help you become wiser in loving, nurturing, and cherishing your beloved children.

According to this principle's proverb, wise parents discipline their children while there is hope because we don't desire their deaths. Of course, no loving parent desires that. But if we are not disciplining our children during the most hopeful years, there is a sense in which we are, indeed, contributing to their deaths. The proverb is not simply a command meant to prevent parents from being passive in raising their children. It's also a strong warning against neglecting discipline, both corrective and preventative, so that we do not contribute to our children's destruction or even death. Thus, we are reminded again of the small window of opportunity and what is at stake—the very soul-lives of our children.

Parenting Principle 22
Wise Parents Teach Their Children How to Not Fight

Keeping away from strife is an honor for a
man, but any fool will quarrel.
Proverbs 20:3

This proverb encourages us to accept the fact that kids, since they are born foolish, are also born to fight. But we can work hard to train those feisty children to grow up to be honorable adults; we can teach them how *not* to fight.

The world and our sin nature teach our kids that they must fight (1) for pride's sake and to save face; (2) so they can get what they want because life is all about them—if ever there was a "me first" generation, we're living in it; and (3) to stick up for themselves. If we don't reverse this secular teaching in our children, many of them will grow up ready and willing to fight for what they think is right. On the other hand, heaven teaches us that it is honorable to walk away from a fight and that fighting is not only childish but worldly and stupid. Any fool will fight, whether with fists or words, but the person who has the wisdom of God instilled from childhood knows that "a gentle answer turns away wrath" (Proverbs 15:1).

Proverbs 20:11 says, "It is by his deeds that a lad distinguishes himself if his conduct is pure and right." Therefore, a wise father would say, "Son, don't fight. Instead, distinguish yourself by how you calmly, purely, and rightly carry yourself. Don't follow the crowd. Lead a crowd into righteousness." But that's not an easy lesson to teach in a hostile world, and it's an even harder one to receive and accept. Do we want them to give in to bullies? Are we okay with them getting hurt because they won't fight back and stand up for themselves against abuse? This is a hard call for many of us. Our natural inclination is to teach our children to fight back and to defend themselves. But what is right in the sight of God?

In the Sermon on the Mount in Matthew 5:38–39, Jesus said: "You have heard that it was said, 'An eye for an eye, and a tooth for a tooth.' But I say to you, do not resist an evil person; but whoever slaps you on your right cheek, turn the other to him also." It is much easier to practice an eye for an eye than to turn the other cheek. It's also easy for us to relegate this teaching to the future kingdom and excuse it as not applying to ourselves and to our children in this age of hostility; however, I don't believe that's allowable. This is God's truth and mandate for every culture and generation—in God's kingdom now in us during the present church age as well as in His kingdom to come. Notice that Jesus wasn't teaching in the future tense, but in the present. As a younger, not-so-wise man, I had hoped that our Lord's teaching here was not for today, but now I know better.

So how in world do we teach this principle to our sons and our daughters? While boys generally tend to express their aggression through physical combat, girls are more likely show their aggression through silent treatment, cold shoulders, vengeful friendships with other girls to hurt the friend that hurt them, spreading rumors and gossip, and just plain, petty meanness—although they can get physical, too. Whether boys or girls, how do we teach them to *not* fight in a fallen world where everyone is prone to fighting, quarreling, striving, striking, and the like?

Here are some proactive precepts on the subject.

1. Raise Your Children in a Countercultural Environment

Don't be surprised to find your children thrown into a world where survival of the fittest reigns, even in a Christian school or Sunday school class or nursery, because worldlings are everywhere. For this reason, your children should learn and be content with the fact that your family swims against the tide of the world around them. Like us, they are—or will be—*in* the world, but they must learn to be not *of* it (John 17:13–19). And who would be better than their wise parents to teach them that they are otherworldly, that they belong wholly to the King and His kingdom? Swimming against the tide of the world sounds difficult, but when we go the way of the Spirit in the power of the Spirit, it's more like letting go and flowing with His current. Galatians 5:16 calls this "walking by the Spirit." The difficulty lies in initially letting go of the world's way, but once you do, it's smooth swimming, caught in the current of the Spirit of God. Teach your children that there is a better way than fighting against the world; it's walking (or swimming) in God's way.

2. Teach Your Children to Let God Fight for Them

The premise of the excellent movie *War Room* (subtitled *Prayer Is a Powerful Weapon*) is that we, as Christians, are to let God fight for us. Any fighting we do should be done in the prayer closet, known in the movie as the "war room." It is not our place to retaliate; instead, we are to commit our case to the Lord, who will one day set all things straight (Romans 12:17–21). Jesus exemplified this in His life on earth, teaching us to follow His example. His apostle put it this way in 1 Peter 2:18–23:

> Servants, be submissive to your masters with all respect, not only to those who are good and gentle, but also to those who are unreasonable. For this finds favor [with God], if for the sake of conscience toward God a person bears up under sorrows when suffering unjustly. For what credit is there if, when you sin and are harshly treated, you endure it with patience? But if when you do what is right and suffer for it you patiently endure it, this finds favor with God. For you have been called for this purpose, since Christ also suffered for you, leaving you an example for you to follow in His steps, who committed no sin, nor was any deceit found in His mouth; and while being reviled,

> He did not revile in return; while suffering, He uttered no threats, but kept entrusting Himself to Him who judges righteously.

Wise parents teach their children to *entrust* themselves to the Father, who will set all things right in His time. Teach your children to take the fight to the Lord in prayer instead of fighting back. Teach them to let Him fight on their behalf in His way and on His timetable.

3. Train Your Children by Your Own Example

Wise parents follow Peter's inspired words and the Lord's perfect and powerful example, because it is helpful if we can say to our children in all integrity, "Follow me as I follow Christ." No, you may not always be able to follow Him perfectly, but you can follow Him well most of the time through total trust and dependence. We must teach our children early to trust in the Lord with all their hearts so they can have the spiritual guts to entrust themselves to Him in the midst of trouble, including in the face of a bully or provocation. This is how they become men and women of honor. It may be a challenge to teach them that God is sovereign and that we can always trust His sovereignty, but by precept and example, we must train them in this critically important, doctrinal truth.

4. Raise Your Children to Be Humble and Selfless

I have long worked with a young woman who grew up in an abusive home where she learned that if she didn't take care of herself, defend herself, stand up for her rights, and protect herself, she wouldn't survive. No one else was going to look out for her, so she learned to look out for herself. People like this young woman learn early to devote their energy, intelligence, skill, and ability to remain as safe as possible—without realizing that *safe* is an illusion. I can testify from working with her that, even as a saved person, it's difficult to grow in humility and selflessness. But it can come hard for children who grow up in spiritually and emotionally healthy environments, too. Somewhere along the way, if our children are not going to grow up defending themselves, they will have to become broken and humble, for only broken and humble humans are selfless. Only the selfless can put down their swords, especially the deadly sword called the tongue. Brokenness, humility, and selflessness can be taught consistently by precept, example, and corrective discipline, but ultimately, it must be brought to your children by the power of the Holy Spirit. In addition to teaching, exemplifying, and correcting, the wisest thing we can do for our children is to regularly retreat to our war room to intercede on their behalf—until they are ready to stop making war and instead make peace with God, with themselves, and with others, including their enemies.

5. Make Your Home as Secure and Safe as Possible

I often wonder what that young woman's life would be like today if she'd grown up in a home where Jesus was Lord, love was supreme, and parental (and, therefore, emotional) security was the norm. It is much easier to teach your children not to fight when they mostly know safety and security. But an insecure person… Wow, can they be feisty! No one else will defend or fight for them, so they have to fight for themselves. They get good at it, too, and often it is quite ugly in its manifestations. This precept is not only vital, but for wise parents, it's easy. When we have a secure and safe relationship with our Lord and are secure in who we are in Christ and in our marriage, we can supernaturally bring up our children in safety and security, where they learn that they don't need to fight. Instead, God will fight for them, and their parents will do their best to protect them.

6. Teach Your Children to Love Their Enemies

Will your children eventually have enemies? You bet, just like we all do. We live in a fallen world, and we're all fallen people, even Christians. Let's go back to the Sermon on the Mount, where Jesus instructs His followers on loving our enemies in Matthew 5:43–48:

> You have heard that it was said, "You shall love your neighbor and hate your enemy." But I say to you, love your enemies and pray for those who persecute you, so that you may be sons of your Father who is in heaven; for He causes His sun to rise on the evil and the good, and sends rain on the righteous and the unrighteous. For if you love those who love you, what reward do you have? Do not even the tax collectors do the same? If you greet only your brothers, what more are you

> doing than others? Do not even the Gentiles do the same? Therefore you are to be perfect, as your heavenly Father is perfect.

Perfect? Really? Yes, perfect in the sense of being fully mature in Christ and complete in His holiness. As children of God the Father, we should strive to be called "like Father, like son." (Read also Luke's additional thoughts on loving our enemies in Luke 6:35–38.) Wise parents begin early to train their children to love their enemies. It is harder to fight with them when we love them the way the Father loved us while we were yet His enemies (Romans 5:8). While we were His enemies, His Son died for us—it is the ultimate demonstration of His unfathomable love. And since Jesus died for us, His enemies, perhaps our children can learn from us to *not* fight with theirs.

7. Teach Your Children That Walking away from a Fight Takes Courage

Fathers, teach your sons that walking away from a fight is not the cowardly or the weak thing to do, but the strong thing, the honorable thing, the truly manly thing because, as our proverb says, any fool can quarrel. Mothers, teach your daughters that fussing and fighting with other girls, including with their friends, is shameful behavior, whereas treating others the way they would want to be treated—with dignity, kindness, and even preference—is pure, lovely, and Christlike. None of this is natural, is it? It's supernatural, and in a wise, godly, submissive-to-Christ home, this principle can be both *taught* and *caught*!

Honorable men and women are not fighters but lovers who live by this biblical code: "If possible, so far as it depends on you," do whatever it takes to "be at peace with all men" (Romans 12:18), even if that means turning the other cheek. This takes brokenness, humility, and selflessness, and they must be found in us parents first if we ever hope to see them transferred into our children's sinful little hearts. Remember, the window is small, so begin early to teach your children this biblical and wise principle from Proverbs.

Before I close this principle, I am compelled to give an important caveat. I don't want you to think that a person should *not* stand up against physical or sexual abuse. First, ours is a nation of laws, and illegal abusive activity should be reported to authorities immediately. Second, anyone who is caught in an abusive situation should be able to seek immediate help from you. When you teach your children to turn the other cheek, be sure they know the difference between that and being abused. Make certain they know this is something they can freely talk to their trusted parents about, even if an abuser has told them otherwise. Also, if needed, seek immediate help and support from church leaders. A child (or an adult) caught in an abusive situation—whether at home, at school, at church, or anywhere—must not turn the other cheek or act like nothing serious has happened. Unfortunately, church authority figures who practice heinous activity prey upon children who are taught to absorb the hurt instead of report it. There are situations where fighting back or telling adults is the appropriate and acceptable action. God hates violence and abuse, and so do godly people. As a church leader, I stand with the abused and against abusers. That action is pleasing to God, for the psalmist declares, "Defend the poor and fatherless; do justice to the afflicted and needy" (Psalm 82:3 NKJV). Wise parents stand up for their children against abuse and the abuser.

Parenting Principle 23
Wise Parents Display Great Confidence in God

Man's steps are ordained by the LORD, how then can he understand his way?
PROVERBS 20:24

This proverb doesn't mean that because God is sovereign, we shouldn't make plans for our lives. In fact, Proverbs encourages wise planning. Plan for your life and for the life of your family, but plan wisely with your standard, the Word of God, in hand, in mind, and in heart. Remember that God is God, and like it or not, He has the divine right, worth, and wisdom to have the ultimate, sovereign say in the outcome of your plans. Personally, I love this truth. I have learned over the years, through good times and bad, that His sovereign care and control over my entire life can be fully trusted. I know I can trust His sovereign direction in my life and in the life of my family and church family. Do you?

If you are wise, you are moving through life with full confidence in God. You know, as I do, that He orders, ordains, and directs our steps perfectly, for He is God. Our lives and choices are far from perfect, but His plans for us are. Jeremiah 29:11 gives us that assurance: " 'I know the plans that I have for you,' declares the LORD, 'plans for welfare and not for calamity, to give you a future and a hope.' " If the Lord could say that and mean it to His people who were in Babylonian captivity for seventy years because of their obstinate rebellion against Him, then He can certainly say it and mean it to us as well.

We can surrender and fully submit to His plans for our well-being. We don't have to always know where we are going; we only have to confidently know that He knows. To the confident, that brings unshakeable peace and joy all along the way.

Since God ordains our steps, the proverb then questions our futile attempts to understand everything that happens in our lives. We often can't understand—but again, we don't need to; we need only to trust in God's goodness. Romans 8:28–29 is ever true for those who believe in Him, live for Him, and trust Him: "We know that God causes all things to work together for good to those who love God, to those who are called according to His purpose.… [And His purpose is that we] become conformed to the image of His Son," progressively becoming more and more like Jesus. Parents, you can and must have confidence in His sovereignty. If you want all to go well and end well for your family, then trust His good and sovereign plans for you.

But what if you don't have confidence in Him and you keep kicking against the goads in persistent attempts to order your own steps? Or what if your plans include God only as a divine prayer source that you consult only to request He bless your way and your plan? If that's been your plan, how's it working out for you? Good so far? Just wait... Trying to do life your own way will, if it hasn't already, bring fear, frustration, confusion, and chaos.

When we leave God out of the planning process—except to ask Him to bless the plans we've made—we have become a god unto ourselves, and God never blesses idolatry. Trying to be captains of our souls and of our own fate is an idolatrous root issue. When that is how we live, then usually along the way and certainly in the end, our plans come to ruin.

It is always wise and certainly best to get on the good side of God's will by dying to our way and fully accepting and trusting His way alone. We may not always understand our good Father's ways, but we can always trust Him. We can always believe that He providentially superintends all of life's events in order to get us home, completely sanctified to His everlasting glory and for the blessing and benefit of our lives and our homes.

To further drive home the principle that God ordains our steps, Proverbs 21:1 says, "The king's heart is like channels of water in the hand of the LORD; He turns it wherever He wishes." That proverb reminds us that no matter the person—no matter how powerful or weak he is, no matter how good or wicked, no matter his station in life, including ruling sovereigns—his heart doesn't belong to him. It belongs to the Lord, the sovereign King of heaven and earth, who turns it as He wishes wherever He wishes. If the person is wicked, that biblical truth should be his worst threat; if the person is wise and godly, that truth is his deepest comfort. Wicked or wise, God channels what is in one's heart wherever He wishes.

For example, if I choose to walk toward evil, God will direct my heart to accomplish His will through my sin. However, if I choose to walk toward godliness, He will direct my heart to accomplish His purposes through my righteousness. This is the doctrine of God's sovereignty. If we fully trust Him and, by precept and example, teach our children to trust Him, then God's sovereignty becomes our greatest comfort. We can delight to be on the right side of God's plans. If we do not trust His sovereignty, there will be a day when we regret being on the wrong side of His plans. But either way, He will sovereignly accomplish His plans in and through us.

So how important is it for parents to display before their children absolute confidence in the sovereignty of God? Examine yourselves to make sure you truly believe this principle where the rubber meets the road—in your daily walk in God's way. And then train your children to see how each of their circumstances play out, considering these verses from Proverbs and Romans 8. Remember, life is short, and our window of opportunity to prepare our children to make wise choices as adults is small. Be wise parents who display before your beloved children great confidence in God.

In retrospect, I am so thankful that Jason and Lindsay loved the Lord's way for their lives and were clearly confident in Him. That allowed them to walk on His way without fear. I'm also thankful that they didn't know murder was ahead on the road before them. Further, I delight in the reward that awaited them because of their confidence in God's sovereign and good plan. They were on the good side of it, and now and forever, their reward is great.

I also think of the wicked man who pulled the trigger two times on that dark night in August 2004. His heart was ultimately directed by God to accomplish His will, even through his great evil. (I remind myself, as Martin Luther said, that "even the devil is God's devil.") At the same time, God directed the hearts of our children to accomplish His will for their short lives through their faithfulness.

I think further of our California sheriff friend and how God used our tragedy to bring him to salvation. Because of our children's murders, he and his family have given their hearts and lives to Jesus as their Savior and Lord. Among many others, this entire family came to Christ because God used good *and* evil on that fateful night to work out His perfect plan, and I am perfectly at peace with His plan and His way for our daughter and Jason…and even for their killer.

Wow! How reassuring is it to trust God's sovereign plan for our lives.

Heavenly Father, keep turning our hearts wherever You wish. Continue to use good and evil for our eternal good and for Your eternal glory. We trust You completely. In Jesus's sovereign name I pray and praise. Amen.

How can I say and pray any of that with sincerity of heart? It is because I dare to have nothing but God-confidence in His sovereign plans for us. And I like to think that this God-confidence was not only *taught by me* to Lindsay (precept), but that it was *caught from me* (example) as well.

You can bring that same God-given power into the lives of your children. However, three things must take place. First, by faith, you must wholeheartedly take hold of His sovereign care and control. Don't ever doubt it and don't try to fully understand it—no one sees the whole picture all at once except God. Simply receive and accept it by faith. Second, teach it confidently and consistently to your children. Precept upon precept and principle upon principle, teach them that God is sovereign. And then, third, boldly live out this truth before your children so they can't miss seeing it in you, so that they will have no excuse if they turn away from having your kind of God-confidence. For your children's sake, don't give them any excuse. Instead, give them this from James 4:13–17:

> Come now, you who say, "Today or tomorrow we will go to such and such a city, and spend a year there and engage in business and make a profit." Yet you do not

> know what your life will be like tomorrow. You are just a vapor that appears for a little while and then vanishes away. Instead, you ought to say, "If the Lord wills, we will live and also do this or that." But as it is, you boast in your arrogance; all such boasting is evil. Therefore, to one who knows the right thing to do and does not do it, to him it is sin.

Since your children's lives are just vapors, and since your window to train them well is so small, teach them now and remind them often that their lives must be all about *if the Lord wills*, fully and confidently trusting in Him and His way for their lives.

Parenting Principle 24
Wise Parents Teach Their Children to Fully Cooperate with God

There is no wisdom and no understanding and no counsel against the LORD*. The horse is prepared for the day of battle, but victory belongs to the* LORD*.*

PROVERBS 21:30–31

In Acts 26:14, as Paul retells his conversion experience on the Damascus Road, he relates, "When we had all fallen to the ground, I heard a voice saying to me in the Hebrew dialect,

'Saul, Saul, why are you persecuting Me? It is hard for you to kick against the goads.'" Goads are sharp prods used to direct or redirect livestock; to kick against them would be stupid and painful. But it's exactly what fallen humanity outside of Christ does—they kick hard against the goads. Consequently, they live stupidly and in much pain because they continue to fight against God, constantly kicking against cooperation with Him. Our Lord told unbelieving Saul that it's like kicking against the goads of His Word, will, and way. And that is incredibly painful.

Sadly, this principle applies to Christians as well. James, speaking to the church, writes, "You [spiritual] adulteresses, do you not know that friendship with the world is hostility toward God? Therefore whoever wishes to be a friend of the world makes himself an enemy of God" (James 4:4). This teaching takes us back again to the beginning of our study, to the principle that the fear of the Lord is the beginning of wisdom. Our God is loving, ever gracious, and compassionate, but He's also most holy; therefore, "it is a terrifying thing to fall into the hands of the living God" (Hebrews 10:31). We do this when we deliberately befriend the world and worldly ways, kicking and screaming against God's goads. If we walk in full cooperation with the Lord, striving to live in full obedience to Him, we have nothing to fear; the pain we know will not be a result of noncooperation with God. The goads of God, as it turns out, are there for our protection.

If Christ-followers had the divine power to more fully trust God's big-picture view of everything, if we understood that He is graciously directing us away from terrible trouble ahead, wouldn't we be much more ready to obey Him? The last principle we discussed was about trusting in God's sovereign plans for our lives. This principle is its sister—it is about obedience, about fully cooperating with God for our good always. Instead of fighting against Him through self-willed or ignorant disobedience, let us trust and then obey Him fully. Full obedience is God's way of protecting us from much trouble ahead, even death.

Truth be told, there is absolutely no wisdom, understanding, or counsel against the Lord. How foolish we show ourselves to be and what an awful waste we make of our short lives (and that small window of opportunity with our children) when we live as though we know better than God. When we do that, Proverbs tells us we are leaning on our own understanding, rather than trusting Him with all our hearts. We do not acknowledge Him in all our ways, and we fail to delight to walk in His way through careful and consistent obedience. In this situation, it is impossible for Him to make our paths straight.

Our proverb goes on to say that we may make all the preparations necessary for the day of battle, but in the end, the victory belongs to the Lord. I wonder how many actual battles in the Bible were won when God's leaders and people fully cooperated with Him and obeyed His every command. Well, I don't know the number, but I do know that it was every one. Conversely, how many battles were lost when God's leaders and people didn't obey Him, insisting instead to wage warfare their own way in their own strength? Again, I don't know the number, but I know that it was every one.

Spiritually speaking, then, how many spiritual battles in the Bible and through the centuries up to this day have been waged and won through full-on obedience to God? Only God knows, but we do know that it was and continues to be *every single one*. So, how many were lost?

I'm reminded of Saul's disobedience in 1 Samuel 15. Here, the prophet Samuel gave King Saul specific directions from God to punish Amalek for "what he did to Israel, how he set himself against him on the way while he was coming up from Egypt. Now go and strike Amalek and utterly destroy all that he has" (1 Samuel 15:2–3; cf. Exodus 17:8–16). As the rest of the text makes clear, God meant for *everything* to be destroyed. But Saul did not fully comply with those instructions. In his humanity, Saul thought he was making a wise decision. He destroyed everything that was "despised and worthless," but he kept the livestock and "all that was good" (15:9). Surely, keeping things of value was good? But no, not if it is contrary to God's will. Because of Saul's disobedience, God told Samuel, "I regret that I have made Saul king, for he has turned back from following Me and has not carried out My commands" (15:10). And then, the next morning when Samuel confronted Saul about this failure (15:13–14), the king said to the prophet, "Blessed are you of the Lord! I have carried out the command of the Lord." But Samuel said, "What then is this bleating of the sheep in my ears, and the lowing of the oxen which I hear?"

Reflect carefully on what happened next. The king proceeded to make several excuses for not fully obeying the Lord's commands, including the claim that he had saved the best of the livestock to sacrifice to God. But Samuel said, "Has the Lord as much delight in burnt offering and sacrifices as in obeying the voice of the Lord? Behold, to obey is better than sacrifice, and to heed [is better] than the fat of rams. For rebellion is as the sin of divination, and insubordination is as iniquity and idolatry. Because you have rejected the word of the Lord, He has also rejected you from being king" (22–23). And that was the beginning of the end for Israel's first king.

It looked on the surface as though Saul had won the battle, but a closer look clearly shows that Saul's defeat was final and fatal. Listen to the bleating of Amalek's best sheep and never forget that our best in disobedience, including partial obedience, is nothing but total failure in the sight of God.

So here are some things that wise parents do during that small window of opportunity in which they have time to teach their children to fully cooperate with God.

1. They Understand That Partial Obedience Is Disobedience

Christians may offer excuses and justifications, but what are those to God? He has proven His greatness and trustworthiness to us; therefore, there are no excuses for partial obedience. Several people come immediately to my mind—Christians who would go so far as to say that they are Christ-followers, but who are only partially obedient to the Lord's clear command concerning church attendance and church involvement from Hebrews 10:23–25:

> Let us hold fast the confession of our hope without wavering, for He who promised is faithful; and let us consider how to stimulate one another to love and good deeds, not forsaking our own assembling together, as is the habit of some, but encouraging one another; and all the more as you see the day drawing near.

We must be consistently present and involved, stimulating and encouraging others before the lights go out on our lives and it is too late to worship God and serve others. Wise parents hate their own wretched excuses and steer clear of partial obedience. They are acutely aware that the cost of such rebellion is too awful to consider.

2. They Understand That Victory Follows Surrendered Obedience

Instead of kicking against God's goads, which are more like fences of protection along God's way so that they don't wander off, wise parents stay in the center of the way, allowing distance between themselves and God's protective prodding. Their reward for remaining in surrendered obedience is victory in Jesus, and they love that about the Lord's way.

3. They Understand Their Responsibilities

Wise parents understand that they have a responsibility to fight the evil that is against and within their children; therefore, they understand the need to be prepared for the day of spiritual battle. But they also know that the victory belongs to the Lord. Since God is for them because they are for Him, it doesn't matter who is against them. God will win. Thus, wise parents lean heavily on the Lord and allow Him to direct their paths. When the victories come, small and large alike, they give all the glory to Him. "Lord, this victory in the life our child, like all victories, belongs to You. As always, we glorify Your good and glorious name!"

4. They Understand That They Must Train Their Children to Obey

It is not enough for wise parents to teach their children about obedience. They know they must train them to live strictly obedient lives before the all-knowing and all-seeing God. With this knowledge implanted in their minds and hearts, they then consistently, diligently, and passionately bring corrective discipline to their children every time they cross over into disobedience. They fear that if their children can't obey their parental God-given authority over them, how are they going to obey God's ultimate authority over them when they come of age and are effectively removed from under that parental authority?

5. They Understand the Consequences of Disobedience

Wise parents understand from Scripture and experience that there are consequences to both disobedience and partial obedience; therefore, they train their children accordingly, doing their level best to prevent them from paying a high and hard price for these offenses. Frankly, I am weary of adult Christians who live as though they can get away with partial obedience. It not only makes me tired, but it breaks my heart. I do my best to faithfully preach to them that there are consequences for partial obedience, but some Christian adults never get it, even in the face of personal and severe consequences. It is especially grieving to me when those Christians are parents who have children living in their homes. They just don't seem to understand that it is stupid and painful to kick against God's goads. But wise parents do understand; consequently, they deliberately train their children to walk in obedience to God at every turn and at every command so that they will know only victory instead of consequence.

6. They Understand That Obedience Isn't Legalism

Strict obedience to God isn't simply keeping a list of *dos* and *don'ts*. Obedience to Him cannot be an external thing alone; it must be a thing of the heart. Wise parents love to obey God because they love Him. Their overwhelming devotion to Jesus Christ is what makes them tick. They love Him because He loved them first and continues to prove His love to them every day of their lives. For them, "the love of Christ controls [them], having concluded this, that…He died for all, so that they who live might no longer live for themselves, but for Him who died and rose again on their behalf" (2 Corinthians 5:14–15). True Christianity comes from the heart. Out of our compelling love for Jesus Christ, we delight to obey, and when we delight to obey, there is much joy in the journey.

7. They Understand That Disobedience Is Equivalent to Rebellion

Wise parents understand that, not only is disobedience equivalent to rebellion, but rebellion is equivalent to idolatry. The last thing wise parents want in their lives and in their homes are those grave abominations against God. With Joshua, they declare, "As for me and my house, we will serve the LORD" (Joshua 24:15). When God is our God, there is no room for any other gods. King Saul was a god unto himself, so he did what was right in his disobedient heart. The hearts of wise parents worship the Lord alone—they gladly do what He commands and train their children to do the same. Why? Because the Lord, He is God. There is no other!

8. They Understand the Nature of the Fight

Wise parents understand the spiritual nature of the fight—that the spiritual battle is waged against their children, to deceive them into rejecting God all their lives, including during that small window we have to raise them. Faithful Samuel said to faithless Saul, "Because you have rejected the word of the LORD, He has also rejected you from being king" (1 Samuel 15:23).

We need to know that this is a spiritual battle that we might not always win. It is possible that we could lose a child to rejection. There are no ironclad guarantees that our children will live obedient lives. There is the danger and fear that some will reject the Lord. But wise parents faithfully fight the battle against their children's rejection because they understand that rejecting the Word of the Lord means that He will also reject them from being His beloved children. We cannot guarantee our children's ultimate safety, but we can remain faithful even if our children turn out faithless. Keep in mind that if Jesus could have a rebellious disciple who betrayed Him because he rejected Him, it is possible for us to have rebellious children as well. Take nothing for granted—do your best; pray like crazy; and leave the rest to our good and gracious Father because, as 2 Peter 3:9 says, "the Lord is not slow about His promise, as some count slowness, but is patient toward you [and your children], not wishing for any to perish but for all to come to repentance."

So, since there is no wisdom, understanding, or counsel against the Lord, and since every spiritual victory in life belongs to Him, wise parents train their children to fully cooperate with God. Their victory in Jesus depends upon our obedience and theirs. Therefore, we do our level best to fully cooperate with God and lead our children to do the same. How important is this? Wise parents know that nothing is more valuable than the souls of their children.

Parenting Principle 25
Wise Parents Pass Along the Family Legacy

A good name is to be more desired than great wealth;
favor is better than silver and gold.
Proverbs 22:1

A good name is synonymous with a good reputation and is rooted in good and godly character. What is more important—a good name before God, our family, our church family, and our community…or wealth? Asked another way, is high favor (or esteem) from a good reputation better to us than material prosperity? Or than anything else, for that matter? The best way to answer that is by asking God what He favors. From His perspective—which is the only perspective that counts for anything—a good name is to be more desired than anything this world has to offer.

Luke's gospel gives us brief insights into the childhood of Jesus. For example, Luke 2:40 speaks of Jesus as a young boy and says of Him, "The Child continued to grow and become strong, increasing in wisdom; and the grace [the favor] of God was upon Him." Then, in verses 51–52, when Jesus was twelve, after an astonishing visit to Jerusalem where He was found in the temple teaching the teachers, we read, "He went down with [his earthly parents] and came to Nazareth, and He continued in subjection to them; and His mother treasured all these things in her heart. And Jesus kept increasing in wisdom and stature, and in favor with God and men." Jesus was born into a poor family, but look at His stature before God and mankind. So what is more important to God? What is more desirous for us in the sight of God—favor or worldly wealth and possessions?

We know, of course, that Jesus's parents had very little to do with Jesus growing up perfect in character. Since He was God's Son, He could have been raised in the worst of homes and still turned out perfect because, before His conception and birth, He was perfect. He was, therefore, born without the ability to sin; little credit can be given to Joseph and Mary for Jesus's character. However, they had other children who turned out well, including James and Jude. Jesus didn't need godly parents to be perfectly godly; nonetheless, on a human level, Jesus's good name before His community reflected on His home and His parents. They had a good name before the community, and Jesus didn't do anything to stain or embarrass that name. The people of Nazareth never forgot that Jesus was "the carpenter's son" (Matthew 13:55). Later, when He was revealed to the world as God the Father's "only begotten Son" (John 3:16), Jesus continued His divine legacy of a perfectly good name, the name of God.

Having a good name is important to God; therefore, it must be important to us. I wonder how we—God's other sons and daughters—are doing with the legacy passed on to us as children of the Father. Wise people think much about their legacy; their passion for a good name is greater than anything else. Wise parents are passionate about passing along their good name to their children so that they can pass it down to their children, and they will pass it down to their children, generation after generation, until Jesus returns. Think legacy. Think good name.

When we think of a person's name, whether a divine Person or a human person, it's not just their name that comes to mind. In an instant, the entire person—his personality, his idiosyncrasies, his mannerisms, his looks, his conduct, his deeds good or bad—they all come to mind. For example, "the name of the Lord" (Proverbs 18:10) represents God Himself—exactly who He is and what He has done and is doing and will do in all His perfections. In like manner, your name represents you yourself before God and the world; it represents exactly who and what you are and what you have done and are doing and will do. In other words, your name is your testimony that you live out every day of your life. So think legacy. Do you have a good and godly name? Are you working in cooperation with God to pass down your good and godly name to your children?

Years ago, a television commercial featured tennis star Andre Agassi in the prime of his career. Multiple shots were taken and shown of Andre in action. At the end of the commercial, he peered over his sunglasses at the television camera and said, "Image is everything." That pretty well describes our culture. It's all about the image of yourself that you create or project. But there's no real substance to image; it's all about exteriors and appearances. And because that's okay with our world, we have an entire system of image makers. Oftentimes, people in the limelight with questionable character try to reinvent themselves by recreating their image, and they hire professional image makers to help them do it. We often see it in the political scene—a not-so-likable political figure invests much in repackaging himself. But it is all surface and superficial.

God isn't into false image creation; He's into godly, Christlike character development—the process of sanctification.

King David confessed to God in his prayer of pardon, "You desire truth in the innermost being, and in the hidden part You will make me know wisdom. Purify me with hyssop, and I shall be clean; wash me and I shall be whiter than snow" (Psalm 51:6–7). In God's economy, outward image is utterly nothing. Before he repented, David worked hard to make himself look good before the nation, but what was that to God? In His economy, inner integrity and purified character are everything. Therefore, one of the greatest gifts we can give our children is a good and godly name.

If you have inherited a good name and you are continuing that legacy yourself, count yourself most blessed of God. Keep the legacy going in your children and grandchildren. Pass along to them a true and eternal legacy because a good name is more to be desired than great wealth, and favor is so much better than silver and gold.

For some people, however, the name passed down to them from their parents may be a source of pain or even shame, especially in light of eternity. I loved my grandparents on my dad's side, but my great-grandfather's god was his wallet, and my grandfather's god was alcohol. Both he and my grandmother were alcoholics. In the last few years before my father's conversion to Christ, he was following the same pattern—becoming like his father, moving toward an alcoholic lifestyle, drinking more heavily and increasing in discontentment and anger. In all honesty, that was the Cutshall name...until God broke through with the amazing grace of Jesus Christ and saved my dad when I was eighteen. I'm extremely thankful for that, but it was too late for my childhood. The damage was already done. I was saved by God primarily through the influence of my godly mother, but I was not very sanctified. Anger had already set in. By God's grace, however, my father's name was salvaged, and sometime later, so was mine.

What I'm saying is that if you have no spiritual inheritance passed down to you from your grandparents and parents, if you have not been given a godly legacy in Christ Jesus, you can change that legacy for yourself and for your children and grandchildren. You can have the privilege of beginning a legacy in your own life that pleases God and blesses everyone around you. You will then be able to pass along to those who come after you your high and holy and eternal heritage in Christ.

Many of you have already allowed Christ to break you out of the cycle of spiritual deadness and foolishness; you've allowed Him to make you alive and capable of passing down a real and godly legacy. What a privilege—changing the family legacy for your progeny! If you haven't already, don't stick with the status quo. Allow God to change your name and reputation in Christ and then pass along that new name to your children so they can move confidently forward into adulthood, knowing who they are in Christ. Think legacy. Remember that time is short and the window of opportunity is small.

When Lindsay flew out to California to serve alongside her fiancé at Rock-N-Water adventure camp, she left our home and presence in love with Jesus Christ and with firm confidence in her heavenly Father. It was hard for her mother and me to say good-bye to her, but we knew early in her life that our beloved daughter had been called to serve the Lord in ministry. Now she was off to fulfill that calling. We couldn't have been more proud of her.

At the end of her summer of effective ministry, on the next to the last weekend of her life, she called us, most excited about how God had used her in the life of a teenage girl who was deeply troubled about her broken home and broken life. Shortly after arriving at camp, the girl was drawn to Lindsay, and they spent long hours together, with Lindsay counseling, encouraging, and comforting her. By the end of the next weekend, Lindsay was gone.

I don't know exactly what she would say to her mother and me for giving her a good name and godly legacy. But I think it would be something like this: "Thank you, Mom and Dad, for raising me up in Christ and building within me the character of Christ that enabled me to triumphantly pass from this life only to stand before the Lord of glory in life eternal."

That's our task as godly parents, isn't it? We're to transfer God's truth from one generation to the next, building the kind of character within our children that will enable them to face the storms of life and yet remain faithful to their Savior and Lord, for His glory, to the end of their lives. But how can wise parents make sure they have and are maintaining a good name and that they are passing on to their children this eternal legacy? Following is a three-point strategy.

1. Establish and Maintain an Accountability Relationship

Temptations to sin are everywhere in the world. Mutual accountability with a godly brother or sister (a man with a man and a woman with a woman) is an essential measure that too few Christians take in preserving their testimony and the testimony of their accountability partner. Solomon was right when he wrote, "Two are better than one because they have a good return for their labor. For if either of them falls, the one will lift up his companion. But woe to the one who falls when there is not another to lift him up.... And if one can overpower him who is alone, two can resist him. A cord of three strands is not quickly torn apart" (Ecclesiastes 4:9–10, 12). In fact, it's impossible to tear that cord apart if the third strand is the Holy Spirit.

We need accountability relationships in our lives if we are to maintain our good names and reputations before God and others.

2. Deliberately Keep the Spiritual Fires of Your Devotion to God Burning

Accountability is an essential discipline because, to use an analogy, a hot coal that is kicked out of a fire will soon grow cold. It takes other hot coals to keep a single coal hot. But other spiritual disciplines must be regularly practiced as well, such as daily time in the Word and in prayer. Faithful assembling together with your church family to worship the Lord in community and to encourage one another in Christ is also important, "all the more as you see the day drawing near"

(Hebrews 10:25). Time is short; if we put this off, saying we'll start tomorrow, we might find tomorrow never comes.

3. Above All Else, Love the Truth, Which Is Jesus Christ and His Word

If you love the truth, then you will pursue the truth of His Word, embrace it, and live it out in your daily life. Jesus said, "I am…the truth" (John 14:6). He also said, "If you continue in My word, then you are truly disciples of Mine; and you will know the truth, and the truth will make you free" (John 8:31–32). In His high priestly prayer for us, He prayed to the Father, "Sanctify them [set them apart] in the truth; Your word is truth" (John 17:17). In Ephesians 6:14 NIV, we're told that the first piece of the armor of God is truth: "Stand firm then [against the schemes of the devil (6:11)], with the belt of truth buckled around your waist." If we are to stand firm against the satanic scheming that incessantly comes against us, we must allow the truth of God's Word to control our minds. That is why wise parents love the truth with all that is within them.

A good name is more to be desired than great wealth, and favor is better than silver and gold. What will it take to create within you a good name so that you will have a testimony that pleases God and blesses others? Whatever it takes, give yourself to it so you can pass your good name along to your beloved children. The window is small. Remember:

I took a piece of living clay,
And gently formed it day by day;

And molded with my power and art,
A young child's soft and yielding heart.

Be diligent in doing so, so that when those children grow up, they will be fully prepared to face real life in a fallen world with a good name. May it be so in Jesus's most worthy name. Amen.

CHAPTER 7

Wise Parenting Principles 26-30: The Treasure That You Seek

Proverbs 22–25

THERE WAS ONCE AN OKLAHOMA farmer who, above all else, coveted striking it rich. During the California Gold Rush, he left all behind—his home, his farm, his family, his livelihood, his integrity, everything—in his insatiable quest for wealth. However, as often was the case, instead of striking it rich, he experienced nothing but misery, heartache, and one failed gold mining scheme after another. And then, the one time he was somewhat successful in unearthing gold, he was robbed. In the end, deathly sick and penniless, he requested that his partner return his body home to be buried on the farm that his wife and children had somehow maintained without him.

His partner kept his word and returned him home. When they dug a grave to bury him a little distance from the house, amazingly they struck oil—a gusher. Just six feet beneath the surface of the land he had owned, walked, and farmed was incredible wealth. Ironic—the treasure he'd coveted, sought, and died trying to discover was buried in his own backyard.

When you look at your home—your wife, your husband, your children—what do you see? Is your family the treasure that you seek? Do you have the spiritual ability to see beneath the surface to what is most precious? Is your sharpest focus on your children's eternal souls? Are your time, attention, and energy are fully invested, first in their salvation and then in their sanctification until their glorification?

When Lindsay died, what I missed the most at first was the surface of her being—her physical presence, what I could see and touch. I missed her so much that I went through her dresser drawers looking for a strand of hair, something tangible to which I could cling. I found what I was looking for and put it away in a little box where it continues to reside in one of my dresser drawers. Even at the time, my actions as her father seemed rather sad and pathetic to me. But my need to do this was also quite real.

I can tell you from personal experience that the surface of a person is immeasurably valuable. But it is also quite clear to me that the eternal, spiritual elements that lie beneath the surface—the spirit and soul of a person—are so much more valuable! Body, soul, and spirit, may our children be the treasure that we seek! If they are, then we will give ourselves fully to bringing them up in the way they should go. The following five wise parenting principles from Proverbs underline this reality in our thinking.

Parenting Principle 26
Wise Parents Train Up Their Children in God's Way

Train up a child in the way he should go,
even when he is old he will not depart from it.
PROVERBS 22:6

The "way a child should go" is God's way of wisdom that is beautifully displayed throughout the book of Proverbs. Wise parents train up their children in God's way because they are convinced that it's the only way to live life well, now and forever.

Jesus said in John 14:6, "I am the way, and the truth, and the life." Jesus is the only way because He's the only truth; therefore, He's the only true way to a relationship with God. He's also the only way because He is the only life; consequently, He could also declare, "no one comes to the Father but through Me." Contrary to what many people think, there are not multiple ways to obtain salvation. Salvation is available only through Jesus Christ, for He is the way.

From a New Testament perspective with New Testament revelation, the ultimate "way" of Proverbs 22:6 is Jesus Christ. Jesus is *the only way* to know the truth of God, the only way to know God, and the only way to know the eternal life of God. There is no other way. Randy Alcorn, in *The Grace and Truth Paradox*, said this about Jesus's exclusive statement in John 14:6:

> Raised in a culture that condemns such thinking as narrow and intolerant, even many Christians now consider

> it arrogant to say that only Christians will go to heaven. It certainly would be arrogant if we were the ones who came up with it. But we didn't. We're just repeating what Jesus said. We're not trusting ourselves; we're trusting Him. (Multnomah Books, 2003, 41.)

Jesus also said in Matthew 7:13–14,

> Enter through the narrow gate; for the gate is wide and the way is broad that leads to destruction, and there are many who enter through it. For the gate is small and the way is narrow that leads to life, and there are few who find it.

The gate is small and the way is narrow because there is only one gate and one way. So let's be clear as to what God says about the way. Jesus Christ is not only *the way*; He's the *only way*! Based on that reality, then, to "train up a child in the way he should go" means to train up a child in Christ. Here's what that looks like:

1. Teach Your Children That Jesus Is the Way, the Truth, and the Life

Wise parents raise up their children in this reality so they will know that they must receive Him as their personal Savior in order to be eternally *in the way*, to eternally *know the truth*, and to eternally *belong to the life*. It's not difficult to teach young children that Jesus is the way. If parents can teach their children to believe in a mythical Santa Claus who takes gifts to children throughout the world in a single night, they can teach them to believe in Jesus as the only way. It is only when children get older and begin to reason things out in fallen, faulty reasoning that they may wrongly reason that there are other ways. This is why it is critically important to implant the truth about Christ in their tender hearts at an early age.

2. Teach Your Children to Love the Lord because He First Loved Them

Our children need to know that the greatest motivation for love, devotion, and service to Christ is Christ's love for them. First John 4:10 (NIV) rightly says, "This is love: not that we loved God, but that He loved us and sent his Son as an atoning sacrifice for our sins." There is nothing in the world like love-motivation. Wise parents teach their children to love Jesus because He first loved them so that when they grow up in Christ, they can say "it is no longer I who live, but Christ lives in me; and the life which I now live in the flesh, I live by faith in the Son of God, who loved me and gave Himself up for me" (Galatians 2:20).

3. Show Your Children Early and Often What Love for Christ Looks Like

In Jesus's own words, love for Him looks like this: "If you love Me, you will keep My commandments" (John 14:15). And His "new commandment" is "that you love one another, even as I have loved you, that you also love one another. By this all men will know that you are My disciples, if you have love for one another" (John 13:34–35). Did you catch His reiterated point: that we are to love one another? Love for Jesus Christ means obedience to Christ's commands, including and especially His new commandment to love His other followers.

If we are to bring up our children in Christ, we must do so in an atmosphere of love, both in our homes and in our churches. They need to grow up loving God's people who are the church. The church is also known in Scripture as the body of Christ. How can we love our Head if we don't love His body? We can't! If we try to love the Head only, we are only giving lip service to our love for Christ, and we are living in disobedience. We must train our children to prove their love for Jesus by loving His people, the church, His body.

My daughters grew up as PKs (pastor's kids). It's pretty much all they knew growing up—Kerry was six and Lindsay was four when Kathy and I entered full-time pastoral ministry. Unfortunately, many PKs have watched how churches treated their parents and have grown up to hate the church. Not my girls. We constantly strive at our church to be a true family in Christ, a faith family, God's family. Sadly, that is not distinctive of every church, but by God's grace, it was and continues to be at ours.

Our girls grew up with a positive church experience that caused them to love the church—and they love it still. One loves it perfectly from heaven, and the other loves it imperfectly but passionately from earth. We brought our daughters up to love the church and to be loved by the church. When

Lindsay died, a godly elder statesman of our church, Sam Wyler, said to me, "Chris, we lost a daughter too." When he said that, he was speaking the truth. She'd grown up in our local church family—we loved her and she loved us in return. Be sure to raise your children to love and be loved by the church of Jesus Christ. It is how we train them up in the way, and it is how they prove their love for Christ, who is the way.

4. Train Up Your Children to Know Christ

Too many of our children know only *about* Christ. They might have all the Bible stories and even many Bible verses stored up in their heads, but if they don't have Jesus stored up in their hearts, their religion will not change their lives from sinners to saints who truly love, worship, and serve their Redeemer King.

I have long been delightfully held captive by Paul's words in chapter 3 of Philippians. I recommend you read and study the whole chapter, but let's look at verses 7 and 8 here:

> But whatever things were gain to me, those things I have counted as loss for the sake of Christ. More than that, I count all things to be loss in view of the surpassing value of knowing Christ Jesus my Lord, for whom I have suffered the loss of all things, and count them but rubbish so that I may gain Christ.

Wise parents so treasure their children that they teach them by precept and example that Jesus Christ is the greatest treasure they will ever find. But if He's only in one's head and not firmly established and cherished in one's heart, what good is that?

These points are part of what it means to train up our children in the way they should go. And when they are old—that is to say, all grown up and moved out of the home—they will be among the few who hear the words of Christ and act upon them. And then, God promises that lives built on that foundation will be stormproof—even, in Lindsay's case, bulletproof! Hear the words of our Lord in Matthew 7:24–27:

> Therefore everyone who hears these words of Mine and acts on them, may be compared to a wise man who built his house on the rock. And the rain fell, and the floods came, and the winds blew and slammed against that house; and yet it did not fall, for it had been founded on the rock. Everyone who hears these words of Mine and does not act on them, will be like a foolish man who built his house on the sand. The rain fell, and the floods came, and the winds blew and slammed against that house; and it fell—and great was its fall.

And because this is the absolute truth, wise parents train up their children in the way they should go.

It is important to understand that Proverbs 22:6 is a rule to life that is generally true. In the larger context of God's Word, we are to take into account that there are prodigals among us, and exceptions occur. Raising children born with sin natures in a fallen world where Satan is the god of this age is risky business. In light of fuller biblical revelation, then, it is a mistake to judge parents of a wayward child (or children) without full knowledge of why their child walked away from God's way. Throughout history, children of godly parents have walked away from the faith. It is not unusual to see a child who was raised in a godly home eventually turn completely away from his or her spiritual upbringing. As I said earlier, even God the Father has had many prodigals throughout human history, and none of us in our right spiritual minds would question the Father's goodness. Let us not add to a grieving parent's burden by casting blame and leveling judgment. In many cases, the parents are not to blame but deserve praise for doing their best to train up their children in the way they should go.

It is, however, typically true that when parents train up their children in the way they should go, the children do not depart from it when they are grown; rather, they stay the course all the way home. Thus, wise parents who are forward-looking and upward-striving start their children on the way early, with the end clearly in view. They persistently strive to give their children a good start on the way so they will have a solid middle and a strong finish at heaven's shore. But it all begins with the start. If our children do not have a good early start, the odds that they will have a good middle and finish diminish greatly.

Parents, examine that which you are giving your life to. Imagine for a moment the nearly unthinkable—you, standing at the side of your child's grave. Some of us have already experienced this, but for the rest, stand there in your imagination. Then look back and ask, "What I lived for and strived after while my children were in the home—was it worth it?" The answer can be "Yes, absolutely!" if, having fully invested in their spiritual inheritance, the treasure you sought was the salvation and sanctification of the souls of your children. To you, Jesus Christ is the greatest treasure of all, and you have passed that treasure on to your children.

Parenting Principle 27
Wise Parents Are Sold on Corrective Discipline

Foolishness is bound up in the heart of a child;
the rod of discipline will remove it far from him.
PROVERBS 22:15

Unlike the previous proverb, the first statement in this one is not just generally true—it is absolutely and always true. We know this based on the whole teaching of God's Word concerning the inherent, fallen nature of all humanity. Make no mistake about it; foolishness *is* bound up in the heart of a child, every child. This bound-up foolishness is the innate sin nature within every child that is made evident in their bent toward acts of foolishness. Children will exhibit unwise, imprudent, irrational, selfish, and stupid behavior because they think their way is the best, if not the only way. It is a serious problem that every parent faces.

The second statement in the proverb, unlike the first part, is usually true, but it is not absolutely guaranteed. As we know from Scripture and experience, some particularly wayward children will not respond positively to discipline of any sort. However, it is generally true that the rod of discipline will remove the bound-up foolishness far from a child. Can that instrument of discipline mean anything other than a literal instrument of spanking—a paddle, if you will?

To me it is obvious; yet, I have heard a thousand times: "But Chris, you don't understand—spanking doesn't work with my child. I've tried it, but it just doesn't work with him." That may be true for a scant few, but it's much more likely that the parent isn't correctly and effectively using the rod of discipline. If you've said that spanking doesn't work, or if you believe that statement to be true, I would strongly encourage you to think it possible, even probable, that you have not used the rod correctly. Let me give you some pointers on how to spank correctly and effectively.

1. Spank Your Children in the Atmosphere of a Loving Relationship

When corporal discipline is administered to a child by an unloving, uncaring parent who is seldom engaged in the child's life, or by a parent who disciplines in anger, the opposite effect of the proverb almost always occurs. Instead of removing foolishness far from the child, the parent will effectively provoke the child to anger (Ephesians 6:4). That only fuels the foolishness that remains bound up in his or her heart. Children must know, without a shadow of a doubt, that the daddy or mommy who spanks them is the daddy or mommy who loves them and who proves it through tender loving care.

2. Be Sure You Spank for Biblically Motivated Reasons

Wise parents administer corrective discipline for the same reasons that God administers it to His children. Hebrews tells us, "Those whom the Lord loves He disciplines, and He scourges every son whom He receives...God deals with [us] as with sons; for what son is there whom his father does not discipline" (12:6–7). The primary motivation is a parent's massive love for his child. It's like this: "I love you just the way you are, but I love you too much to leave you the way you are. So I discipline you, my beloved child, because of my great love for you!" It's got to be like that—rightly motivated by an overwhelming love for your children.

Further, because God loves us, He always disciplines us for our good. Wise parents do the same: "For [our fathers] disciplined us for a short time as seemed best to them, but He disciplines us for our good, so that we may share His holiness. All discipline for the moment seems not to be joyful, but sorrowful; yet to those who have been trained by it, afterward it yields the peaceful fruit of righteousness" (12:10–11). Wise parents apply the paddle of discipline for the same reasons—we desire the good and godly outcomes of holiness and righteousness that bring peace to the home, to the parents, and to the children.

When I spanked one of my girls, I would leave her on her bed until she had time to cry and think about what she had done. (This didn't take long.) Then I would return, sit on the bed beside my daughter, hold her close, and explain *why* she'd been disciplined. Because of my great love for her, I was most desirous to remove the foolishness that was bound up within her that caused her to do what she had done. I wanted to displace her foolishness with holiness and righteousness. And if holiness and righteousness were followed with right attitude and behavior, then wonderful peace also followed.

3. The Spanking Should Be Appropriately Painful

God's chastening, even scourging, of His beloved children is not soft, but it's not abusive either. Corporal discipline, balanced by tenderness and love, must be severe enough to bring appropriate pain before it will be effective. The purpose of administering appropriate pain is this: "I am hurting you now so that you won't hurt yourself later." Of course, I'm speaking to wise parents who know the difference between a good spanking on the backside of their child and a beating that has clearly crossed the line. Once again, "Fathers, do not provoke your children to anger, but bring them up in the discipline and instruction of the Lord" (Ephesians 6:4). This requires a proper balance between being lenient and being harsh, which can be equally harmful to our children. I say *equally*, because I am convinced that leniency has the potential to be just as abusive as harshness. Both are lacking in wise, parental love for our children.

4. Understand the Need for Diligence and Consistency

To effectively use a paddle to remove foolishness from their children, wise parents understand the need for diligence and consistency. Back to Proverbs 13:24: "He who withholds his rod hates his son, but he who loves him disciplines him diligently." Diligent, consistent discipline with the rod of discipline equals love, because diligent, consistent discipline for every foolish act every time is what will consistently remove the foolishness bound up in your child. It may remove foolishness only a little at time, or at times, none at all; wise parents must understand the need to be diligent and consistent. If the foolish act was wrong thirty minutes ago, it is wrong now, and it will be wrong thirty minutes from now. The correct way to use the rod of correction is to keep using it often enough and painfully enough, inflicting temporary pain, until the child's foolish self-will loses and God's righteousness wins.

There was a short season in my daughter Kerry's young life when I had to use the paddle on her every day because of her strong self-will. Actually, there were days when I had to use it more than once, and I had to keep using it daily and often and effectively until I won—because if Kerry had won, everyone would lose, including Kerry. If you knew Kerry today, you would know that I didn't break her personality or her person, for she has personality galore! But I kept on using the rod often enough and tough enough until her self-will lost and God's righteousness won.

5. Always Spank Your Children with a Paddle

Use a paddle, not your hand. God has reasons for instructing parents to use an instrument of corporal discipline as opposed to the parent's hand. Does it even need to be said that a paddle on the backside constitutes discipline, while a parent's fists to the body or slaps to the face clearly constitute physical abuse? Some argue that parents should not spank with their hands because it is an extension of their body, and the child might equate the discipline as hitting rather than spanking. I don't know about that; I think it is a weak argument. What I do know though is that the hand is far less effective than a paddle—using your hand may hurt you more than it hurts your child. The hand is too soft. Corrective discipline must be loving but effectively tough. If the Lord wanted us to use our hands, He would have told us so; instead He was careful to give us a weapon, so to speak, in the war against bound-up foolishness within our children. Wise are the parents who trust God and His Word and discipline His way rather than their own way.

I've given you these five pointers so that you will understand that if God's method of spanking is not working for you, most likely the problem is not with the method but the lack, misuse, or inconsistent and inappropriate use of the method. Follow God's instructions. Be wise enough to understand that the problem may lie within you rather than with the method itself. Also, take time to read carefully other Scriptures that clearly show that the method, rightly used, is effective in removing foolishness, but the misuse or the lack of use of it is quite destructive. I recommend Proverbs 23:13–16 and 29:15–17.

Creation scientist Dr. Henry Morris wrote, "The Bible clearly teaches that judicious corporal punishment is necessary to child raising, if administered appropriately, carefully, and lovingly. This is, of course, contrary to modern, humanistic child psychology" (*The New Defender's Study Bible*, World Publishing, 1995, 964). Secular humanism has chipped away at biblical psychology to the point that there is now enormous pressure on modern parents to abandon it altogether. Unfortunately, many Christian parents have either caved to the pressure or allowed the pressure to shape their psychology until the biblical call to spare not the rod is replaced by a timeout. In my day, a timeout was the time I spent on the bed waiting for the spanking. It was very effective. Today about the only thing a timeout does is give parents a ten-minute break.

Wise parents are sold on corrective discipline, which is primarily comprised of diligent spanking. Discipline must be effective in delivering sufficient pain so that the correction will be more painful to the child than the delight in the foolish act. Parents must give their children good reason to forsake their folly. Don't be afraid; your children won't break. They must be broken, however. Foolishness must be driven out far from them. What will it take? How much and how often must corrective discipline be practiced? What must you do to correct the child's path, redirecting them to the way they should go? Wise parents figure it out; they're determined to discipline often enough and tough enough out of enormous love because foolishness and wisdom are in the balance, and holiness in our children is the treasure that we seek.

Parenting Principle 28
Wise Parents Lead in Spiritual Discipline by Example

Apply your heart to discipline and your ears to words of knowledge.
PROVERBS 23:12

Parents must practice spiritual discipline in their own lives if they expect their children to be spiritually disciplined. "Do as I say, not as I do" has no positive power in the life of a child. There's a wretched hypocrisy to teaching something to our children that we are not practicing ourselves. There's only one way to be an effective parent-leader: before you instruct your children in the way they should go, you must lead by example, walking in the way before them. It is only when you practice the wise parenting principles from Proverbs that you have the power to speak these truths into your child's life. If you consistently apply your heart to discipline in the Lord per this proverb, then you can say to your son or daughter, without hypocrisy, "Follow my example. As I apply my heart to discipline, you do the same."

Applying your heart suggests an inner drive and desire for spiritual discipline, which can also be translated as "instruction." To apply your ears to words of knowledge is to say, "Pay careful attention to the knowledge of God found in His Word." There is no growth in spiritual understanding unless we diligently apply ourselves to spiritual instruction. Likewise, there is no growth in personally and passionately knowing God unless we pursue the knowledge of God. The more passionate the pursuit, the more one acquires the knowledge of God.

Wise parents are driven by a holy desire to know God, with godliness as the glorious result. If that describes you, then you will teach your children first with your life, which gives power to your words. It's not either *a strong example* or *words of instruction*—it's both. The apostle Paul's inspired counsel to his son in the faith, Timothy, is for all of us, including parents who are passionate about being godly and wise: "Discipline yourself for the purpose of godliness; for...godliness is profitable for all things, since it holds promise for the present life and also for the life to come" (1 Timothy 4:7–8). There cannot be any doubt that Paul lived that out in life, so he could instruct Timothy in integrity.

Good parents work hard to protect their children the best they can, but only godly parents know that the best protection for their children is to protect their hearts and souls by grounding them in Christ and in His Word. So, parents, be wise. Teach your kids first by example—personally and passionately apply your heart to instruction and your ears to words of knowledge. And then, with your godly example as the backdrop for all that you say, instruct them to be as passionate for God and His Word as you are. Teach them by practice and precept to be disciplined in the spiritual.

One spiritual discipline that I have given myself to for years is the production of the fruit of the Spirit in my life. The Holy Spirit is the One who produces His fruit in us, but I have learned that I must "walk by the Spirit" with the promise that if I do, I "will not carry out the desire of the flesh" (Galatians 5:16). I have also learned that the only way to walk *by* the Spirit is to be fully surrendered and submissive *to* the Spirit so that I can be totally dependent and obedient to Him. Only when I am walking by the Spirit can I cooperate with Him in the production of His fruit in my life. Notice that the evidence of the fruit of the Spirit (5:22–23) follows the command to walk by the Spirit.

Years ago, I attended a local men's breakfast. I don't remember the man's name who shared the devotion with us, but I haven't forgotten the "Fruit of the Spirit Test" he gave us. We were asked to put our names in the following sentence: "[My name] is especially sensitive to the Spirit as it relates to," and then it listed the nine characteristics of the fruit of the Spirit: love, joy, peace, patience, kindness, goodness, faithfulness, gentleness, and self-control. We were then asked to evaluate ourselves on a one-to-ten scale, putting the number in the blank that best indicated how deeply each aspect was embedded in our lives. If you would like to apply the test to yourself, it looked like this:

____[My name]____

is especially sensitive to the Spirit as it relates to love. ______

is especially sensitive to the Spirit as it relates to joy. ______

is especially sensitive to the Spirit as it relates to peace. ______

is especially sensitive to the Spirit as it relates to patience. ______

is especially sensitive to the Spirit as it relates to kindness. ______

is especially sensitive to the Spirit as it relates to goodness. ______

is especially sensitive to the Spirit as it relates to faithfulness. ______

is especially sensitive to the Spirit as it relates to gentleness. ______

is especially sensitive to the Spirit as it relates to self-control. ______

That was tough...but it got worse. He then asked us to take the test home and have our wives evaluate us with the same one-to-ten scale. I did as the speaker asked, and I will tell you that it was a sobering, painful, and life-changing exercise. I told

Kathy, as we were instructed, to be painfully honest. To my delight, Kathy honestly rated me high on peace, faithfulness, and self-control. However, to my pain and shame, she rated me not so high on others, in particular, patience, kindness, and gentleness. But here's the glory in it: that little exercise pinpointed specific areas in my life where I was falling short of being like Christ, and it began a process in me of walking by the Spirit and not carrying out the desire of the flesh. I don't do it perfectly, of course, but I am growing in the fruit of the Spirit, and it continues to this day.

Now, each day of the week, Monday through Friday, I take one aspect of the fruit and concentrate on it in my morning prayer. If, for example, this morning's fruit-focus is peace, then tomorrow's fruit-focus will be patience, which was at one time one of the weakest fruit characteristics in my life.

A couple years after the original testing, I asked Kathy to retake the test. Thankfully, by the Spirit's power, there was significant progress in each area. But I was not satisfied, so I stuck with it, and I continue to consistently give myself to the process every week of my life. I encourage you to do the same. It is a spiritual discipline that will progressively change your life into the image of Christ and will make you a much more effective husband or wife and parent.

Here's how I do it: I use the list below that contains the nine aspects of the Spirit's fruit to help focus me in prayer on that day's characteristic. Perhaps you are ready to follow my example to discipline yourself for the purpose of godliness. If so, ask your spouse to test you, using the above test. Then diligently and consistently use the list below in your daily prayers.

Just a caveat here: you may not agree with how your spouse scores you on some of the characteristics. That's okay—those scores reflect how she or he sees you, so accept that perception and get to work!

Love

"The love of God has been poured out within our hearts through the Holy Spirit who was given to us" (Romans 5:5) at the point of our salvation. This *divine love* is in me but needs to grow up in me, for it is not natural to me. Rather, it is supernatural, unmerited love for the people in my life, and therefore it's supernaturally unconditional and sacrificial. It is the kind of love that highly values what God values—the lives and souls of other human beings...even the ones I don't like. It's the kind of love that willingly gives up my rights and wants to serve God by serving others with His love. It is only when I die to my own self-centeredness that I begin to love as Christ loved me and gave up His life for me.

> *Lord Jesus, teach me to love others in the same way You love me, selflessly, without conditions or expectations. Amen.*

Joy

"The joy of the Lord is your strength" (Nehemiah 8:10). The joy of the Lord is the abiding inner gladness, delight, and satisfaction in me that comes from knowing, trusting, delighting in, depending on, and obeying the Lord. When my joy is in the Lord Himself, trial and circumstance cannot touch my joy.

Dear Lord, may I be so satisfied with You that Your joy will be my constant companion and strength. Amen.

Peace

"Let the peace of Christ rule in your hearts" (Colossians 3:15). I know I am involved in this process because there's something I must do: I have to *let* the peace of Christ rule (umpire, or call the shots) in my heart. The peace of Christ brings inner tranquility and rest that quiets my mind and heart. It defies human understanding, even in the midst of circumstances that ordinarily cause me anxiety.

Holy Spirit, empower me to allow the peace of Christ to call the shots in my heart. May I intimately know inner tranquility and rest so that my circumstances cannot disturb my inner peace. Amen.

Patience

"Therefore be patient, brethren, until the coming of the Lord" (James 5:7). Patience is suffering long (long-suffering) with aggravating and demanding people. I learn to suffer long with difficult people by accepting the fact that the Holy Spirit sovereignly brought into my life the person who is causing me to suffer because He knows exactly the personalities He needs to use in the process of refining me into the likeness of Christ.

Spirit of God, remind me that difficult people are sovereignly given to me for a divine purpose: to refine me into the likeness of Christ. Teach me to not only accept suffering caused by a difficult person but to welcome it with open arms. Please, Lord, make me like Jesus. Amen.

Kindness

"Be kind to one another, tender-hearted, forgiving each other, just as God in Christ also has forgiven you" (Ephesians 4:32). Kindness is compassion, consideration, and respect that is rooted in God's grace within; it's grace in action—a tender heart toward all people that manifests itself in great concern, not for myself but for others. It is behaving kindly toward all others as God has behaved kindly toward me.

Holy Spirit, make me so selfless that I will be content with being kind even in the face of unkindness. And teach me to allow You, not people, to control my responses to them. Amen.

Goodness

"Your word I have treasured in my heart, that I may not sin against You" (Psalm 119:11). This is the inner goodness and uprightness of the soul that hates evil and refrains from doing it. Goodness is about being good (moral goodness), but *being* good will result in *doing* good. Only a godly person is a good person.

Lord, make me godly good so that I will not sin against You. Amen.

Faithfulness

"For the eyes of the Lord move to and fro throughout the earth that He may strongly support those whose heart is completely His" (2 Chronicles 16:9). Faithfulness expresses itself in dependability, reliability, trustworthiness, and loyalty. It means I keep my promises and fulfill my responsibilities before a faithful and holy God. Being a bondslave to Christ makes it much easier to be faithful, for bondslaves willingly lay down their rights for God's glory and for the benefit of others. Only those whose lives are all about God—not about themselves—will be counted among the faithful.

Lord, may my life be all about You, so that I may be counted among the faithful. May You be able to trust me because my heart belongs completely to You. Amen.

Gentleness

"Walk in a manner worthy of the calling with which you have been called, with all humility and gentleness, with patience, showing tolerance for one another in love" (Ephesians 4:1–2). The Greek word used for "gentleness" describes an animal that has been broken, tamed, and brought under control. So a gentleman or a gentlewoman is one whose self-will and self-way has been broken by the Spirit of God. A gentleperson then is constantly under His sovereign, gracious control.

Holy Spirit, break me down and free me from my selfish self; tame me and control me, thereby making me gentle toward all. Amen.

Self-control

"Everyone who competes in the games exercises self-control in all things. They then do it to receive a perishable wreath, but we an imperishable" (1 Corinthians 9:25). To be self-controlled is to be self-disciplined. Mind, emotions, passions, and will are mastered and under control. As a self-controlled person, I must allow myself to be thoroughly conquered by the Holy Spirit so that I will say yes to God and no to my enemies—the world, the flesh, and the devil.

Spirit of God, grant me the grace to consistently walk by You in strict self-discipline so that I will not carry out the desires of the flesh, but rather will please You in every way. Amen.

The fruit of the Spirit makes one like Christ, and a Christlike life is powerful. It comes only to those who walk in full cooperation with the Spirit, those passionately pursuing His fruit. As a wise parent, discipline yourself for godliness because you know that godliness is caught as well as taught. The souls of your children are the treasure that you seek, so be a wise parent-leader by first exemplifying spiritual discipline within yourself.

Parenting Principle 29
Wise Parents Show Their Children What a God-Fearing Life Looks Like

Do not let your heart envy sinners, but live in the fear of the LORD *always. Surely there is a future, and your hope will not be cut off. Listen, my son, and be wise, and direct your heart in the way. Do not be with heavy drinkers of wine, or with gluttonous eaters of meat; for the heavy drinker and the glutton will come to poverty, and drowsiness will clothe one with rags.*

PROVERBS 23:17–21

Wise parents show their children what a God-fearing life looks like by applying the four directives of this passage to their lives and to their children's lives.

Directive 1: Do Not Let Your Heart Envy Sinners (Proverbs 23:17)

There is no future goodness or godliness in envying sinners and wanting what they want or have. If you pursue what they pursue, you will find only hurt, harm, destruction, or death.

Sometimes I wonder why Christian parents go after the same things the world pursues. When we seek worldly gain and pleasure, aren't we teaching our children that our values are the same as those of the world?

We needn't covet these things because God promises He will provide everything we need. And then He goes further and blesses His children with so much more—not necessarily worldly treasure, but with blessings that we may not have imagined or even known existed. The trappings of His wealth are so much better than those of the world. And yet, He knows our physical needs here, too. That's why Jesus reassured His followers in Matthew 6:31–33, "Do not worry...for your heavenly Father knows that you need all these things. But seek first His kingdom and His righteousness, and all these things [that you need] will be added to you."

Directive 2: Live with an Eternal Perspective (Proverbs 23:18)

Live in the fear of the Lord always. *Don't* envy sinners in your heart, but *do* live zealously in the fear of the Lord. Those who do not fear the Lord instead pursue what they want in life. But those who fear the Lord first, pursue Him and the things that He desires us to pursue—His righteousness, His kingdom, and His glory. Our Lord beautifully states this eternal perspective in Matthew 6:19–21:

> Do not store up for yourselves treasures on earth, where moth and rust destroy, and where thieves break

> in and steal. But store up for yourselves treasures in heaven, where neither moth nor rust destroys, and where thieves do not break in or steal; for where your treasure is, there your heart will be also.

The eternal perspective always questions what the heart desires. It then makes corrections when necessary to align with a God-fearing life.

In the first two directives, the contrast is between a heart that is envious for what the world has and a heart that is passionate for the things of God. Obedience to these two directives comes with the promise in verse 18: "Surely there is a future, and your hope [your confidence in a glorious future] will not be cut off." The fleeting pleasures of sin are contrasted with the ultimate future that belongs to those who fear the Lord... and that contrast is immense. So, wise parents whose treasure is the eternal souls of their children store up for themselves and their family treasures in heaven. With that heavenly pursuit, there comes a present future on earth as well.

Directive 3: Listen and Be Wise (23:19)

Children are to listen to their wise parents' instruction and to direct their hearts in the way. When they seek the right and righteous way of godly thinking and behavior given to us by God and exemplified in Christ, they will be exceptionally wise. However, many sons and daughters naturally and foolishly tend to think they know better than their wise parents. Their natural bent is toward doing whatever it takes to get what they think will make them happy. But they are too immature to know what is best for them, so they strive for what they think is best. Wise parents train their foolish sons and daughters through corrective discipline and verbal reproof to learn to listen to them. Then they prove over time that they are far wiser and know much better than their children what is best for them. Children must learn to listen to their wise parents in order to gain wisdom and to direct their hearts in the way.

Directive 4: Be Careful of the Company You Keep (23:20)

This directive comes from wise parents to their children, instructing them not to belong to the company of certain people, implying that if they are in association with them, they most likely will become like them.

The first company of people to avoid are "heavy drinkers of wine." There are those among us who have a strong bias against alcohol, and for good reason. Alcoholism brings destruction to our culture and our families. I understand that strong bias—alcoholism was present in my family when I was a child. Yet, let us be careful not to make God's Word align with our biases and, in the process, make it say what it doesn't say. This is most dangerous because it gives our opinion equal authority with God's Word.

If total abstinence from alcohol is a principle you live by, I applaud you for that. But there are two things you shouldn't do: One, don't claim it as a biblical command, because it's not. Two, don't make your personal convictions everyone else's conviction to live by.

As we've seen, the Old Testament teaches that we shouldn't drink heavily or keep company with heavy drinkers. We find the same teaching in the New Testament. For example, there's this command: "Do not get drunk with wine" (Ephesians 5:18). Further, 1 Timothy 3:8 instructs that elders and deacons, the spiritual and moral officeholders in the church, must not be "addicted to wine." Nothing in Scripture strictly *prohibits* drinking, but much is said about *abusive* drinking. However, while it is not biblically honest to say that all drinking is sinful, the Bible does clearly speak of the evils of addiction, drunkenness, and excess. So what we are to hate and to teach our children to hate is the *abuse* of alcohol. This and every other excess in life is not only sinful but destructive and must be hated and avoided at all cost.

Because of the excessive abuse of alcohol in our nation and families and because of the spiritual weakness of humanity, it is easy for well-meaning people to move moderate drinking into the category of biblical sin, even though it's not. Drinking wine in moderation is only a cultural sin, not a biblical one. In Bible times, God's people drank wine for four purposes: purification of water (historical fact); medicinally (1 Timothy 5:23); enjoyment (as in many other cultures); and celebration, like at the wedding of Cana (John 2:1–11).

This is a hard truth for those raised in churches where godly leaders instructed their people that the Bible teaches total abstinence from alcohol. It's also a hard truth for those deeply and negatively impacted by its abuse. But it is a biblical truth nonetheless: drunkenness, excessive and abusive drinking, and an addiction to alcohol are strictly prohibited. Moderate drinking is not.

Having said that, let me be quick to add that many of us should never drink wine because we cannot drink it in moderation. In that case, abstinence is the only wise course of action. If you are this type of person, don't ever drink. Doing so will easily lead to excess and even alcoholism. Wise people who have addictive personalities know not to go there. Further, wise parents with addictive personalities will practice abstinence because they are aware their children may share their addictive nature. For these families, it is wise to never introduce alcohol of any form into your home.

The second company of people we should avoid are "gluttonous eaters." This teaching doesn't instruct us to stay away from those who eat—we all eat. It does say, however, that we shouldn't *keep company* with gluttons. This implies that we could easily become gluttons ourselves. Gluttony, as it relates to food, is the habitual practice of eating too much; it is usually seen as a greedy and excessive indulgence in eating.

It's fascinating to me how passionate Christians are when in it comes to excessive drinking, but excessive eating is barely a blip on a spiritual radar screen. I have come to believe that gluttony is perhaps the most overlooked and permissible sin in the evangelical community. It's more than tolerated—it's often encouraged.

Obesity is a destructive problem in our country. Dangerous illnesses related to overindulgence in food (like heart disease and diabetes) plague our nation and our churches. In fact, childhood obesity is now a prevalent problem in our society, a serious issue that begs for physical activity and healthier eating habits.

Since excessive eating is a sin and poor eating habits are unhealthy, wise parents do not ignore or downgrade the problem to something less than it is. If there are eating issues in the lives of wise parents and/or their children, they evaluate those lifestyles to determine the reasons for their abusive eating, eating disorders, or unhealthy habits. As parents, are they too busy to eat properly and to train their children to eat properly? Do they and their children deal with the pressures and pains of life by turning to food? Are their children absorbed in the world of electronic devices to the point that they no longer take part in active, physical play? Is the family not one that plays and exercises regularly? Are there compulsive behaviors in the family that stem from other unresolved issues?

Wise parents carefully evaluate the eating habits, lifestyle, and activity levels of their family, and they become proactive in making effective changes to unhealthy habits in their lives and homes. If they need help in dealing with these issues, wise parents turn to healthcare professionals, and/or to the church for counsel, encouragement, and prayer. Wise parents understand that eating issues must be addressed, not ignored.

The consequences that accompany the habitual abuse of both alcohol and food are very serious. They are clearly stated in the final verse of our proverb: "For the heavy drinker and the glutton will come to poverty, and drowsiness will clothe one with rags" (23:21). Ephesians 5:15–18 gives parents wise counsel and practice to pass along to their children:

> Therefore be careful how you walk, not as unwise men but as wise, making the most of your time, because the days are evil. So then do not be foolish, but understand what the will of the Lord is. And do not get drunk with wine, for that is dissipation, but be filled with the Spirit.

With all this in mind, wise parents will demonstrate a God-fearing lifestyle to their children. They will instruct their children to zealously live in the fear of the Lord; they will keep before them the promise that there is an extraordinary future in such living; and finally, they will remind them that their blessed hope and assurance will not be cut off by the enemies of their souls. So, wise parents, say to your sons and daughters, "Listen, children, and be wise. Let us together direct our hearts in the upward way." May it be so! Amen.

Parenting Principle 30
Wise Parents Train Their Children to Practice Moderation

If you find honey, eat just enough—too much of it, and you will vomit.
Proverbs 25:16 (NIV)

The old saying, "moderation in all things," is not found in the Bible; however, moderation is a principle that's clearly taught in Scripture. We see it here in this proverb, as well as in other passages that I will reference a bit later. But while the Bible recommends moderation in many things, that does not include all things. Specifically, it does not apply to the spiritual realm of life. We are not to *moderately* love God and others, nor are we to extend *in moderation* mercy and grace to the undeserving. No, we are commanded to love the Lord our God with our *entire* being—in fact, we're told the world will know we are Christians by our overwhelming, Christlike love for one another (see John 13:34–35). Further, as children born of the Father, His extravagant mercy and grace are built into our spiritual DNA. Thus, biblical teaching does not encompass moderation in spiritual things.

Moderation does apply, however, to all things that are of this world. These include what we consider the pleasures of life—such things as wine, food, and sweet indulgences like honey or chocolate. The proverb gives a consequence if moderation is not practiced: if you eat more than just enough, you will probably vomit.

Obviously, the opposite of moderation is excess and overindulgence. Ever since man fell into sin, people have disregarded God's *enough* and have chosen to live by the philosophy, "Let us overeat and overdrink and be overmerry, for tomorrow we die." And they wake up the next morning with a hangover or nausea or both. But wise people who are in an intimate relationship with God know that God's *enough*—that is to say, His boundaries—are established for our good. He's out to protect us; therefore, those who are wise practice moderation in all good and pleasurable things of life so that those things will remain wholesome and good.

In James 1:14, the apostle warns of the grave danger of being "carried away and enticed by [one's] own lusts." He goes on in verses 16–17 to say, "Do not be deceived, my beloved brethren. Every good thing given and every perfect gift is from above, coming down from the Father of lights, with whom there is no variation or shifting shadow." But every good thing given by God can effectively move from a good desire to an insatiable lust, and when this happens, corruption of the partaker follows. The *excess monster*, if you will, will gobble him or her up.

We live in a society that excels in blowing past boundaries like they're not there. We promote excess at every turn and don't know the meaning of "enough." How important, then, does it become for Christian parents to walk in wisdom by creating in their homes—long before children arrive—an atmosphere of moderation in all things that bring pleasure in this life? Part of the reason God's people are so deeply in debt today is that we don't say no to ourselves or to our children. We've bought into the world's cry—the "American dream!"—that we *deserve* the best. The best cars, the best homes, the best clothes, the best of everything temporal, and all that's immediately satisfying! But that's not a kingdom-of-God mentality. It's keeping up with the Joneses instead of promoting and living for the things of God. It is only when our treasures are in heaven instead of on earth that we will raise our children to be moderate in the things of earth and to be passionately, excessively, over-the-top immoderate in the things of God.

Some in Christianity would call this radical thinking. But a missionary friend of mine, Tom Zurowski, simply calls it the "normal Christian life." He believes and teaches that the normal Christian life *is* a radical life—we should be radically different from the world around us. I think wise parents would agree with Tom and would set out to be radically, spiritually *normal*, which includes moderation in all things that pertain to this world. If you knew Tom, his wife Elli, and their six children, you would know that they are on fire for all things eternal. One cannot be on fire for all things eternal and all things temporal at the same time. Wise parents choose that which will outlast their earthly lives and then lead their children in this eternal way.

Proverbs 25:17 says, "Let your foot rarely be in your neighbor's house, or he will become weary of you and hate you." This proverb speaks of moderation in conduct and actions toward neighbors. In other words, don't wear out your welcome because too much of a good thing—even good neighborly relations—will eventually breed contempt. If your neighbor proves to be highly social and clearly enjoys your company, then by all means go as often as you are invited. If he or she is not a believer, then go as a faithful but not intrusive witness. If they don't mind you popping in on occasion, then occasionally pop in. Of course, if you pop in on them, they may pop in on you, so be sure that arrangement agrees with you. Practice the commonsense principle of not visiting too much in order to prevent bad feelings and negative attitudes.

Here are some more passages that teach moderation in all things not eternal. Proverbs 25:27 says, "It is not good to eat much honey." Verse 28 warns that whoever has no rule over his own spirit is "like a city that is broken into and without walls." In other words, a person of excess who has no self-control has no protective walls from the sin and penalties of overindulgence.

Galatians 5:23 tells us that one aspect of the fruit of the Spirit is self-control. We gain self-control as we learn to submit to the Spirit's control and become dependent on Him. So once again, parents must be wise by leading the way. If our children are to be schooled in self-control so that their lives reflect moderation in all things pertaining to the world, they must learn it in the home first—both through our example and through biblical instruction and corrective discipline.

As we've already seen, Ephesians 5:18 instructs us to "not get drunk with wine, for that is dissipation, but be filled with the Spirit." God is not a stick-in-the-mud. He wants us to enjoy the things of this world, but He wants us to enjoy in moderation what He supplies, not what we selfishly and excessively pursue in the lust of the flesh. Any excess, even if it is good in and of itself, will make you vomit, either literally or figuratively.

Here are some other areas where we must practice moderation.

Sleep. Too much of this good thing can produce laziness. Conversely, too little sleep is also an issue. We homeschooled our oldest daughter, partly because she struggled with asthma and getting up early to meet the school bus wore her out and made her physically ill. She simply needed more sleep. A wise parent knows his children and lets them sleep enough—but not too much. A healthy spiritual exercise would be to read through Proverbs and take note of all the verses that speak strongly against laziness and slothfulness. At the same time, note the verses that speak of the rewards of being active and industrious.

Television. There are two dangers with television: *what* our children watch and *how much* they watch it. Even if it is good programming, too much of a good thing is too much. Of course, wise parents are aware of the lack of good programming today. Even much of what is considered programming for children must be carefully monitored. And then there are the commercials that regularly cross the line of what is morally acceptable for Christian adults to watch, let alone our children! Kathy and I record shows that we deem appropriate for our grandchildren, but even then, there are commercials that promote materialism. Children's shows are peppered with consumerism—commercials that target children. During the last Christmas season, our four-year-old grandson responded to nearly every commercial with "I want that!" Over and over, "I want that!" It was a teaching moment because greed can come early and easy.

Stuff. Our American culture has created a love affair with material things. Much of our society has an insatiable appetite for more and more of what we have enough of already. The Lord Jesus warned in Luke 12:15, "Be on your guard against every form of greed; for not even when one has an abundance does his life consist of his possessions." And then He told a parable about greed and its terrible consequences for "the man who stores up treasures for himself and is not rich toward God" (12:16–21).

Clothes, shoes, jewelry, golf clubs, fishing tackle, guns… Whatever it is you overindulge in, remember: little (and not so little) eyes are watching your every move. Wise parents practice strict self-discipline and control. Instead of greedily accumulating stuff, they maintain a focus and pursuit that is rich toward God. They keep their real earthly treasures—their spouse and children—constantly on their minds.

Now, let me say something here. Do not be quick to judge—not everyone who is rich is greedy and can be accused of excess, just as not all people who are considered overweight can be accused of overeating. Some people have medical conditions that make it easy to gain and difficult to shed pounds. Likewise, not everyone who possesses much is excessive in his pursuit. Some people are simply good at making money. In fact, some of the most generous people I know are those who have much. They are good stewards of what God has given them, and they give much to the church, to missions, and to those in need.

Games. You don't need me to tell you that video gaming is all the rage today. For many people—children and adults—gaming can be addictive and far too excessive. Limiting the time your children play video games is necessary to protect them from excessive and hard-to-break habits. Of course, this must begin with you. If you are a parent who enjoys gaming, be sure you lead by example in limiting the time *you* spend playing games. In addition (and it shouldn't need to be said, but I'll say it anyway), the types of games we allow our children to play are just as important as the time they spend playing them. Wise parents are discerning in the selection of the games allowed into their homes and into their children's hearts and minds.

Electronics. In this age of electronics, there is a line that can be crossed into the world of *way too much.* I'm old-school, I know; therefore, I'm not a good judge on how early and how much children should have access to these devices. I will leave that up to the discernment of wise parents who are in touch with the scary realities that our amazing technological advances present. It is safe and true to say, however, that too much of a good thing is too much. Included under this heading is free access to too much information too early. This is extremely dangerous. Wise parents are aware of such things and carefully control what devices their children are allowed to use and what they may access on the Internet.

Sports and other extracurricular activities. Without moderation, many parents allow their children to be involved in way too many activities. They seem to think their kids will somehow be deprived of something if they aren't participating. Some children are involved in just about everything their schools and other organizations offer. Consequently, parents constantly run their children here and there, longing for the day when their children will be able drive themselves to their activities. Wisdom says that too much of such things will rob the family and the church of quality and quantity time with their children. Our church youth ministry is doing quite well; however, I can't help but think how many more young people we could influence for Christ if everything else they were involved in wasn't more important than their involvement in youth ministry. We lose the involvement of youth in winter retreats and summer mission trips because of other, seemingly more important activities. What are we teaching our children about priorities when family and church are not in their appropriate places in the lives, hearts, and minds of our teenagers?

Again, it's all about moderation, except in that which is spiritual and eternal. I trust that the parents who read this will be wise in their discernment. What is best for your family? You may have to wisely reevaluate here.

God is out to protect us, and wise parents are out to protect their children. Protection comes in maintaining moderation in all things not spiritual and eternal. The Word of God warns against all excess that does not pertain to Him. So, wise parents, train your children to be disciplined in all areas of life where *enough* is good and enjoyable but *too much* of the same thing is destructive and deadly.

An important question to consider is this: If we simply let our children do whatever is right in their own eyes, will they practice self-moderation on their own? We've all seen children who wield control over their parents—they have learned to manipulate their parents to get what they want. Those children are out of control. They desperately need parental training and accountability to rein them in until they grow up in Christ to be mature people who depend on the Spirit for greater growth in self-control.

If we want our children to grow up to practice moderation on their own, we must follow the same biblical formula in child training that was noted earlier and is restated here. Wise parents:

- Teach self-control in all things, first by their own example.
- Teach it in precept through careful instruction from God's Word.
- Reinforce the teaching through corrective discipline when necessary.
- Reward obedience through praise and encouragement.
- Continue to wisely lean hard on God throughout the parenting process.

Is God your priority of priorities? Do you seek Him fully so that you are truly and eternally rich toward Him? When you look at your family, what do you see? Second only to God, are they the treasure you seek? Amy Carmichael once said, "We will have all of eternity to celebrate the victories, but only a few hours before sunset in which to win them." We have only a few hours before the sun sets on our short season of bringing up our children in the discipline and instruction of the Lord. Wise parents keep eternity's values in clear view. In Christ and through the power of the Holy Spirit, they strive to strongly establish their children in the way they should go. They have learned that nothing is more valuable than the eternal souls of their children, and nothing is more important than the glory of the Lord, both in their own and in their children's lives.

CHAPTER 8

Wise Parenting Principles 31-35: Stay on Mission

Proverbs 25–28

A MISSION STATEMENT IS A clear, concise statement that communicates the purpose and goal of an organization. Churches, businesses, and nonprofit organizations all use mission statements to help them prioritize their actions and remain focused on their goals. Mission statements can also be helpful for wise parents who wish to keep their eyes on the heavenly prize of raising godly children.

While our girls were in our home, Kathy and I thought it important to have a family mission statement to help keep us focused on our mission as parents. We decided to adopt a Bible verse as our statement, and it's one I have referenced several times already. We chose Ephesians 6:4: "Do not provoke your children to anger, but bring them up in the discipline and instruction of the Lord." We found this verse a helpful reminder of what we wanted to achieve through our parenting efforts.

It is easy, however, to drift from that mission. The busyness and distractions of life, as well as the innate challenges of marriage and parenting, can pull our attention away from our goals and away from Christ. Some people set a specific, spiritual mission for their families, and they stay on mission throughout their lives. At the end of their journey, they can say, "Mission accomplished!" But there are others who set similar missions and who begin the journey well, but somewhere along the line, they begin to drift off mission. In the end, these families fall apart spiritually. Oftentimes, too, the family unit breaks up, and they all drift away from each other. Long-term mission focus is a strategy to prevent mission drift.

I would encourage you to create your own mission statement for your family. You can write one yourself, or do like we did and adopt a Bible verse as your statement. A family mission statement will give you clarity of direction and help you remain focused on your parenting mission. Whatever you decide to be your family mission statement, make sure it is Christ-centered, and then carefully guard against mission drift. It does no good to adopt a family mission statement if you pay less and less attention to it until you completely drift away from it. It's too late for many families—they are long lost and most likely will never recover. But you and your family have a marvelous hope in Christ. Maintain your focus on Him.

I seriously doubt that you would be this deep in this book if you were not on a mission to carefully bring up your children in the Lord. As you proactively and diligently apply the wise parenting principles from Proverbs to your lives and homes, my prayer is that God will give you grace to raise up your children in the Lord for His eternal glory and their everlasting benefit. May God empower you to stay on mission!

Parenting Principle 31
Wise Parents Think before They Speak

Like apples of gold in settings of silver is a word spoken in right circumstances. Like an earring of gold
and an ornament of fine gold
is a wise reprover to a listening ear.
PROVERBS 25:11–12

PART 1: USING WISE WORDS

"Like apples of gold in settings of silver..." In fine jewelry, settings of silver enhance the beauty and value of apples crafted out of gold. In the same way, a wise, encouraging, and edifying word is beautified and valued when it is spoken in right circumstances. In applying this proverb to parenting, wise parents are careful about two things: One, they are careful to speak *right words* (likened to apples of gold); and, two, they are careful to speak them in *right circumstances* (likened to settings of silver).

Right Words

Have you ever said something you regretted, either immediately or later on? We all have. There are times when wisdom isn't our present companion, and we speak without thinking about how our words will negatively impact the person who receives them. Oh, we might think, but we do it too little or too late or both. This happens often in a family dynamic where everyone is comfortable with each other and used to freely speaking their minds. Parents sometimes find frustration from the day exiting their mouths as unwise and hurtful criticism of their children. It's important, then, when we realize we have spoken first and thought last, that we offer a sincere apology, even to our children. The apology should be accompanied by true repentance so we don't repeat the same mistake again.

I have discovered that children are quick to forgive their parents for the sins they commit against them. However, wise parents will learn from their mistakes and be quick to think before they speak. They will ask themselves, "What are the right words for my child? How can I in wisdom say what needs to be said so that it is helpful and not hurtful?"

Right Circumstances

Sometimes the words you speak to a family member are right and appropriate, but the circumstances are wrong. I learned in my marriage that, no matter how necessary it seemed that

I speak a constructive but critical word to my wife, doing so just before bedtime was (and still is) the absolutely wrong circumstance and time. I used to unwisely think that I should speak whatever was on my mind (including things that were negative and probably not as constructive as I thought) whenever it was on my mind. I didn't consider how tired she might be or how inappropriate my saying it might be at the moment. It might have been a right word (maybe…most likely… Okay, almost assuredly not!), but it was most definitely the wrong time. Wisdom teaches us that at times, timing is everything!

Right words are, by necessity, often negative in nature, but in this proverb, right words at the right time are mostly positive and encouraging. We learned earlier in Principle 12 about the destructive power of negative words to our children. But this verse speaks about wise words that build up and encourage. Godly parents who are growing in Christ and walking in the wisdom of Christ learn to know what and when to say what is needed to encourage, instruct, and edify their children. This requires careful thought because an unthinking parent doesn't inspire anything positive in his or her children.

It is often said that hindsight is 20/20. Too often, while we're in the moment, we aren't thinking clearly enough to have 20/20 vision. It's only after something happens that we look back with much-improved vision and wish we would have handled a situation differently. We all live with regret in this area, but learning to think before we speak will help us to live with much less of it.

How do we learn to wisely and carefully think first? Here are some questions that will get us thinking and moving in the right direction and then help us remain there, right on mission.

1. *Are you working in cooperation with the Spirit in the production of His fruit in your life; namely, the fruit of patience, kindness, gentleness, and self-control?*

Under Principle 28, where wise parents lead in spiritual discipline by example, I encouraged you to allow the Spirit to work out in you as you work with Him to produce the fruit of the Spirit in your life. If you haven't started that holy process, I strongly encourage you to go back and do so now. The fruit of the Spirit brings Christlike character, and it will cause you to see situations clearly so you will more easily think before you speak.

2. *Are you walking in the light of Christ and His Word?*

Jesus Christ is the true Light, and He came into the world to enlighten mankind (John 1:9). The apostle John testified in 1 John 1:5–7:

> This is the message we have heard from Him [the Christ] and announce to you, that God is Light, and in Him there is no darkness at all. If we say that we have fellowship with Him and yet walk in the darkness, we lie and do not practice the truth; but if we walk in the

> Light as He Himself is in the Light, we have fellowship with one another, and the blood of Jesus His Son cleanses us from all sin.

Light illuminates and enlightens; it allows us to see what we could never see while living and walking in the dark. Notice that the inspired apostle of Christ says that if we walk in the Light, we have fellowship with one another, including with our children. When we walk in the Light, we see clearly and we learn to think clearly, so that we will speak wisely. This allows us to walk in intimate fellowship with God and with our families.

3. ***Are you daily presenting your body to God as a living and holy sacrifice?***

Our bodies include our entire being, including our hearts, our brains, and our mouths. Romans 12:2 is an absolute necessity if our hearts, heads, and mouths are to know spiritual transformation. However, we can never intimately experience verse 2 if we don't first effectively and continually apply verse 1.

> Therefore I urge you, brethren, by the mercies of God, to present your bodies a living and holy sacrifice, acceptable to God, which is your spiritual service of worship. And do not be conformed to this world, but be transformed by the renewing of your mind, so that

> you may prove what the will of God is, that which is good and acceptable and perfect.

Between the *and* of no longer being conformed to the world and the *but* of being transformed by the renewing our minds, we must every day present our whole selves as living and holy sacrifices to God. It is in that humbled, surrendered, submissive, and sacrificial state that we stop conforming and start transforming. And then, with transformed and renewed minds, we will know how to wisely think before we wisely speak.

4. ***Are you consistently allowing God to purify your heart?***
   Jesus said in Luke 6:45,

> The good man out of the good treasure of his heart brings forth what is good; and the evil man out of the evil treasure brings forth what is evil; for his mouth speaks from that which fills his heart.

An impure mouth is a huge problem, but it's not the root problem. The root of the problem is the heart. According to Jesus, if we purify our hearts, then whatever comes out of our mouths will be good and godly.

5. ***Is your life clean before God?***
   Asked another way, are you humble, like Christ, so that through confession, you get clean quickly when you sin with your lips? 1 John 1:9 gives us this promise:

> If we confess our sins, He is faithful and righteous to forgive us our sins and to cleanse us from all unrighteousness.

Think about what the verse promises and provides: The Father is faithful and righteous (or just) to forgive us our sins and to cleanse us from all unrighteousness because Jesus fully paid the penalty of our sins on the cross. This means the Father *must* forgive a true confession, or He would be unfaithful, unrighteous, and unjust! But since He is altogether perfect, suddenly the forgiveness of our sins and our purity of heart and life become all about Jesus Christ and the cleansing power of His blood shed on our behalf so that we might become and remain "the righteousness of God in Him" (2 Corinthians 5:21). And, suddenly, "blessed are the pure in heart, for they shall see God" (Matthew 5:8). If our lives are pure and remain pure in Christ, our tongues will be tamed and our words will be like apples of gold in settings of silver—right words in right circumstances—so that we wisely think before we wisely speak.

Part 2: Using Wise Reproof

"Like an earring of gold and an ornament of fine gold is a wise reprover to a listening ear" (Proverbs 25:12). The second proverb under this principle speaks of reproof, which is verbal correction. Children typically need reproof in large measure if they are to be led to accept Christ and then grow up in Christ.

But there are two wise people in this proverb—the reprover (the parent) and the listener (the child).

The Wise Reprover

Wise parents are not afraid to reprove or rebuke their children when they need it. Reproof is an essential aspect of tough, loving, corrective discipline. But wise parents must be *wise reprovers*—their reproof, like finely crafted gold jewelry, is stunningly beautiful and appropriate. It is never too little or too much. It doesn't tear down because it's harsh, critical, cutting, or caustic. Instead, it lovingly but effectively corrects and builds up, and in the end, it brings encouragement to both the wise parental reprover and the wise listening child.

In Principle 12, we discussed Paul's counsel in Ephesians 4:29–30. It's worth revisiting here:

> Let no unwholesome word proceed from your mouth, but only such a word as is good for edification [building up] according to the need of the moment, so that it will give grace to those who hear. Do not grieve the Holy Spirit of God, by whom you were sealed for the day of redemption.

We grieve the Spirit of God with unwholesome words that tear down rather than build up and encourage. For God's sake and for the sake of your family, think under the impact of the Holy Spirit. Then choose your words carefully and wisely speak them into the life and heart of your beloved child.

The Wise Listener

A wise listener will see the enormous value of a wise reproof, especially if it is given by a wise reprover. To him, the needed reproof is more valuable than fine gold jewelry. But for most children, a listening ear is nurtured into them, not born into them. Critical to that nurturing process are the parents who are careful not to provoke their children to anger through harsh and uncaring words or unfair and inappropriate treatment. Instead, wise parents create an atmosphere of safety and trust so that their children grow up to know that their parents have their best interests in mind. Our desire is that our children will come to know and even say, "Dad and Mom may not always approve of what I say and do, but they sure do approve of me, and they prove it with their tender loving care!" That atmosphere is most conducive to creating trust and a sense of safety.

However, tender love is seldom, if ever, enough. Our children are born with foolish hearts. Wisdom is not natural to them—foolishness is. So along with corrective, loving reproof must come the corrective rod of discipline: the paddle. I have said much about this, so it's not necessary to dwell on it here; I will only remind parents that tender love is never enough. Tender love effectively creates a trusting and caring environment. Tough love is needed to effectively remove foolishness from the child's heart so he can learn to be a wise and ready listener. Left to himself, a child will think he knows best and will not be transformed into a wise listener who is ready to receive wise counsel.

Our children desperately need their parents to be reprovers, but we must be wise ones who bring with our reproofs the wisdom and knowledge of Jesus Christ under the power of the Holy Spirit. Trained well in that holy environment, a wise child will find the wise reprover a valued treasure, like jewelry made of fine gold.

If the mission statement is Ephesians 6:4, and if wise parents are determined to stay on mission, then they must wisely and carefully think before they deliberately speak in right circumstances. For Christ's sake and for the sake of our children, may we be and stay on point!

Parenting Principle 32
Wise Parents Pass On to Their Children the Gift of Grace

If your enemy is hungry, give him food to eat; and if he is thirsty,
give him water to drink; for you will heap
burning coals on his head,
and the LORD will reward you.
PROVERBS 25:21–22

Giving grace (undeserved favor) to our enemies is just the opposite of what is natural to us and is completely foreign to what the world practices. What is natural to us is the desire for revenge. However, as Christians who are compelled and controlled by the love of Christ, we are new creations. The old things that controlled us have passed away, and new things have come. (See 2 Corinthians 5:14–17.) We no longer need to be slaves to our old nature and ways. We are now free in Christ to behave in brand-new and supernatural ways. Behold, the new has come! What a gift from God that wise parents have the privilege of passing on to their children. If we want to stay on mission by bringing up our children in the discipline and instruction of the Lord, then we must extend to our children the gift of grace so they can channel it to others—even to their enemies.

If the proverb sounds familiar to you, it is. The apostle Paul included it in his admonitions and instructions concerning the application of grace to the undeserving in Romans 12:17–21, a passage that I have returned to more times than I can count.

> Never pay back evil for evil to anyone. Respect what is right in the sight of all men. If possible, so far as it depends on you, be at peace with all men. Never take your own revenge, beloved, but leave room for the wrath of God, for it is written, "Vengeance is Mine, I will repay," says the Lord. "But if your enemy is hungry, feed him, and if he is thirsty, give him a drink; for in so doing you will heap burning coals on his head." Do not be overcome by evil, but overcome evil with good.

Now, attitudes and actions like these are not natural. Only new creations in Christ can respond in such a magnanimous and gracious manner.

An enemy can be simply defined "someone who hates you." Many might be surprised to find the transcendent grace of God here in Proverbs, flowing through His ancient covenant people to those who hate them. We expect to find such teachings of grace in the New Testament, but the Old Testament? And, yet, here it is, clear as a cloudless day: grace and loving kindness extended to the one who hates you instead of revenge. Now, that's not natural in any Testament, is it? It's supernatural!

There is a man still out there somewhere who hated the Allens' son, Jason, and our daughter, Lindsay. What should be our supernatural response to that as it relates to grace? As children of our heavenly Father, we are to love kindness and to do justice—that which is right, fair, and just. (See Micah 6:8.) Further, because "God is just" (2 Thessalonians 1:6 NIV), we ourselves are to love justice. If the murderer of Jason and Lindsay is ever captured, we will love the justice he receives. But even now, we pray for God to be gracious to him and to save his poor, wretched soul before it is eternally too late, so that the justice he receives from God is the forgiveness of his sins because he trusts in the substitutionary death of Christ. (See again 1 John 1:9.) We love justice, but our desire is for grace and the justice that flows from the cross, even toward the man who hated our children. We especially love that kind of justice.

Now, when it comes vengeance, wise and godly people, including wise parents, know that vengeance belongs to God, not to us. We are not permitted to take matters into our own hands; we are not to be like God in vengeance. Instead, our calling is to be like God in grace. Vengeance is God's prerogative and place, not ours. What we must do then is to entirely trust God to judge righteously. Then, in His patient and sovereign time, if there is no repentance, He will set all records straight. I can honestly say—and it's only by the wonder of God's amazing grace—that there has never been even a moment when I wanted revenge for my daughter's and Jason's murders. I can only raise my hand in praise to God because that is not of Chris Cutshall. It is only of Jesus Christ. And it has been my passion to pass that grace along to my family and my church family and to the church at large, as God has given me opportunity to testify of His grace.

It should be evident by now, as it has been consistently taught in this book, that before we can pass on the gift of grace to others, including to our children, we must be filled up and overflowing with grace ourselves. Grace is the power of heaven that flows down to us, into us, and then through us. Obviously, we can't manufacture it; we can only be conduits of divine love and grace. What a privilege to channel that marvelous grace to our children so that they will learn from us how to channel it to others.

Extending grace to others is our calling, especially when we extend it to those who hate us. Look at the cross of Jesus Christ. God's grace put Him there. God's grace kept Him there. And God's grace flowed through that cross from His gracious heart to ours. His grace flowed to those who hated Him as He said, "Father, forgive them, for they do not know what they are doing" (Luke 23:34). His grace flowed to the one criminal who confessed Him as He said, "Today you shall be with Me in Paradise" (23:43). When Jesus died, His pure grace flowed like a torrent out of His sacrificial, substitutionary death. Through it the church was born and salvation was made available to all people. The book of Acts details the story of how the early church was formed, grew, and spread throughout the known world. It was all by God's amazing and incomprehensible grace!

We cannot neglect the consequence of rejecting that grace, however. The criminal who rejected Christ experienced the vengeance of God because that was what he deserved for rejecting God's Son. Vengeance was God's alone to give. Governing bodies have the authority of God to mete out judgment and justice on earth (see Romans 13:1–7), but only God has the power and right to extend full vengeance. Again, we are not permitted to go there, for vengeance belongs to Him alone.

Since we are to be Godlike in grace but not in vengeance, let's take a closer look at our proverb: "If your enemy is hungry, give him food to eat; and if he is thirsty, give him water to drink; for you will heap burning coals on his head, and the Lord will reward you" (Proverbs 25:21–22).

If we read this proverb without background information, it might seem to say that being gracious toward your enemy is the best way to gain revenge. He might hurt you through his hate-filled unkindness, but your love-filled kindness will, in the end, multiply hurt upon him because your kindness heaps burning, hot coals on his head. We might see this as a win-win situation: he will get his just desserts, and you will get a great reward from God. That's what it sounds like at face value, but that's not what verse 22 means.

In ancient times, to give a person a heaping load of live, fiery hot coals in a pan to carry home "on his head" was a kind and neighborly thing to do. Imagine a chilly night and your neighbor, who is also your enemy—he actually hates you—has settled down for the night. Sometime in the night, because he is sleeping so soundly, he fails to wake up to fuel his fire, and it goes out. He finally awakens with a chill, rolls off his sleeping mat, realizes what has happened, and knows it will take a long time to make a new fire that will warm his house. So he comes next door to your little home, hoping to get a pan full of hot coals from you to restart a fire that will be quickly hot. Being a gracious neighbor, you roll out of your comfortable bed and give him your hottest coals. Now, as he carries it home, even though he's placed an insulating pad between his head and the pan to protect himself, the heat from the pan warms his head. You hope that perhaps the heat will remind him of the way he has shamefully treated you, his gracious neighbor, in the past.

This is what it means to heap burning coals on your enemy's head. It's not only a neighborly act of kindness, but also an act of unexpected grace. Your enemy probably thought, "He knows I hate him, so it's not going to happen—he's not going to give me the coals. But I need to warm my home quickly;

I have to have his coals!" Maybe he even did something he's not accustomed to doing on the way to your house—maybe he prayed to God that you would extend grace to him. He knows he doesn't deserve it. And your actions toward him might possibly even make a friend out of an enemy.

In the same way, providing sustenance to a hungry and thirsty enemy may make him ashamed of hating you and may cause him to repent, turning your enemy into your ally, friend, and brother. But even if your grace doesn't accomplish shame and repentance and fellowship with your enemy, the Lord *will* reward you for channeling His grace to the utterly undeserving.

Because they know their children will live in a fallen world with broken people who need God's grace, wise parents will ask themselves, "What kind of children do we want to raise in our home—children who believe in an eye for an eye, or children who are powerful witnesses of the wonders of divine grace extended to the undeserving?"

Christianity well lived by gracious Christians is the best way to attract others to the truth. If we are fully committed to fulfilling our mission to raise children who are Godlike in grace, then we will raise them in homes where we, their parents, extend much grace to those who hate us, even as we consistently teach our children to be just as gracious as we are. Grace toward haters will come to our children only through combined parental practice and biblical precept.

Here are some precepts that you may find helpful in training your children to be givers of grace.

1. Train Them to Love with the Love of God

The love of God is unconditional, unmerited, and sacrificial. John 3:16 says, "For God so loved the world, that He gave His only begotten Son, that whoever believes in Him shall not perish, but have eternal life."

The world doesn't need more anger, hatred, rudeness, smugness, pride, or even the best that human love can muster—they have too much of what human love offers already. What the world desperately needs from Christians is love from above—love divine, love and grace that flow from heaven into us and then through us to them.

Imagine this scenario:

> "Dad! Joey hit me and told me that he's not my friend anymore. So I hit him back!"
>
> "Son, that was not a loving response to Joey, was it? What have your mother and I been teaching you about God's love being in you, so that you love others like He loves you?"
>
> "But Dad, he started it."
>
> "Son, you can't control Joey. You can't even control yourself. But God can control you if you let Him. Now, let's talk about how Jesus would have responded to Joey and what your love should look like the next time you see him."

Train your children in the love of God.

2. Train Them to Seek the Pleasure of God through Obedience

Listen to the words of our Lord from Luke 6:27–29 and 35–36.

> But I say to you who hear, love your enemies, do good to those who hate you, bless those who curse you, pray for those who mistreat you. Whoever hits you on the cheek, offer him the other also; and whoever takes away your coat, do not withhold your shirt from him either... But love your enemies, and do good, and lend, expecting nothing in return; and your reward will be great, and you will be sons of the Most High; for He Himself is kind to ungrateful and evil men. Be merciful, just as your Father is merciful.

That is not a divine suggestion. It is a divine command from the Lord Himself. Train your children to be Godlike through their obedience, which will cause the pleasure of God to be upon them, and their reward from Him will be great.

3. Train Them to Entrust Themselves Fully to God as Jesus Did from the Cross

I love the most instructive words of Jesus's faithful apostle in 1 Peter 2:21–23, regarding how we should respond to personal injustice.

> For you have been called for this purpose, since Christ also suffered for you, leaving you an example for you to follow in His steps, who committed no sin, nor was any deceit found in His mouth; and while being reviled, He did not revile in return; while suffering, He uttered no threats, but kept entrusting Himself to [the Father] who judges righteously.

Suffering is our lot in life. The question is not whether we will suffer; it's how we will receive and respond to the suffering that counts, for now and for eternity. We can either choose to be Christlike or we can place our trust in ourselves and do what is right in our own eyes. When we entrust ourselves fully to God when we are abused by hate-filled people, we will grow through the experience into the likeness of Christ. If we choose to trust in our own strength, however, we should be prepared to suffer the consequences of living a faithless life.

As parents, we must get entrusting right for ourselves first, and then faithfully pass it along to our children.

4. Train Them to Expect Trouble, Trial, and Awful Treatment from the World

On the eve of His death, Jesus gave His disciples instructions that they would need in His absence, since He would soon be going back to heaven to be with His Father. He concluded His instructions on their coming persecution for His sake with this encouraging word from John 16:33:

> These things I have spoken to you, so that in Me you may have peace. In the world you have tribulation, but take courage; I have overcome the world.

Notice the contrast between being in Christ (having peace) and being in the world (experiencing tribulation). Bad news: In the world, you have tribulation. Good news: In Christ, you can have peace, for He has overcome the world. Without bad news, you can't have good news. And that good news should greatly encourage us. However, we can expect Satan to use our human tendencies to live life in denial or with bad theology to deceive us and our children into expecting nothing but good news and peace in the world. But that's not what Jesus taught, is it? He taught us that this isn't heaven. In heaven, we can expect heavenly bliss and blessings forevermore—it is our blessed, future hope. But He never taught us to expect heaven on earth from the world and the worldly. It's a terribly false expectation. But don't be discouraged—there is substantial power in realistic expectations. Wise parents fully possess them and carefully and consistently pass them along to their children.

Wise parents, be careful to stay on mission. What your children need from you is not more of the natural, but an ongoing infusion of supernatural grace, channeled through you to them and then to all others—even to your enemies. Especially to your enemies. Teach your children that by showing grace, we might change the minds and hearts of those who hate us. But even if we don't, we will most certainly be like God and He will be pleased and glorified. Then, at just the right time, we will receive our reward from the Lord Jesus Himself. Since He has called us to be Godlike in grace, He will reward the faithful. Teach your children that it doesn't get any better than that. Be fiercely determined to stay on mission.

Parenting Principle 33
Wise Parents Do Not Tolerate Destructive Behavior

A whip is for the horse, a bridle for the donkey, and a rod for the back of fools.
PROVERBS 26:3

How do wise parents break foolish, destructive thinking and behavior in their children? With determined, consistent intolerance!

Since "foolishness is bound up in the heart of [every] child" (22:15), wise parents begin early to consistently apply verbal reproof when foolish behavior crops up. And when their children reach the age that they understand the difference between right and wrong, then wise parents consistently back up verbal reproof with physical discipline when necessary. This begins the long process of removing foolishness far from those children. Consistency in corrective discipline is critical; understand from the proverb that the rod, consistently applied when needed, is designed to effectively address foolish thinking and behavior.

A horse is motivated by a whip, a donkey is controlled by a bridle, and a fool is corrected by the rod because foolish people do not respond positively to reason. The rod as physical punishment in this verse is to be understood as corporal punishment for those old enough to receive it—primarily, adults. As we apply this text to our children, then, let's be sure we understand that what we administer to them is not corporal punishment to their *backs*, but corporal discipline to their *backsides.* It is certainly much more profitable to spank consistently and effectively while our children are young fools so they don't grow up to be older fools who eventually become old fools, where only harsh treatment will control and subdue them.

Foolish children must be consistently and lovingly controlled by the rod of discipline if their foolish behavior is to be effectively removed from their hearts. Appealing to their immature and foolish intellect will only frustrate parents and will prove to be ineffective in dealing with their child's foolishness. The only language a foolish child understands is the language of painful discipline, firmly and lovingly administered. Wise parents will consistently speak this language to their children because they are quite aware of the destructive nature of foolish attitudes and behavior.

Wise parents can look down the road to see the destructive end of a foolish child who is wise in his own eyes and who insists on going his own foolish way. They know that when insistent childish foolishness happens, that is not the time for a passive response, but active, effective, and consistent action. They also know they needn't become too alarmed when they see foolishness in their children, for they expect it. What does alarm them is knowing what will surely happen if they passively ignore bad behavior instead of aggressively and effectively addressing it.

Before we continue, I want to say that I realize I am being a bit repetitious in returning again and again to corrective discipline. It is true, yes, but the primary reason for the emphasis is because Proverbs is also repetitious concerning many teachings, including how to deal effectively with fools and foolish behavior. Perhaps Solomon learned from experience that repetition is a great teaching tool—it's how he wrote under the inspiration of the Holy Spirit. Another good reason that the Spirit may have inspired him to repeat himself is because of our human tendency to look outside of Scripture for other less painful but more effective techniques for disciplining the foolishness out of our children. But according to Proverbs—which means, according to God—it is an effective technique.

So, like Proverbs, I'm revisiting the topic to encourage consistency in disciplining our beloved little fools God's way because the last thing wise parents want from their children is destructive behavior. I pray that you are being convinced—not by me, but by the Holy Spirit-inspired Scriptures. May the Scriptures motivate you to motivate your children early in life to abandon foolishness, and may your motivating tough love successfully convince them that their foolishness simply isn't worth the pain of discipline. As I said earlier, it's okay to hurt them a little now so they won't hurt themselves a lot later.

With that said, let's get back to the wisdom from our text. Proverbs 26:4 says, "Do not answer a fool according to his folly, or you will also be like him."

This proverb is a warning to the wise not to be drawn in and down to the level of a fool by arguing with him or her. Remember, not even the wise can reason with a fool. Wise and discerning responses will only be met by silly and foolish rebuttals. Pursuing such an argument puts the wise person on the same level as the fool. Have you ever witnessed a parent arguing with his or her child? Back and forth they go at each other, gaining no ground but escalating the temperature of the argument. It's an ugly and painful thing to watch. In fact, it makes one wonder who's the greater fool, the child or the parent?

The next proverb parallels the previous one by giving the appropriate response to a fool: "Answer a fool as his folly deserves, that he not be wise in his own eyes" (Proverbs 26:5).

If you argue with a fool, he will see you as the fool and will continue to be wise in his own eyes. If the foolish person is an adult, instead of arguing, you should rebuke him with the Word of God. If the foolish person is your child, the same kind of response is in order. You must bring a quick and decisive rebuke from God's Word. If the foolishness continues through an argumentative response or an attitude or posture of rebellion, then you back up the rebuke with corrective discipline. Quickly, effectively, and consistently (meaning every time), answer your little fool as his or her folly deserves. Do not allow your child to continue as wise in his or her own eyes and thus continue in his way toward destruction. Proverbs 26:11–12 says,

> Like a dog that returns to its vomit is a fool who repeats his folly. Do you see a man wise in his own eyes? There is more hope for a fool than for him.

Is there anything more disgusting than a dog that returns to eat its own vomit, the thing that made it sick in the first place? Well, the Bible says a fool who repeats his foolish behavior is just as revolting. It goes on to say, however, that there is someone even stupider than that kind of fool—a person who thinks he is beyond instruction, the know-it-all kind of fool who has arrived and is wise in his own eyes. There is more hope for the fool who acts like a dirty dog than there is for him!

These teachings are powerful incentives to nip foolishness in the bud. Every child has the potential to go over the edge into destructive thinking and behavior that will eventually lead to an awful and tragic end. For this reason, I shall continue to be an advocate for parental wisdom. I will teach stubborn consistency in bringing the necessary verbal rebukes and physical discipline to not only control our children, but to correct and protect them from their own foolishness. This is what will eventually remove it far from them.

Go ahead and talk—but talk less and talk appropriately. Address the foolishness quickly and briefly with a rebuke based on the Word, but never expect talking to your foolish child to be enough. Since our children's temporal and eternal well-being is at stake, please get on mission and stay on mission.

Parenting Principle 34
Wise Parents Teach Their Children about Consequences

He who digs a pit will fall into it, and he who rolls a stone,
it will come back on him.
PROVERBS 26:27

This proverb states an absolute, indisputable fact that is based on a divine law that our sovereign God has built into His world. When a person schemes against another with the intent to trap him and to bring him harm, that harm will, in God's sovereign time, turn back upon the scheming person. Make no mistake about it: the sins of a man that are meant to harm another will boomerang back to harm him. God has given ample warning in His Word as to the reality of this divine law. This proverb is one of many that teach this precept.

Proverbs 28:9–10 brings the additional thought that righteousness is the path that leads straight to reward:

> He who turns away his ear from listening to the law, even his prayer is an abomination. He who leads the upright astray in an evil way will himself fall into his own pit, but the blameless will inherit good.

An especially egregious sin to God is when a person deliberately turns away from listening to the law of God and then deliberately leads a righteous person to stray with him into an evil way. Such wicked plans will backfire, and he will fall into his own trap. On the other hand, the person who walks blamelessly before the Lord in obedience to His law will receive an inheritance of goodness from Him. We can count on this because God said so, and God's Word is as good as God.

Proverb 28:18 also teaches this principle: "He who walks blamelessly will be delivered, but he who is crooked will fall all at once." The person who walks in God's upright way is without blame before God. To be sure, there will be opportunities for him to fall away into sin. But if he continues to walk in the blameless way, he will be delivered from the crooked way and will, therefore, remain safe from the awful consequences of wickedness and immorality—he has God's promise. But the one who is crooked will not be delivered. He is not at all safe, and when his consequential fall comes, it will be sudden and fatal, like the bottom abruptly falling out from underneath him—he has God's promise.

It's the divine law of reaping what is sown. The classic passage for this teaching in the New Testament is Galatians 6:7–9 (NIV).

> Do not be deceived: God cannot be mocked. A man reaps what he sows. Whoever sows to please their flesh, from the flesh will reap destruction; whoever sows to please the Spirit, from the Spirit will reap eternal life.

> Let us not become weary in doing good, for at the proper time we will reap a harvest if we do not give up.

A person reaps what he or she sows. The harvest may come soon, or it may come late, depending on God's sovereign timing, but it will come. This is a hard principle for many Christians to wrap their heads around. They look at their own experiences and the experiences of others. Then, based on these experiences, doubt creeps in concerning the truth of this law of God. When doubt creeps in, faith in God and His Word creeps out.

The primary reason for this serious spiritual issue is rooted in a Christian's starting point of view. If the starting point is shortsighted, if it is mostly horizontal and focused on the temporal, if it is an earthly perspective—these things will allow doubt to creep in. But if the Christian's starting point is longsighted, if it is vertical and sharply focused on the eternal, if it is predominately a heavenly perspective—then faith will triumph over any temptation to doubt.

When Lindsay's and Jason's young lives were cut short by the appalling crime of double murder, a shortsighted point of view would make it appear that they'd received very little for loving Christ and walking blamelessly before Him and giving themselves to faithful Christian service. However, a longsighted point of view sees and knows that they have missed out on nothing. We who know and love them are missing out on having them with us, but they are not missing out. They have lost nothing. We have lost much, but they have not. To

Lindsay and Jason, to live was Christ but to die was and is and always will be gain (Philippians 1:21) because death means we are absent from the body and at home with the Lord (2 Corinthians 5:8).

What is better for the Christ-follower—a long life on earth with very little of the eternal to speak for it, or a short life on earth walking with and for Jesus, only "to depart and be with [Him]" in heaven forevermore (Philippians 1:23)? Jesus Himself said in Matthew 13:43, "Then the righteous will shine forth as the sun in the kingdom of their Father. He who has ears, let him hear." The people of faith have ears to hear Jesus, and we gladly take everything by faith because we have learned to trust God and have firmly adopted His eternal view on life. We continue to walk by faith on earth, not by sight (2 Corinthians 5:7), but Jason and Lindsay no longer need faith, for their faith has become sight!

The real loser in this entire episode is the evil man who killed my daughter and Jason. If he is one of the men on our detectives' suspect list, and we believe he is, then he's still very much alive. We have come to terms with and have accepted the real possibility that he may never answer for his crimes on earth. But unless he repents, he has an appointment at the great white throne judgment. There he will receive his reward, eternal punishment in the lake of fire, also known in Scripture as hell. (See Revelation 20:11–14.) That's why we are motivated to pray for this man's soul—his projected destiny is eternally awful.

Who would you rather be—Jason and Lindsay, whose earthly lives were cut short by evil but who eternally dwell in heaven with the Father, Son, Holy Spirit, and all the heavenly hosts, or the one who will never step foot in heaven but, instead, will know nothing but the everlasting pain of punishment in hell for his sins? The wise person, the person who walks by faith in Jesus Christ, totally gets it; he is not deceived, for he knows beyond the shadow of a doubt that "God is not mocked; for whatever a man sows, this he will also reap" (Galatians 6:7).

Consequently, wise parents deliberately and firmly take hold of the long point of view. They keep eternity's values in clear view and believe with all their might that the blameless will inherit nothing but good from God. They clearly see it and trust it and train their children in it: "Son, Daughter, you will reap what you sow! There are temporal and, most importantly, eternal consequences to be reaped, depending on what you sow."

How do we best teach our children this universal principle that is backed up by the promises and power of an almighty and sovereign God?

1. Take Them to the Word

Take them to Proverbs and Galatians and plant this teaching from the Word into their hearts and minds. Memorizing Galatians 6:7–9 together as a family would be a wise and helpful spiritual exercise. Teach this principle first by implanting the Word.

2. Illustrate the Truth from the Word

Take them to stories in the Bible that clearly illustrate the truth that a person reaps what he sows, whether corruption and destruction or divine blessing and reward. From the book of Esther, contrast Mordecai's exaltation for his faithfulness with Haman's awful demise for plotting against Mordecai. Mordecai received the reward that Haman had planned for himself—the place of highest prominence. Haman received the punishment that he had planned for Mordecai—he was hanged on the gallows he'd prepared for Mordecai. In this amazing true story, Mordecai, the blameless, inherited much good, while Haman, the wicked, fell into his own pit.

3. Illustrate the Truth with Your Life

If there was a time in your life when you were not walking with the Lord, you can share with your children how terribly that worked out for you, how you regretfully reaped what you'd sown. Show them that you learned from your mistakes and that you want them to learn from them as well, so they don't have to do it the hard way. And then show them from your life how walking spiritually and morally blameless before the Lord now is working out for your great good and His great glory.

There are plenty of prosperity blessings that come just from living in the United States. Despite ourselves, God "causes His sun to rise on the evil and the good, and sends rain on the righteous and the unrighteous" (Matthew 5:45), "for He Himself is kind to ungrateful and evil men" as well as to the grateful and righteous (Luke 6:35). When you speak of blessings for obedience, be sure to accentuate the spiritual, relational, and eternal blessings that God has lavished upon you and your family personally. Wise parents teach their children that health and wealth aren't special blessings from God; these blessings can fall on the righteous and unrighteous alike. Neither is it proof when a person is poor or ill that God has withheld His temporal and eternal rewards. Proverbs 28:6 instructs, "Better is the poor who walks in his integrity than he who is crooked though he be rich." Teach your children by the Scriptures and through personal examples that real wealth and reward are measured in an eternal inheritance—one with present, as well as eternal, blessings, benefits, and rewards.

4. Illustrate the Truth from Their Own Lives

Wise parents discipline their children for foolish behavior even while they encourage and reward wise behavior. There are natural consequences for a child's foolishness, but in the same way, natural blessings flow from behavior that is pleasing to God, their parents, and to the righteous. Take time to point out that they are living proof of the principle's reality.

5. Illustrate the Truth from the World Around Them

Another way to illustrate the principle is by using the agricultural sowing and reaping analogy given in Galatians 6. I live in a farming community; in fact, there is a field directly across the road from our house. The farmer who works that field rotates his crops from corn one year to soybean the next. It is helpful to take a child to a field in the spring when the crop is just pushing through the soil and ask what is growing there.

Ask them why that crop is what is growing and what harvest the farmer will reap in the fall from that crop. Then point out the same reality in his or her own life: "Son, Daughter, if the farmer sows corn in the spring, he will not reap soybeans in the fall. And if you sow righteousness in your life by living a life that pleases the Holy Spirit, you will not reap corruption and destruction in your present and future life; instead, you will most certainly reap eternal life with all its present and eternal rewards."

6. Teach Them by Your Built-In Discipline-Reward System

Consistently discipline for foolishness and consistently reward your children for being good. Reward them especially through praise and affirmation; tell them that you are most pleased with them. Remind them that if you, as a godly parent, are pleased with them, then God is also. On occasion, do something special with your children as a reward tell them that this special family event is what they have reaped for sowing righteousness. This is vital to the health of your children, as we all have a driving need to please others. Too many children grow up and leave their homes knowing that, even though they tried, they couldn't please their parents. Don't let this happen—be vigilant in catching them being good and be sure they are rewarded with your pleasure. Your pleasure in them will delight and encourage their souls.

The earlier you begin training your children in this principle, the better. Since wise parents are on a holy mission to bring up their children in the discipline and instruction of the Lord, they start early and stay on mission until it is accomplished. The reward for you as a parent is watching your children grow up into adults who walk blamelessly before the Lord. Then, with your parental mission accomplished, you can take a deep spiritual breath and thank God for His amazing grace toward you and your children. "I have no greater joy than this, to hear of my children walking in the truth" (3 John 1:4). I delight in knowing that my beloved blameless ones will inherit nothing but good.

Parenting Principle 35
Wise Parents Culture Their Children in Christ

Do not boast about tomorrow, for you do not know what a day may bring forth. Let another praise you, and not your own mouth; a stranger, and not your own lips.
PROVERBS 27:1–2

Several years ago, I was sitting in my dentist's waiting room. While I waited, I leafed through a magazine and was suddenly taken aback by the words in a Nike ad. In big, bold print the ad declared, WE ARE HEDONISTS, meaning that the all-out pursuit of personal pleasure is the most important thing in life. It shouldn't have surprised me because hedonism has become the American way. We are taught early and often in our culture to pursue personal fulfillment—whatever it is that will make us happy, we should go for it. So why was I so surprised? In retrospect, I think I wasn't prepared to see it proclaimed so boldly, so in-your-face and without shame or apology. But there it was in black and white: *We are hedonists.*

Shortly after, I began seeing a bumper sticker that frankly and matter-of-factly stated, IT'S ALL ABOUT ME! When I saw that sticker the first time, I was once again surprised by the audacious pride that the statement seemed to communicate. I'm fairly confident that the people who deliberately purchased that sticker and plastered it on their bumpers for everyone to see were not displaying it in shame, as if it were an honest confession of their core sin issue. I'm pretty sure they weren't announcing, "I hate to admit it but, honestly…and God forgive me for this…it's all about me!" No. Rather, it's a proclamation of prideful self-importance: "I am the center of my world. The most important person in the world to me is me. Therefore, my life is all about me!"

Right about the same time, a local pastor friend of mine, Ned Horsfall, spoke on the topic with a talk he entitled, "It's All About God!" Wow, what a contrasting message to that of the world! I was so excited about that contrasting message that we made it a slogan of our church. From the platform, I would loudly declare, "It's all about—" and in unison, the response from the congregation was an even louder, "GOD!" We no longer make that proclamation. It was a countercultural statement for that time. But it was something we needed to loudly proclaim for our own encouragement, to the glory of God. We are still surrounded by a blatantly prideful and selfish secular culture, but in the Christian world where Jesus is Lord, life is and always will be all about God.

In the world, of course, it naturally becomes all about me. It's been that way ever since the headlong fall of mankind into sin recorded in Genesis 3. In the past in our country, it was said more subtly, if said at all. In our present American culture, however, where the fear of the Lord is nearly nonexistent, the wholehearted pursuit of selfish pleasure and prideful gain is clearly and unashamedly declared. It is socially acceptable to arrogantly and selfishly pursue personal happiness. This philosophy is stated in many ways as we live by the motto, "Whatever makes you happy." In today's worldly culture, pride is a virtue rather than a vice. Consequently, our proverb doesn't make sense to the worldly.

The world doesn't understand what could be wrong with boasting about tomorrow and praising oneself. Children are encouraged to say things like, "When I grow up, I'm going to make a lot of money and be famous." Prideful statements, plans, and pursuits are not only strongly encouraged, they are enthusiastically applauded. It is socially acceptable to be proud about what you are going to do and who you are and who you are going to become. The worldly, false assumption is that each person is the captain of his own ship—that we are in control of our own destiny. Too many of us see ourselves as sovereigns and gods unto ourselves. We do not consider the hidden reality that there is only one Sovereign in the universe. Clearly, "the god of this world has blinded the minds of the unbelieving so that they might not see the light of the gospel of the glory of Christ, who is the image of God" (2 Corinthians 4:4). This is the world we live in and where we are raising our children.

Unfortunately, this worldly culture has also slipped into the church. Even in His time, Jesus had to confront religious pride that had crept into the Jewish culture and corrupted it quite thoroughly. Luke 14:8–11 recounts a time when Jesus was invited to a Pharisee leader's home to eat dinner. There, He noticed how some of the invited guests had seated themselves at the table in places of honor. That had become normal in their religious culture. But the Lord didn't hesitate. He boldly took advantage of the opportunity to teach the true culture of God. He began speaking a parable to the invited guests, telling them that when they were invited to a wedding feast, they were not to take the place of honor; instead, they should humbly keep in mind that a more distinguished guest might arrive, and the one who invited them might have to say to them, "Give your seat to this man." In disgrace, they would have to move to a much less dignified place. But then, Jesus went on to say (14:10–11),

> When you are invited, go and recline at the last place, so that when the one who has invited you comes, he may say to you, "Friend, move up higher"; then you will have honor in the sight of all who are at the table with you. For everyone who exalts himself will be humbled, and he who humbles himself will be exalted.

What a contrast! Wise parents understand the world around them and know that pride is a virtue only to the worldly. Therefore, they make certain that in their homes, a paradigm shift has effectively taken them away from the norms of this world and solidly placed them in the world of Christ. There it is *culturally unacceptable* for them and their children to adopt the prideful, self-seeking ways of the world. They have heard their Lord say that all who exalt themselves will be humbled, and all who humble themselves will be exalted. For that reason, they have quietly humbled themselves before the Lord and remain there, day by day.

Wise parents know it won't be easy to train their children to resist the enormous pressure placed upon them to be socially acceptable and not be considered odd or different. However, as they raise their children, they train them in the understanding that they have the high and holy pleasure of belonging to a heavenly, holy culture where they are totally different from the world. In fact, 1 Peter 2:9–11 makes it clear that, as Christians, we are to humbly and gratefully glory in our differences.

> But you are a chosen race, a royal priesthood, a holy nation, a people for God's own possession, so that you may proclaim the excellencies of Him who has called you out of darkness into His marvelous light; for you once were not a people, but now you are the people of God; you had not received mercy, but now you have received mercy. Beloved, I urge you as aliens and

> strangers to abstain from fleshly lusts which wage war against the soul.

We are a people called out for a purpose; the purpose is not about us, but all about Him, so that we may proclaim His excellence for calling us out of awful darkness into His marvelous light. Instead of passively allowing our children to *fit in* with the world, we must deliberately train them to glory in their differences. But in teaching them this, take care they do not become proud of being aliens and strangers in and to the world. Instead, teach them to be humbly thankful for God's grace toward them.

Now, let me say this. We want our kids to be different from the world, but we don't want them to be socially awkward or relationally dysfunctional. If we are raising them in a spiritually and emotionally healthy environment, they will be aliens and strangers to the world, but they needn't be graceless or uncomfortable in society. In fact, they should be the most graceful, gracious, and comfortable people on the planet. Wise parents train their children in the social graces, but that's where any sameness with the world ends and training to become socially acceptable in the spiritual world begins.

In the culture of Christ, instead of boasting about tomorrow, wise parents teach their children to walk humbly before the Lord, entrusting all their tomorrows to Him, for He is the only One who knows for sure what tomorrow will bring. To what we've already learned in Proverbs 27:1–2, James 4:13–16 adds this counsel:

> Come now, you who say, "Today or tomorrow we will go to such and such a city, and spend a year there and engage in business and make a profit." Yet you do not know what your life will be like tomorrow. You are just a vapor that appears for a little while and then vanishes away. Instead, you ought to say, "If the Lord wills, we will live and also do this or that." But as it is, you boast in your arrogance; all such boasting is evil.

In the culture of Christ, there is no place for arrogant boasting. "Look what I'm going to do" or "Look at what I will accomplish" or "Look at who I am and what I have become" should not be our cry. There is no place for that because in the culture of Christ, there is no such thing as a self-made man or woman. There are plenty in the world, yes, but there will be a day when that will be their shame. In the kingdom of God, there are only God-made men and women, so the only boasting to be done is in God for His amazing, miraculous grace. Paul himself could only boast in the grace of God for his high place of leadership in the church. In 1 Corinthians 15:9–10, the apostle said,

> For I am the least of the apostles, and not fit to be called an apostle, because I persecuted the church of God. But by the grace of God I am what I am, and His grace toward me did not prove vain; but I labored even more than all of them, yet not I, but the grace of God with me.

It really *isn't* about us, is it? But it *is* all about Him! Therefore, instead of boasting about tomorrow, we humbly entrust ourselves to the Lord. Instead of boasting in ourselves, we are humbly grateful for His grace. Only by His grace are we what and who we are in Christ. That is what it means to be socially acceptable in the culture of Christ. All our boasting and praise belong to Him who owns our very lives, who possesses our every tomorrow, and who deserves all the glory for what He has and will accomplish in and through us.

It's not an easy assignment to culture our children in Christ while living in a powerfully influential world. According to the apostle John, "The spirit of the antichrist…is already in the world." But "you are from God, little children, and have overcome them; because greater is He who is in you than he who is in the world" (1 John 4:3–4). No, it won't be easy, but if we fully immerse ourselves and our children in Christ and in the culture of Christ, they may overcome the world with us. But we'd better start early so they will be ready to stand up under and against the bombardment of immoral pride and unbridled selfishness that they will quickly be exposed to in the world.

How do we do this? Since it's all about God, wise parents culture their children in Christ in their Christ-centered homes, in their Christ-centered churches, and in the Word. These are the primary resources with which we combat this world's corrupting influences. Many today also choose to send their children to Christ-centered schools, which can be a terrific resource. In this Christ-centered culture, wise parents teach their children to listen to the wise—which begins with listening to their parents. They teach them to listen in the sense of hearing, receiving, obeying, and applying the words of wisdom to their lives. According to 1 John 4:5–6, those who possess the spirit of the antichrist

> are from the world; therefore they speak as from the world, and the world listens to them. We [the apostles] are from God; he who knows God listens to us; he who is not from God does not listen to us. By this we know the spirit of truth and the spirit of error.

Wise parents teach their children the Word and train them to study and listen to what Jesus and the apostles have to say, rather than the world. Then they will be able to discern the difference between the spirit of truth and the spirit of error; that will protect them from the evil one and from evil, worldly ways.

When Jesus was brought before Pilate by the Jews to be crucified (John 18), the Roman governor asked Him if He was the king of the Jews. Jesus answered in verse 36,

> My kingdom is not of this world. If My kingdom were of this world, then My servants would be fighting so that I would not be handed over to the Jews; but as it is, My kingdom is not of this realm.

There will be a day when His kingdom *will* be of this world, but until that day, His kingdom is in us. So if our King's kingdom is not of this world, then the kingdom of this world doesn't belong to us either. Therefore, wise parents, teach your children to be socially acceptable in the spiritual world alone. Thoroughly culture them in the kingdom of Christ our King.

Life is all about God! If your children believe that and live it, then you are doing your job well. You can glory in Christ because, by His grace, your children are Christ-followers and your mission is well on its way to being accomplished. For Christ's sake, for your home's sake, and for the church's sake, stay on mission. If the world is to find any hope in us, we must stay on mission!

CHAPTER 9

Wise Parenting Principles 36-40: No Regrets

Proverbs 29–31

HARRY CHAPIN'S SONG, "CAT'S IN the Cradle," hit number one in the United States in 1974. I watched a YouTube video of him performing when he first introduced the song to a live audience. He told his audience the song was for his son, and he admitted that the premise of the song scared him to death. Really? What's so scary about it? Well, if you are familiar with the song, then you understand why he was scared. If you are not familiar with it, look it up and read the lyrics.

The song presents a father-son relationship, beginning with a boy's childhood. It tells how the son loved his father and longed for his company, but his dad was absent for most of his growing-up years. Yet, he admired his dad and committed himself to grow up to be just like him. And sure enough, as a man with a family, he turned out to be just like his dad.

The end of the song shows the dad older and retired; the son moved away. Dad calls the son one day, wishing to see him soon, but the son is too busy to make a visit happen. He sure does like briefly talking to his dad, though. As the father hangs up the phone, he realizes that his son has, indeed, become just like him.

For me, that's the saddest thing about the song—the father is now living with regret. He understands that it's too late to recover the time and attention that he *didn't* spend on his son in his childhood years because his other responsibilities trumped what should have been a far greater one. Now that he's retired and has time on his hands, he has no one to spend it with. Not only is his son distant from him, but so are his grandchildren. I assert to you that that's incredibly and irrevocably sad!

The saddest thing about any regret comes when it's too late to fix it. In the song, now the clock is ticking on the dad's son, but it's probably already too late for him as well, because he turned out to be just like his dad. In a typical cycle of life, one day he will be old and in his father's place—looking back. He will likely live to regret all the lost and misspent time that he cannot recover. No wonder Harry Chapin said the song scared him to death. It should sufficiently scare all of us into repentance now, if necessary, before it is eternally too late!

In these last five wise parenting principles we will look at from Proverbs, I want to focus on *time well spent*, so that parents will wisely spend their time on their children while they are young and in the home. That way, when the parents are old, they will be able to look back with no regrets. *No regrets*? Is that possible? Perhaps. In Christ, it's even probable.

Wise parents, spend your time establishing these final five principles in your home so you will have nothing serious to regret in your old age.

Parenting Principle 36
Wise Parents Train Their Children to Be God Pleasers

The fear of man brings a snare, but he who trusts in the Lord *will be exalted.*
Proverbs 29:25

"I'm a people pleaser." I hear and see this all the time. People who come into the Christian faith with that awful condition tend to stay there, at least for a time. When I'm confronted with it in Christian people, I am obligated to point out to them that it is a spiritual stronghold that will effectively hold them back from being a God pleaser.

It's a most serious problem in a believer because *freedom from* the power of man and the consequent *freedom to know* the power of God are at stake. We can't have both—we can't fear man and fear God at the same time. We can't trust man for what we need and, at the same time, also trust God. We can't be ensnared by the fear of man and experience the exalted safety of God. Being man pleasers means we're not God pleasers. We cannot be both.

Further, we can't be man pleasers without serious consequences. According to our proverb, the fear of people brings a snare. Fearing people is being overly concerned about what they think about us. It makes us to try to please them, and that is the awful snare. It's the exact opposite of trusting in God for approval, which will lead us to pursue pleasing Him.

It should be obvious that we can't please everybody—there are some people who simply will never be pleased. What an awful snare it is to try to please people even as we are controlled by the fear of not pleasing them! And while we may succeed in pleasing some, how long will that last? And what will we have gained? Far worse, what will we have lost? We'll have lost the ability to please God and His righteous ones! However, if we are pleasing God, we will then be pleasing the *right* people—those who are *righteous.*

The solution is to trust in the Lord with the promise that the person who trusts in Him will be exalted. The New American Standard version translates the Hebrew verb in Proverbs 29:25 as "exalted." The New International Version translates it as "kept safe." Which is right? Both English words are entwined in the Hebrew meaning; the Hebrew verb gives the sense of being elevated to an inaccessibly high place, beyond human reach, and there in that high place, the trusting person is safe—he has been exalted to safety.

Based on that explanation of the proverb, here is some direction on how to train your children to be God pleasers rather than people pleasers. In this way, they will be elevated to the place of safety.

1. Grow in Your Own Trust in God

Grow in your trust in God until you trust in Him with all your heart. It is the only way to be certain that you and your home will be safe from the awful snare of fearing people. Having such trust will place your family far out of the reach of their control, intimidation, and manipulation. Said another way, when you live to please the Lord by fully trusting Him, He will lift you up into a security that is utterly foreign to this world. Then, from that secure location, the Lord will enable you to teach your children that He is the only One they have to please. Remind them that if God is pleased with them, then you, their parents, will be pleased with them, along with all the other righteous people in their lives.

I need to add a caveat to this point. Your children must know that they are loved and accepted by you just the way they are and that you are most pleased with them simply because they are your beloved children. When we talk about your pleasure in and with your children under this principle, we are not talking about their personal value to you. That should be a given because you have already strongly established in them the reality of their immense value to God and to you. Thus, it's not their personhood we are talking about, but rather their attitudes, beliefs, thoughts, words, and actions. If they want to please you with how they are thinking, behaving, and living, they need to know that they most certainly can do so. Here's how: when they please God in how they live, then you are most pleased with them.

2. Teach Your Children That They Will Strive to Please the One They Fear

If your children fear God, then more than anything else, they will desire to please Him. If they fear what people think and what they can do to them—like accept or reject them—then they will ultimately do whatever it takes to please those people. Either way, the compulsion will be strong, but one leads to a snare while the other leads to a safe and secure place. I'm reminded of a powerful proverb we visited earlier: "The name of the Lord is a strong tower; the righteous runs into it and is safe" (18:10). How do we run into it? Through steadfast faith in God; the one who trusts in Him will be lifted into that impregnably strong place. Teach your children that when they trust in and fear the Lord alone, they will strive to please Him. Subsequently, they will personally know freedom, security, and relief by taking up residence within His infinitely strong tower.

3. Teach Your Children What This Safety Means

First, being elevated to a safe place *doesn't* mean that we are safe from persecution. We will still suffer the anger, malice, hatred, and slanderous lies of those who hate us; they will still falsely speak evil against us for the sake of righteousness

(Matthew 5:10–11). Frankly, man strongly dislikes *not* being trusted or feared; therefore, we are not safe from physical and emotional abuse. What this safety *does* mean, however, is that we are free from the power of people to control what we think, how we respond, and how we act. Consequently, in obedience to Christ, we may "rejoice and be glad, for [our] reward in heaven is great; for in the same way they persecuted the prophets who were before [us]" (Matthew 5:12). When we are safe from the control of human power but not safe from physical and verbal hurt and harm, we are in good company. And when that is our place and perspective, who cares what mere man thinks?

4. Teach Your Children to Trust in the Lord for What They Need

In our proverb, *fear* and *trust* are nearly synonymous. "The fear of man brings a snare, but he who trusts in the LORD will be exalted." Teach your children that fearing people means they trust people for what they think they want and need. Fearing God means they trust Him for what they truly need. It is normal for children to be concerned about what their peers are doing and what they think of them. Along with those concerns comes the natural temptation and pressure for them to fit in. Teach them that everything they need, God will provide—*if* they fear Him and trust Him to meet their needs. Also teach them that what they *think* they need might not be what they truly need. This is a hard lesson for some children, but stick with it until they get it.

There is, of course, a real need for human acceptance, so remind them often that the only acceptance they need is from those who are godly. If they are godly and if they have a couple of godly friends, that is enough. They need to know that they can't please everybody, but they can please God and the righteous. Train them to know and trust that that is enough.

Acts chapter 4 gives us a powerful, biblical example of how to be God pleasers. Shortly after the birth of the church in Jerusalem, the apostles began openly preaching the gospel of Christ in the temple. They were doing this in obedience to Christ, but it caused the Jewish Council to be extremely displeased with them. The Council made threats and eventually began arresting the apostles. Now, if the apostles were people pleasers, they would have stopped preaching Christ when Peter and John were arrested for teaching that the resurrection from the dead is only in Jesus Christ (Acts 4:2). The next day, the Council convened and brought the two apostles before them. After a short inquiry, they commanded that the men completely stop teaching in the name of Jesus. But Peter and John said to them, "Whether it is right in the sight of God to give heed to you rather than to God, you be the judge; for we cannot stop speaking about what we have seen and heard" (4:18–19). The Council threatened them further but let them go because they feared the people who were gladly receiving the apostles' message of Christ.

The apostles continued to preach the gospel, and they were soon arrested again and put in a public jail. But during the night, an angel of the Lord paid them a visit and sprung them from jail. The angel commanded them to continue to disobey the Council and to stand before the people and declare to them in the temple the gospel of Jesus, their Messiah (Acts 5:20). And because they feared God rather than man, at daybreak they were right back at the temple, preaching Christ.

The Council convened that morning and sent men to bring the apostles from the jail. They found the jail securely locked and the guards still standing at the cell door, just as they should be. But when they opened the door, the cell was empty! Word returned to the Council that the apostles were actually back in the temple, doing their thing. Let's pick up this fascinating true story in Acts 5:25–29.

> Then the captain [of the temple guard] went along with the officers and proceeded to bring them back without violence (for they were afraid of the people, that they might be stoned). When they had brought them, they stood them before the Council. The high priest questioned them, saying, "We gave you strict orders not to continue teaching in this name, and yet, you have filled Jerusalem with your teaching and intend to bring this man's blood upon us." But Peter and the apostles answered, "We must obey God rather than men."

You should turn to Acts 5 and read the whole story again, as though for the first time; it continues to be wonderfully amazing! But let's jump to the end in verses 40–42.

> [The Council] flogged [the apostles] and ordered them not to speak in the name of Jesus, and then released them. So they went on their way from the presence of the Council, rejoicing that they had been considered worthy to suffer shame for His name. And every day, in the temple and from house to house, they kept right on teaching and preaching Jesus as the Christ.

Ha! Of course they did! People strive to please the ones they fear, and since the apostles feared God alone, the Council of Jerusalem had no power to control them. These faithful men of Christ were in a most secure and safe place—spiritually, emotionally, mentally, and relationally. Great was their mutual fellowship, and great is their eternal reward. Teach your children to be God pleasers, for there is eternity in it!

One last word from the apostle Paul in Galatians 1:10: "For am I now seeking the favor of men, or of God? Or am I striving to please men? If I were still trying to please men, I would not be a bondservant of Christ."

There was a time when Paul did work to please men. But once he became a bondservant of Christ, Christ was the only One he needed and desired to please. What a powerful life God pleasers live! Paul's mindset is a biblical one that needs to be passed down from generation to generation. If you want to be parents who have no regrets, invest your time and effort in deliberately, carefully, and frequently teaching your children to be God pleasers.

Parenting Principle 37
Wise Parents Know That Corrective Discipline Gives Wisdom

The rod and reproof give wisdom,
but a child who gets his own way brings shame to his mother.
Proverbs 29:15

To expand on that proverb a bit, corrective discipline (the rod) coupled with verbal correction (reproof) are the God-given parental tools that will impart wisdom to a child. But a child left physically and verbally undisciplined will get his own foolish way and, in turn, will disgrace and shame his mother.

I'm sure you have noticed the embarrassment that comes when an undisciplined child is determined to get his own way. A child who works long and hard enough at it not only gets what he wants, but he ends up being strongly encouraged to continue that wretched way since it worked for him. This begins a cycle that will continue to bring the consequence of shame. However, it's not the child who is embarrassed. An undisciplined child cannot be shamed; the shame is on the one who is responsible for permitting the child to get his own way.

Let's imagine that you are enjoying an evening out with your family when you are distracted by the unruly behavior of a child at a nearby table. You find yourself embarrassed—not for the child, but for the mother who is frantically enabling her out-of-control son by giving him whatever he loudly demands. She is caught in an all-out effort to calm him down and to prevent herself from being further embarrassed. She might even sheepishly look your way and mouth a word of apology. We've all experienced this. But if you're like me, you want to respond by pointing out the direction to the restroom so she can correct the problem there, in private.

Wisdom from above has taught us that an undisciplined child knows only the innate drive of the sin nature to get his or her own way. The child is not shamed because he foolishly believes that his agenda is right. But wisdom from above has also taught us that to withhold corrective discipline from one's child is unthinkably horrible treatment. The combination of the rod of discipline and corrective reproof are necessary to impart wisdom—the very wisdom of God—to our children.

These teachings from Proverbs are based on the biblical truth that children are inherently sinful and do not need to be taught to strive to get their own sinful way. When we combine the teachings of Proverbs 22:15 ("Foolishness is bound up in the heart of a child; the rod of discipline will remove it far from him") with our current Proverb 29:15, we learn that not only does consistent, diligent, and corrective discipline remove inherent folly from the child's heart, it also imparts wisdom to the child. Further, it gives quiet peace and pleasure to the parents...and all public places become shame free. In fact, on the way out of the restaurant, the wise mother might say to her son, "You behaved very well! I'm so proud of you!" And that is the child's reward for his respectful, quiet obedience—his parent's pleasure.

Proverbs has consistently taught us throughout this study that wise parents faithfully discipline their children because they believe God when He repeatedly says that corrective discipline redirects wayward-by-nature children from their way onto His way. When wise parents are consistently obedient to this teaching, Proverbs 29:17 becomes their blessed reality: "Correct your son, and he will give you comfort; he will also delight your soul."

Comfort and delight are the opposites of shame, and wise parents surely desire the comfort and delight that comes to them because their children are well mannered and behaved. But there's a greater motivation for disciplining our children than that. Who among us doesn't want to see our children well mannered, behaved, and growing in the goodness and godliness of Jesus Christ? Because we love them so much, we discipline them diligently.

Consistently correcting the direction of our children so they don't bring shame to us is an excellent, biblical motive. And because it's a biblical motive, it's a logical one. But it cannot be our greatest motive. The greatest motive should be our enormous love for our children. That is why wise parents bring up their children in the discipline and instruction of the Lord. We love them! Love is why wise parents always discipline their children in love—never out of anger, never because they had a bad day, and never *ever* over the top because they lack self-control. The rod and reproof are tools of love, not instruments of abuse.

The most important parenting skill you can have is the ability to discipline your children in an atmosphere of love. Listen, if our children are going to become spiritually and emotionally stable and strong, it is imperative that they grow up in homes where they intimately know love and discipline. Without loving parents who are not afraid to correct and discipline their children in love, they will grow up without the ability to be functionally disciplined and truly loving themselves. This lack has already resulted in massive problems in today's marriages.

Mark it well: if our children are to become fully mature, stable, and strong in Christ, they must grow up fully experiencing the great stability of love and discipline from godly and wise parents who are determined to live with minimal parental regrets.

Before closing this principle, I want you to notice the order of instruction in the proverb: the rod is first; the reproof is second. Often, we reverse that order in our homes. The reproof is first and happens often. It is only after much exasperation that the rod is applied. There are times when a verbal reproof is the only action necessary to correct a child, and in many instances, a reproof alone is effective. But it is too easy for parents who hate using the rod to think *reproof, reproof, reproof* before they think *spank*. I said it earlier; I'll say it again. Sometimes parents talk too much, only to find that the more they talk, the more they rebuke and reprimand and the more the unacceptable attitude and behavior persist. In that case, wise parents will reverse the order to line up with the inspired proverb: the rod and then the reproof.

Because I was careful to physically discipline my children in love, I found that a reproof was more effective when it followed a spanking. Words of reproof, if they are not either preceded or backed up with loving, corrective force, sometimes just become words to a child, kind of like adults speaking in a *Peanuts* cartoon: "*Waa waa waa waa.*" A reproof that is either preceded or backed up with physical discipline may need to be stern and strong, but should not be loud or harsh. The loving force of a spanking removes the felt need for a loud and harsh rebuke. A loving but firm spanking followed by a loving but stern rebuke comes across as more loving, even with a strong-willed child.

Here's what I've found to be the most effective order in a disciplinary episode: the rod, then reproof, then a loving embrace. The wonderful result is the removal of foolishness, effectively imparted wisdom, and no need for anyone to be ashamed. If we are wise, we will be faithful, consistent, diligent, and always loving in corrective discipline. When we follow this direction, we will live with few to no regrets. And that is music to the ears of a wise parent.

Parenting Principle 38
Wise Parents Know How to Minimize Regrets

Where there is no vision, the people are unrestrained,
but happy is he who keeps the law.
Proverbs 29:18

"Vision" in this proverb refers to prophetic vision: divine revelation received by a prophet of God and then communicated to His people. In Israel's history, prophetic vision was at its height when God's people were moving progressively away from Him in their rebellion. As they rebelled, God intensified His prophetic revelation, calling them back to Him through repentance. But the people seldom received or heard those revelations in dark times. That led to darker times, when God rarely spoke to Israel at all. First Samuel 3:1 tells us this was the case when Samuel was a child: "Now the boy Samuel was ministering to the Lord before Eli. And word from the Lord was rare in those days, visions were infrequent."

Historically, God has spoken loudly in dark times, but few have listened. So God allowed darker times to come—times when He rarely communicated to His people because they had become stiff-necked, stone deaf, and totally blind to God and to His prophetic Word.

In our nation, we fall under the first sad scenario. The Word of God is readily available to anyone who wants it. We are free to read it, receive it, and apply it. A hard copy may be purchased in any city and probably every county in our country. Even if there isn't a local store where a Bible may be purchased, we can order a copy online. And if a person can't afford a copy of the Bible or lacks the initiative to purchase one, Gideons International would be pleased to give them one at no cost. Further, in our day of great technological advancements, if all these avenues fail, you can turn to your smartphone to find an electronic copy of the Word of God.

The Word has never been more accessible and available, yet here in America, there is little prophetic vision or revelation from God because we are a people of stopped-up ears, blind eyes, and rock-hard hearts. The awful result of this failure to attend to God's Word is an increase of people who are unrestrained in their sinful, wicked ways. We have successfully cast off the spiritual and moral restraints that held back the floodgates of lawlessness against God Almighty…and disastrous consequences have already begun.

Beyond the lack of vision in our country, what alarms me more is how very little prophetic vision is proclaimed in the churches of our day. The pulpit, where divine revelation was once faithfully expounded on, has been replaced by a stage where entertainment is on display—where a prophetic word preached in power has been replaced by a message offered that has more style than substance, if any substance at all. And unfortunately, this is increasingly true, not only in the professing church, but also in the evangelical church. Fewer and fewer churchgoers feel the need to bring a Bible to church; in many cases, if there is a Word from God, it is flashed on a screen to support a point, rather than the point proceeding forth from the Word.

Don't get me wrong—I'm not opposed to modern methods of communication. What I am opposed to is when modern methods displace the unchanging and timeless message of God's Word. It is becoming increasingly harder for God's people to find a church where Jesus Christ and His Word are preeminent. And what's even sadder is that too many church people don't care. The repercussions, in both our churches and our homes, are disastrous.

God is clear: Where there is no prophetic vision, the people are not held back. The King James Version reads, "the people perish." That's not the best translation of the Hebrew word *para*, but it does communicate well the end result: lack of revelation leads to unrestraint, which leads to death. Parents, if you are taking part in this movement, if you are drifting away from the Way, then you are leading your children toward the precipice, where all spiritually and morally deaf and blind people plunge to their awful demise. God is clear. It is a strong warning to all of us—if we desire to remain in good standing with God and avoid disastrous results in our churches and in our homes, we must protect ourselves from any slippage away from and then off the Way.

As you know, this book was developed from a sermon series I preached to my church family at Fresno Bible Church. Toward the beginning of the series, I asked our parents to share some of their parenting regrets. I asked them to respond to two questions.

1. What do you wish your parents would have done differently when you were a child in their home?
2. As parents of older or adult children, what do you regret that you did or didn't do during your parenting years?

It was a painful exercise for many of our older parents, though they graciously complied. But I found their replies were painful for me, their pastor, too. Faithful shepherds would rather revel in their flocks' victories than read of their regrets. However, the regrets of one generation can offer an important warning to the generations that follow. Because that's true, I've asked my church family to allow me to share some of their regrets. I gratefully reprint their answers here.

In answering the question, "What do you regret that you did or didn't do during your parenting years?" most parents said they had possessed the Word of God, but had not taken it in hand, had not read and listened to it enough. Consequently, they said they were not able to move into the future alongside their children with their spiritual eyes wide open. They had not walked before the Lord in the wisdom of His Word like they wish they had. Please learn from the following regrets:

- There were times when I should have said things and didn't, and times when I should have listened more.
- If I had it to do over again, I would have read the Bible in my children's presence and been a better example of gentleness.
- I regret not seeking God's advice more, especially during my children's teen years. And I regret not being a better example.
- I wish I would have listened more and spoken and controlled less—I should have thought things out first, seeking God's guidance above all for the situation.

- I regret disciplining in anger and being a perfectionist; I allowed emotionally crippling things from my childhood to carry over to my marriage and child-rearing.
- I would not have worked seven days a week.
- I would have spent more time with family.
- I would have spent more time with my child in church.
- I would have been more patient with my children and appreciated them more; I would have spent more time playing with them instead of worrying about cleaning the house.
- I would have spent more time with them. I wasn't saved when my children were small, so that says it all.
- I regret not staying involved with the Lord and raising my family with Him.
- I regret not being a Christian mom and teaching my kids about life with Christ.
- I regret not having a spiritual mentor to guide me and hold me accountable during my children's youth.
- I regret not setting aside time for family devotions.
- I regret not taking my children to church from day one.
- I wish I had done more in choosing a mate. And I wish I had taught my children the principle from 2 Corinthians 6:14: "Do not be bound together with unbelievers; for...what fellowship has light with darkness?"

The following are regrets from adult children concerning their childhood:

- My parents didn't deal with their past until I was in high school. Their fears and lack of faith in God translated into my life. Personally, I am quick to anger and to speak.
- There was a lack of quality time together as a family.
- Growing up, there was a lot of TV in my home.
- My parents didn't keep my siblings and me in church when we were young.

One of the primary reasons I preached the sermon series and the reason I am now writing this book is to help younger parents avoid the regrets of older parents. For those who shared their regrets above, it is too late for them—their child-rearing years are behind them. But God is gracious, and there is a place for all of us to turn to receive forgiveness of sin. Sadness may remain, but sin and guilt are washed away "with precious blood, as of a lamb unblemished and spotless, the blood of Christ" (1 Peter 1:19).

These forgiven, older parents bared their souls so that our younger parents wouldn't have to live with their regrets. The bottom line for those living with regret is that there simply wasn't enough attention paid to prophetic vision so that they could then live before their children in the wisdom of God and impart that wisdom to them.

There is a second line to our proverb that contrasts with the first. Proverbs 29:18 finishes by saying, "happy is he who keeps the law." Thankfully, this second line applies to anyone who has ears to hear what the Spirit of God is saying—including those who are living with regret. You may redeem the time God gives you by teaching your grandchildren or the children in your neighborhood or in your church about the happiness of receiving and keeping the prophetic vision of God's Word.

I now want to apply the second line to those who are either in their parenting years or who are looking forward to parenting one day soon, so that they will be careful to be wise parents. It is God's promise that the wise parent who obeys God's protective law will be happy and blessed.

The happy blessing of living in obedience to Christ is that His divine power helps more than we can know to restrain our society, churches, and homes from fully breaking out in rebellion against God. However, we have prophetic revelation that tells us that the societies of the world, including ours, will get worse before the Lord returns and restores His order on the earth. Nonetheless, people of God who are indwelt and empowered by the Holy Spirit are a significant restraining force in the world.

More under our control is the powerful restraining ministry and force that we as Christ-followers may collectively have in our churches. It should be obvious that we cannot control people, including our brothers and sisters in Christ, but wise church members collectively possess the power of the Holy Spirit to prevent their church family from falling away. Perhaps not all church members and attenders, but the church as a whole may experience staying power and know the huge blessing of obedience to God and His Word.

Further, and even more under our control, are wise parents who will do all within their God-given ability to lead their children in listening to, receiving, heeding, and applying prophetic vision—the Word of God. In so doing, they will lead their families into the center of God's blessing by obeying His Word. The wonderful result will be that, when their children grow up and move out of their homes, they will happily minimize their own regrets. But even if some of our children close their eyes, stop up their ears, and harden their hearts against divine revelation, wise parents will know that they controlled what they could, and they will leave the rest to God. Regarding their wayward children, they will live with sorrow and grief but not regret, because they have done everything within their Spirit-given power to lead their children in the way they should go.

Wise parents, be careful to apply this principle's proverb to your home so you can minimize regrets and know the true happiness and blessings of obedience. Below is a checklist based on Proverbs 29:18. Work through it carefully to make sure that you are imparting only the wisdom of God to your children—as the old truism rightly says, only an examined (home) life is worth living. In homes where wise parents preside over their families:

- The prophetic vision of God's Word is faithfully opened and proclaimed.
- Family members carefully listen to this divine revelation and receive the imparted wisdom.

- Family members effectively refrain from breaking out into sinful rebellion.
- Family members exhibit willing obedience to God and His Word.
- The home is a happy one as the members reside in the wonderful blessings of obedience.

The wisdom of God brings blessings, which are the reverse of regrets. And so, wise parents know how to minimize regrets and perhaps even eliminate them completely from their homes. Subsequently, blessed are the homes that obey God's Word.

Parenting Principle 39
Wise Parents Teach Their Children to Trust God's Word

Who has ascended into heaven and descended? Who has gathered the wind in His fists? Who has wrapped the waters in His garment? Who has established all the ends of the earth? What is His name or His Son's name? Surely you know!

PROVERBS 30:4

This proverb underscores, in five rhetorical questions, the infinite distance between God and man. In doing so, it establishes man's inability to know God without divine assistance. The only answer to these questions is God. Go back and read the questions again, but this time answer each one with, "No one but God." Do that little exercise before reading further.

The last question that asks what is God's or His Son's name speaks to the fact that a person is unable to truly know God's covenant name, Yahweh, without divine help. The question means, "Can one truly know the character and nature of God and His Son that is represented by His name?" The inspired and perhaps even sarcastic conclusion is, "Come on, surely you know!" No, you don't! We cannot know the divine Person represented by His name on our own. God is absolutely infinite. Mankind is unquestionably finite. Therefore, we are unable to know Him by ourselves. Further, we are not able to understand His creation without His assistance.

It's strange how smart people think they have figured out the universe. They think they know how creation came into being and how created things work—but they've not consulted the Creator. When it comes to knowledge, these people reach for the stars, and in their own human effort and ability—without divine enablement—they think they know, or at least will eventually figure it out, through human discovery. And yet they never pick up the Bible to see if their knowledge is true or if it passes the test of authenticity. So how in the world can they know anything with certainty? They can't. Consequently, they move through life without having any real knowledge of God or the things of God, including His creation.

Ignorant humanity, those who ignore divine revelation, are perfectly described in Proverbs 30:2–3.

> Surely I am more stupid than any man, and I do not have the understanding of a man. Neither have I learned wisdom, nor do I have the knowledge of the Holy One.

This proverb demonstrates that true wisdom from above and real knowledge of Holy God can never be discovered by mere humans who are too proud to humble themselves before Him and admit their utter stupidity. So what's the answer? Does humanity have any hope of gaining true wisdom and knowledge? Verses 5–6 tell us how we can know God:

> Every word of God is tested; He is a shield to those who take refuge in Him. Do not add to His words or He will reprove you, and you will be proved a liar.

Let's unwrap the meaning of each line:

- ***Every word of God is tested.*** The word *tested* is used to describe the result of a refining process that purifies gold or silver. Likewise, God's Word—in fact, every word of it—has been thoroughly tested and proven to be impeccably flawless and true; therefore, it can be fully trusted. Mankind can know the nature and character of God, and even experience intimacy with God, only because He has revealed Himself in His infallible and trustworthy Word. Wise people come to the realization of just how flawed and limited they are as finite creatures (actually, downright stupid!), and in humility, they understand the absolute necessity of possessing divine revelation from God by trusting every word that proceeds out of His mouth.

- ***He is a shield to those who take refuge in Him.*** Those who trust God's Word trust Him, and from His Word they know that He is the only One who is *truly* safe. They know they can deliberately and confidently take refuge in Him. They trust in Him completely to save, protect, and bless. These people no longer place their trust in the mere knowledge of man, nor do they lean on their own understanding; rather, they heed God's Word and are saved. They are safely brought into a personal relationship with Him, one in which they may know Him and grow in the knowledge of Him and enjoy wonderful intimacy with Him.
- ***Do not add to His words.*** Since God's Word has been thoroughly tested and proven to be impeccably pure and true, how foolish are we to try to add human thought to it? But lost and consequently stupid humans are naturally given to much human speculation that is out of step with divine revelation. Too many are ignorant of the fact that it is always deadly to think thoughts about God or advance theories pertaining to Him or develop theologies about Him that step out of line with or add to the Scriptures. I can think of so many ways people insult and blaspheme Him without even realizing it. They refer to God as "the man upstairs" and speak of dead loved ones as "angels in heaven." Many arrogantly state, "When I die, I'm

dead, and that's it." Even more arrogantly, some say, "Jesus Christ is only one of the ways to God and to heaven," and they add their stupid speculations to the Word of God. These verses contain a strong warning from God Himself. I paraphrase, but God says, "Don't add to My words, or else!"

- ***Or else He will reprove you, and you will be proved a liar.*** God rebukes those who think they know Him outside of and in addition to what He has revealed about Himself in His Word. It is wretched, fallen, human speculation, and it will prove to be false. Further, the person doing the speculating will be proven to be a liar—one who's full of himself and full of conceit. How dare anyone think they know better than God! Without repentance, God's rebuke will be followed by His eternal judgment. Revelation 21:8 declares this awful reality: "But for...all liars, their part will be in the lake that burns with fire and brimstone, which is the second death."

So, upon understanding the proverbs in verses 2–6, wise parents teach their children to trust God's Word. The following are some application points for homes that are under the leadership of wise parents.

1. Wise Parents Are Convinced That Every Word of God Is True

They are careful not to add human speculation to God's Word; they simply trust it with all their heart. They rest their full weight upon it. They stake their lives and the lives of their children on it. It is their standard of measure for what is truth. Along with Christ, it is the one and only foundation upon which they build their theology, their way of thinking, their perspectives, and their lives. It is their only authority for faith and life.

The world of man has developed a theory concerning the origins of the universe that is now taught not as theory, but as fact. The widespread speculation is that so-called science has proven evolution to be true—that the universe and all that's in it, including humanity, has evolved over billions of years. However, the Bible clearly states in Genesis 1 that God Himself created the universe, including humanity and all living things on the earth, in six literal days, and that He rested on the seventh day. In fact, ever since that creation week, the Judeo-Christian world has based their calendars on twenty-four-hour days and seven-day weeks, just as it was from the beginning.

But many in the church today *add* the theory of evolution to God's creating power and come up with manmade alterations to creation—theories like *theistic evolution*, the idea that God created the world using the billions-of-years-of-random-chance evolutionary process. But wise parents believe every word that proceeds from the mouth of God rather than the speculations of man. And God clearly says that He created our world in six literal days.

If a literal six-day creation is a new teaching to you, go back to Genesis 1 and read it with fresh eyes. Take it for what it says rather than what man endlessly adds to it. Read it as it is meant to be read—as twenty-four-hour days—without speculation. For example, Genesis 1:3–5 says,

> Then God said, "Let there be light"; and there was light. God saw that the light was good; and God separated the light from the darkness. God called the light day, and the darkness He called night. And there was evening and there was morning, one day.

If this is a brand-new way of thinking for you, you should know that there are several excellent ministries that exist today for the purpose of answering your questions about creation versus evolution. I recommend that you check out the "Answers in Genesis" website. It offers both biblical and scientific explanations that not only make sense but, more importantly, perfectly align with divine revelation. This ministry website is www.answersingenesis.org. I have found this site to be scripturally accurate and easy to understand.

2. Wise Parents Train Their Children to Trust God and His Word

Wholehearted trust in God and His Word is the only way that children will grow up knowing God, as well as knowing the security of God in a fallen world that is full of infinitely errant human speculation. Wise parents know and train their children to trust that God is a shield only to those who fully trust Him and take refuge in Him.

3. Wise Parents Train Their Children to Trust God's Word for Their Own Protection

They are deliberate in training their children to trust, thus protecting themselves and their children from deep regret. Listen to these laments from some older parents from our church family. Hear their sad regrets:

- We didn't set aside time for devotions.
- If I could do it all over again, I would have done better with family devotions.
- I regret not teaching God's Word more.
- I regret not teaching my kids to hide God's Word in their hearts more.
- I regret that we did not read Scripture together as a family more often.
- We should have set aside more time for daily devotions with our family.

It's the same regret, repeated over and over. Let me amplify it a bit: "Why, oh why, didn't we take the time to hide God's Word away in our children's hearts? Since God's Word always proves to be true, why didn't we train them to test it, to trust it, and to live by it?"

Parents, be wise by listening to an older generation. Learn from their regrets so you won't make the same mistakes. Take it from them—the regrets they live with are an awful burden they've been bearing for years. In fact, they will continue to bear that burden until their dying days. So how, practically, can you do this?

Establish a Family Practice of Learning and Applying God's Word

I give you now deliberate steps that you may take to instill the trust of God's Word in the minds and hearts of your children.

1. Take Family Time to Implant Bible Verses into Their Heads

If your church has an Awana ministry, make sure your children are involved. Set aside family time to work on their memory verses together. If your church doesn't have a Scripture memory ministry, pursue starting one, or implement one in your home.

2. Work with Them to Move the Word from Their Heads to Their Hearts

It is one thing for your children to have God's Word in their heads; it is another thing altogether for them to fully believe it and trust it so that it is embedded in their hearts. The best way to do this is to live it out before them. Be a living witness early in their lives to the reliability of God and His Word. And then, communicate how God has proven Himself faithful to you and to them. Early and often, expose them to a church full of people who wholly trust in the Word of God.

3. Be Careful to Maintain Family Devotions

It is a hard but most critical habit to begin and maintain. It saddens me to know that daily family time in the Word and in prayer is a routine that few Christians regularly practice.

If you are not in the habit, I would encourage you to revisit the above regrets of those older parents. Then contrast those regrets with the following example of another older parent in our church who is not living with regret. I spoke with his son recently, who is in his midforties. His dad is in his late seventies. His father's devotional life came up in our conversation. I asked the son, "Does your father still do what he did when you were a boy in the home?" He told me, "Every morning at the breakfast table, he has his Bible and the same daily devotional he has used for years, *Our Daily Bread*, open, and he does his morning devotions, just like we did when my sister and I were young. Nothing has changed." This elderly man is one of the most respected men in our church, and he's a man who has never had to live with the regret of not having a devotional life with his family. Now alone, he continues the practice himself, enjoying sweet fellowship with His loving and living Savior and Lord.

4. Apply Trust in God's Word to Every Circumstance in Life

If you as a parent are following Paul's example and learning to be content in every circumstance (Philippians 4:11) and you trust in the sovereignty of God, then the Word of God will be on full display daily in your life and home. When you are given to faith rather than fear and worry, you will live a glorious testimony before your children, as the peace of God that surpasses all understanding guards your heart and mind in Christ Jesus (Philippians 4:7). When Lindsay and Jason were murdered, I thought it was vitally important that I was ready to live before my family and church family with steadfast and unshakable faith in the Word of God. It's one thing for parents to say they trust in God; it is another thing to live it out in every circumstance of life, including and especially during the hardest of circumstances.

5. Train Them to Know That God Has Their Backs

Not only does He have their backs, He has every side covered as their shield and stay. Of course, as stated earlier, God's children are not any more exempt from trial and trouble than was His only begotten Son when He came into the world to provide the way of salvation. Like Jesus, we are not safe from the trials and tribulations of living in a fallen world. But when we take refuge in God because we trust Him fully, our souls are safe, and He will keep us safe from physical harm if that is best for us. This is the eternal perspective that wise parents teach their children.

It would be helpful here to turn to Romans 8:31–39 and read about God's protective, everlasting love and amazing grace toward those who love Him. Let's look at just a few of the verses from this incredible passage.

> If God is for us, who is against us? … Who will separate us from the love of Christ? Will tribulation, or distress, or persecution, or famine, or nakedness, or peril, or sword? … I am convinced that neither death, nor life, nor angels, nor principalities, nor things

> present, nor things to come, nor powers, nor height, nor depth, nor any other created thing, will be able to separate us from the love of God, which is in Christ Jesus our Lord (Romans 8:31, 35, 38–39).

When our children trust in that Word of God from Romans with all their hearts, they will have a faith in God that shields them from failing in their faith and falling away. God has their backs and much, much more. And they can trust Him!

6. Take Steps to Guard Their Minds and Hearts from Worldly Speculation

Paul's counsel to the church in Colossians 3:16 certainly applies to the Christian home:

> Let the word of Christ richly dwell within you, with all wisdom teaching and admonishing one another with psalms and hymns and spiritual songs, singing with thankfulness in your hearts to God.

Wise parents who fully trust in God will make sure the Word of Christ is richly dwelling within themselves and their children. At the same time, wise parents are also careful with what they *don't* allow to go into their children's heads that might eventually dwell in their hearts. Specifically, they guard their children against the worldly, trashy speculation that comes at them from every side in this highly technological age. They understand the importance of filtering what goes through their eyes and ears, for these are the windows of the soul. Much of what goes in will never come out.

Listen. You have the God-given parental authority, right, and responsibility to not only know but control what your children watch on television, what they take in from the Internet, what books and magazines they download onto their e-readers, and what songs they save onto their iPods, smartphones, and laptops. You even have the authority to decide whether your children are smart enough in Christ to have such devices! So while you encourage them to let the Word of Christ dwell richly in them, make sure to protect them from the trash of worldly speculation.

David made this firm commitment in Psalm 101:3–4:

> I will set no worthless thing before my eyes; I hate the work of those who fall away; it shall not fasten its grip on me. A perverse heart shall depart from me; I will know no evil.

Think of all the work of those who fall away in our day—movie and television scriptwriters, book authors, songwriters and producers, Internet programmers, video game makers, and the like. Why, David's inspired words might be more contemporary now than when he wrote them! But if David needed to make that commitment in his day, how much more do we need to make it a firm and constant commitment for ourselves and for our children in our day?

When our girls were young, Kathy and I posted that text from Psalm 103 on the stand below our television. Today, as wise parents, you may have to post it below your televisions and make it the log-in screen for all your computers, including the ones your children use. Go back and read it again, and then make it the commitment of your home.

Did you read it? Are you going to make it your family commitment? Thank you!

Now set out to guard your family well from all the wretched, worldly speculation that is so prevalent in our society, both outside and inside of our churches and homes. Be aware that once it enters the mind and heart, it may and often does stay there.

Wise parents, trust in God alone; trust in every word that proceeds out of His mouth, and then teach your children to do the same. In so doing, you will greatly minimize your regrets and the regrets of your children.

Parenting Principle 40
Wise Fathers Teach Their Children to Honor Their Mothers

PROVERBS 31:10–31

The Proverbs 31 woman is a poetic picture of a most excellent woman, wife, and mother. The proverb is an acrostic in Hebrew, with each verse beginning with the sequential letters of the Hebrew alphabet, giving a complete picture of this wise and godly woman. She is a sterling example for women in every age to follow. It is much easier and much more pleasant to honor a woman who is worthy of the honor she receives.

Let's take a close look at the attributes of an honorable woman as they are given in this passage.

She is an excellent wife—Proverbs 31:10.

> An excellent wife, who can find? For her worth is far above jewels.

The Hebrew word *chayil*, translated "excellent" is the same word that Boaz used to describe Ruth, his future wife: "You are a woman of excellence" (Ruth 3:11). The word speaks of valor and strength of character. The woman who possesses it is spiritually and morally strong, noble, courageous, and capable. Therefore, she can accomplish all the things that are set forth in the rest of the poem. The rhetorical question doesn't mean she doesn't exist; instead, it infers that a man who finds such a wife has a rare and precious treasure on earth. If her husband is wise, he will recognize what he's got; he will value and treasure her above all other earthly treasures.

She is trustworthy—Proverbs 31:11–12.

> The heart of her husband trusts in her, and he will have no lack of gain. She does him good and not evil all the days of her life.

This excellent wife has proven her worth and value to her husband; therefore, he has every confidence in her. She is a good and trustworthy wife, and she brings him nothing but good throughout her life.

She is industrious—Proverbs 31:13.

> She looks for wool and flax and works with her hands in delight.

Today's excellent wife may or may not weave and sew, but she does take responsibility for her family and works hard to meet their needs. She delights in doing so because, as a godly wife and mother, her family is the apple of her eye. Her life is not always easy, but she doesn't have time to sit around and feel sorry for herself; she has responsibilities, and she loves fulfilling them.

She is resourceful—Proverbs 31:14.

> She is like merchant ships; she brings her food from afar.

She's a smart and resourceful shopper. She can lay out a spread on the dinner table that her family didn't know could be found in their community. If the budget is tight, she looks for bargains, cuts out coupons, shops at the local discount grocery store, and still surprises her family with delicious meals. She's amazing in her resourcefulness.

She is a servant—Proverbs 31:15.

> She rises also while it is still night and gives food to her household and portions to her maidens.

There's nothing lazy about this woman. If necessary, she rises early before daylight to make sure her entire family is well fed and ready for the day ahead of them. If she's wealthy enough to have servants, she serves them also, so that they say, "She even serves us!"

She is a hard worker—Proverbs 31:16–19.

> She considers a field and buys it; from her earnings she plants a vineyard. She girds herself with strength and makes her arms strong. She senses that her gain is good; her lamp does not go out at night. She stretches out her hands to the distaff [a staff onto which wool or flax is wound for spinning], and her hands grasp the spindle.

Not all women of excellence have a business mind like this one, but they all can figure out how to meet the physical needs of their family, and they set out to do it. In our day, she knows how to stretch a dollar and pay the bills. In caring for her home, she's driven, energetic, hardworking, and capable.

She is compassionate and generous—Proverbs 31:20–21.

> She extends her hand to the poor, and she stretches out her hands to the needy. She is not afraid of the snow for her household, for all her household are clothed with scarlet.

She's not afraid of the coming cold weather because she's prepared for it; she's made sure her family is dressed in warm clothing. Beyond her family and their needs, she is also aware of the needs of the less fortunate, and she compassionately, generously, and selflessly reaches out to help them. In just the same way that she stretches out her hands to provide for the needs of her family, she stretches out her hands to make provision for the poor and needy.

She is dignified in her inward attitude and outward attire—Proverbs 31:22.

> She makes coverings for herself; her clothing is fine linen and purple.

Fine linen and purple signify wealth. She is dressed according to her stature in the community; she carries herself not with pride, but with dignity. She is comfortable in her own skin and doesn't pretend to be someone she's not. Today, whether wealthy or not, the woman of excellent character cares about her dignity of heart and of appearance. Therefore, her dignified outward appearance is an expression of her noble inward reality.

She is the woman behind the man—Proverbs 31:23.

> Her husband is known in the gates, when he sits among the elders of the land.

This woman's husband is a prominent and well-respected leader in their community. Behind this good and godly man is his good and godly wife. She respects her husband and his leadership. And though she is quite capable herself, she never considers overstepping her God-given role and place as a woman and a wife. Instead of competing with him, she does all within her power to support and encourage him, to build him up rather than tear him down. She is by far his strongest support and encouragement.

She is a most wise woman—Proverbs 31:24–27.

> She makes linen garments and sells them, and supplies belts to the tradesmen. Strength and dignity are her clothing, and she smiles at the future. She opens her mouth in wisdom, and the teaching of kindness is on her tongue. She looks well to the ways of her household, and does not eat the bread of idleness.

Wow, what a noble woman—she wears her godly character like fine clothing! She smiles at the future because she's prepared for it and is confident in God. She not only lives wisely; she also speaks wisdom and teaches others with kindness. This is the Hebrew *hesed*, which speaks of the covenant loyal love of God. She's Godlike in her instructions to her family, servants, and friends.

She is blessed—Proverbs 31:28–29.

> Her children rise up and bless her; her husband also, and he praises her, saying: "Many daughters have done nobly, but you excel them all."

The woman of excellence has proven her value to her family. She is, indeed, a rare and priceless treasure. Therefore, her children are inspired by her love and grace to rise up and offer her praise. Her husband cannot remain silent either, for to him she is the most excellent of the excellent, the rarest of the rare, the best of the best, and she excels all others.

She is to be honored—Proverbs 31:30–31.

> Charm is deceitful and beauty is vain, but a woman who fears the LORD, she shall be praised. Give her the product of her hands, and let her works praise her in the gates.

In other words, her work and her worth are publicly rewarded and recognized. Her husband, her family, and her community can't help it—they must rise up and praise her, for she has proven herself to be God-fearing and, therefore, wise, godly, good, productive, and worthy of praise. Wow, what a woman!

These are the characteristics and qualities of a most excellent lady. She is a marvelous example of wisdom herself. If an unmarried man pursues with all his heart the wisdom of God, personified in Proverbs as a woman called wisdom, and if he desires a wife, then he will pursue a wise woman who fears the Lord. And if a man is so blessed of God as to have such a wife, if he's wise like her, he will take her with great gratitude rather than for granted, knowing that he has an extremely rare treasure whose worth is far above jewels.

Now, let's apply this teaching concerning an excellent wife and mother to the final wise parenting principle: Wise fathers teach their children to honor their mothers. Here are some practical things the wise father will do at all times and in all places, but especially in his home before his children.

1. He Will Live with His Excellent Wife with Great Gratitude

A wise father who has a wise and worthy wife will have a heart that is full of thanksgiving to God that overflows in his grateful attitude toward her, his appreciative treatment of her, and his verbal affirmation and praise for her.

How easy it is for even a godly man to take his wife for granted, to carelessly or unwittingly treat her with indifference, and to fail to be constantly thankful to God for the amazing gift she is to him. The Bible contrasts two polar-opposite men: the godless man who is, among other things, ungrateful (2 Timothy 3:2); and the godly man who, among other things, gives thanks in everything because it is God's will for him in Christ Jesus (1 Thessalonians 5:18). The godly man is most thankful for his godly wife, and his careful, loving, adoring, affectionate treatment of her is the ongoing proof of his overflowing gratitude to God for her.

2. He Will Teach His Children to Hold Their Mother in Highest Esteem

Most children naturally love their mothers, but most don't naturally treat them according to their worth. A wise father will train his children to see the immense value of their mother and to know that their home is graced with the highest earthly treasure, a godly wife and mother! He will teach them to appreciate her and to rise up and bless her. He teaches this first by his own example, praising her in their presence.

3. He Will Not Tolerate Disrespect toward Her

He will not allow his children to disrespect his wife in any way. He will not allow them to verbally disrespect her or dishonor her through their disobedience, nor will he allow them to cheapen her worth by copping an attitude toward her. Because disrespect is natural to most children, it is not uncommon for him to say to his daughter something like, "Honey, you need to understand something: you *will not* talk to your mother with that tone and in that manner; otherwise, there will be consequences." And he will tell his son something like this: "Hey, did your mother tell you to do something, and you just didn't do it?" He doesn't wait for an answer, for the question is rhetorical and can only be answered with a yes. "Listen, buddy boy," he continues, "if you mess with her, you're messing with me!" And those verbal reproofs may need to be backed up with corrective physical discipline because the wise father does not tolerate disrespectful behavior toward a woman as worthy of honor as his wife and their mother.

It is ever true that an excellent wife is a rare treasure; her worth is far above jewels. Thus, an important aspect of a wise father's training of his children is to teach them through loving but firm disciplinary reinforcement to always respect their mother. She's capable of teaching them herself, and her husband should encourage her to do so. But when he's around and disrespect happens, he takes over because a precious woman like his wife will be treated according to her worth—she will be well respected, appreciated, and praised. She will never be trashed by her own children.

4. He Often Takes Them to Scripture for Instruction on Honor

The fifth command of the Ten Commandments is very specific. Exodus 20:12 says, "Honor your father and your mother, that your days may be prolonged in the land which the LORD your God gives you." Added to this is Moses's strong warning to the people of Israel before they crossed over the Jordan into the Promised Land in Deuteronomy 27:16: "'Cursed is he who dishonors his father or mother.' And all the people shall say, 'Amen.'" It is restated and commanded again in the New Testament for the church today. Jesus Himself quoted the fifth commandment on two occasions, in Matthew 15:4 and 19:19. Further, Paul quoted the command in Ephesians 6:1–3 when he gave his Spirit-inspired instructions concerning family relations.

> Children, obey your parents in the Lord, for this is right. Honor your father and mother (which is the first commandment with a promise), so that it may be well with you, and that you may live long on the earth. Fathers, do not provoke your children to anger, but bring them up in the discipline and instruction of the Lord.

A necessary way to fulfill the command of verse 4 is for fathers to carefully teach their children to fulfill their responsibilities before God; namely, to obey and honor their parents for their own well-being and that of the home. If a wise father's children are not honoring their mother in accordance to God's Word, all is not well until quick and effective correction is made and then maintained.

5. He Stresses That the Command to Honor Is Unconditional

The passages referenced above do not add a conditional "if" to the command. They do not say, "honor your mother *if* she is honorable and deserving respect." The command is unconditional honor. This is especially important when the children's mother is not the woman of excellence described in Proverbs 31. Unfortunately, not all mothers are noble in character.

This became clear with the survey we completed in our church. One adult in our church responded to the regrets card with these heartbreaking words about his or her mother: "My mother told me she wished she'd never had me. She seldom held me as a toddler. She never prayed with me or for me." Another lamented about how he or she was parented by matter-of-factly saying, "Lack of parenting." Truth be told, not all mothers, even churched mothers, are of noble mind and heart. But a wise husband and father will teach his children that the command to honor their mother is unconditional. If they can't honor her as an honorable woman, they are still to honor her position as their mother.

Let me add that it is, unfortunately, far too common for child abuse to take place in the home. I would classify the words of the mother mentioned above, who wished she'd never had her child, as verbal abuse. Such evil treatment causes much damage in a child. All forms of parental abuse, whether mental, emotional, physical, or sexual; whether negligence, abandonment, or lack of support, defense, or failure to rescue their child from an abuser—whatever the form of the abuse, it is all wretched and remarkably damaging. An adult who was subjected to parental abuse as a child will almost always need biblical counseling to be restored to health. Without it, he or she will never find the ability to honor that abusive parent or stepparent—for their position, if not for their person.

A Proverbs 31 woman will do whatever it takes to be a blessing to her husband and children. But even a woman of excellence who fears and loves God with all her heart can be taken for granted. The wise, godly father will declare, "Not in my house!" Husbands and fathers, if you want to live without regret, make sure you are setting the pace in your home through the way you look at your wife, in what you say and don't say to her, and in how you treat her and bless her with honor, respect, appreciation, and praise. Then, with your example as their guide, demand the same treatment for her from your children. Teach them what it looks like to honor their mother, and then teach them to consistently practice it themselves. Otherwise, people in your household are going have some awful regrets.

There was one person in our church who responded to the regret question about how he or she was brought up in the childhood home by simply saying, "No regrets." Is it possible in Christ to raise our children in the fear of the Lord so that they can overlook our parental mistakes and failures and sincerely say, "No regrets"?

If that is possible—and I believe it is, through Christ who gives us strength, courage, and wisdom—then wise parents will set their hearts on reaching that high and holy goal of hearing their adult children one day say, "Dad, Mom—no regrets!" And they can look forward to hearing their Lord and Savior say, "Well done, my good and faithful servant. Welcome to your reward!"

CHAPTER 10

The Fellowship of the Unashamed

We Christians each have our own favorite Bible characters—men and women of the Scriptures who inspire, challenge, and encourage us personally more than others. For many, Elijah is their favorite prophet, David is their favorite king, and Peter is their favorite apostle. I personally love these guys because all three had major blowouts in their lives and ministries, but all three completely recovered from their failures and, by God's grace, they all finished well. Elijah, after his mountaintop experience, ran from the wicked queen Jezebel. David sinned with Uriah's wife, Bathsheba, and then covered it up with murder. Peter, after arrogantly asserting that he would never deny his Lord, proceeded to deny Him three times. Being sinful humans who fail often, we can relate to these Bible heroes, and they give us hope of being forgiven and still being useable in God's glorious kingdom.

James 3:2 says that "we all stumble in many ways." Isn't that the truth! When we relate that to parenting, we know failure happens. It has happened in the past, it happens in the present, and it will happen again in the future. We Christian parents are saints in our position in Christ, but too often we sin in our practice. Consequently, there is failure in every one of us. But the most encouraging thing that comes out of lives that are strewn with sin, mistake, and regret is that failure doesn't need to be fatal. God is, indeed, the God of grace who awaits our repentance from our foolish way to walk only in His way. The hymn, "Grace Greater than Our Sin," written by Julia H. Johnston, emphasizes this truth and gives us hope.

> Marvelous grace of our loving Lord,
> Grace that exceeds our sin and our guilt!
> Yonder on Calvary's mount outpoured,
> There where the blood of the Lamb was spilt.
> Grace, grace, God's grace,
> Grace that will pardon and cleanse within;
> Grace, grace, God's grace,
> Grace that is greater than all our sin!

Maybe you're a grandparent reading this book with your adult children in mind. Maybe you are concerned about the choices your children are making with your grandchildren because of mistakes you made as a parent. It is not too late to experience the marvelous grace of our loving Lord—grace that exceeds your sin, your failure, your guilt. It may be too late for many things, but it is not too late to fully receive and know the wonder of God's saving, forgiving, and healing grace. That's why James writes in James 4:6, "God is opposed to the proud but gives grace to the humble." "Humble yourselves in the presence of the Lord," he continues in verse 10, "and He will exalt you." Living with regret doesn't mean you have to live in the depths of guilt. Turn now; turn fully to Jesus Christ. There is hope for a new today and tomorrow for all of us because God's grace is greater than all our sin.

If you are in your parenting years—or even if those years are ahead of you—and your life is strewn with sin, mistake, and failure, it is not too late for you to turn back to the Lord right now through repentance to experience that full power and wonder of His marvelous grace. Then you can begin afresh to become the man or woman God has called you to be. You can be the parent that your children need you to be when you allow God to apply His grace daily to your humbled, surrendered, submissive, dependent, and obedient heart. Choose today, through God's grace, to become His wise child so you can be a wise parent to your beloved children. And someday, just maybe, your children will say to you, "Mom, Dad, about your parenting us—we have no regrets. Thank you for raising us up in the Lord Jesus Christ!"

Begin quickly; begin today! The childhood years happen only once, and they pass by so swiftly. It isn't long before our infants turn into toddlers and then they move into their school age years, and then suddenly, they're preteens. Then, just as quickly, they're in the adolescent stage of their lives and moving rapidly toward adulthood. Before you know it, they're off to college or military service or the workforce and into a life of their own. Eventually they will find a spouse and have children of their own.

Wise parents understand that they have only one shot at this. If you want your children to be wise, godly, and fully committed followers of Jesus Christ, the process must begin with you, and it must begin now. You can only take your children into wise living as far as you are willing to go yourself.

When Lindsay was in her late teens, she hung above her bed a poster with a proclamation on it. The author is unknown but believed to have been a young pastor from Zimbabwe who was martyred for his faith in Jesus Christ. The title of the proclamation, "The Fellowship of the Unashamed," became the title of our testimony that we had the privilege to share many times and in many places after Lindsay and Jason were murdered. In closing, I share it with you with the great hope and prayer that you will be the wisest parents possible in Christ, and that you will raise your children in wisdom so that they too will be counted with Jason and Lindsay among the fellowship of the unashamed.

> I'm part of the fellowship of the unashamed. The die has been cast. I have stepped over the line. The decision has been made. I'm a disciple of Jesus Christ. I won't look back, let up, slow down, back away, or be still.
>
> My past is redeemed, my present makes sense, my future is secure. I am finished and done with low living,

sight walking, smooth knees, colorless dreams, tamed vision, worldly talking, cheap giving, and dwarfed goals.

I no longer need preeminence, prosperity, position, promotions, plaudits, or popularity. I now live by faith, lean on His presence, walk with patience, live by prayer, and labor with power.

My face is set, my gait is fast, my goal is heaven, my road is narrow, my way is rough, my companions are few, my Guide is reliable, my mission is clear. I cannot be bought, compromised, detoured, lured away, turned back, deluded, or delayed. I will not flinch in the face of sacrifice, hesitate in the presence of adversity, negotiate at the table of the enemy, ponder at the pool of popularity, or meander in the maze of mediocrity.

I won't give up, shut up, let up until I have stayed up, stored up, prayed up for the cause of Christ. I am a disciple of Jesus. I must go till He comes, give till I drop, preach till all know, work till He stops me. And when He comes to get His own, He will have no problem recognizing me. My banner will be clear.

I'm part of the fellowship of the unashamed. Is that what you want for your children? It begins with you. Join the fellowship of the unashamed and never turn back. Then raise up your children according to these wise parenting principles from Proverbs so that they will be wise and faithful and unashamed, just like you.

May it be so in the strong and gracious and glorious name of Jesus Christ, for His sake and for the sake of your beloved children. Amen.

Made in the USA
Columbia, SC
06 December 2020